Challenging Man-Made Disease

Challenging
Man-Made Disease

THE MEMOIRS OF
HARRIET L. HARDY, M.D.

with the editorial assistance of
Emily W. Rabe

PRAEGER SPECIAL STUDIES • PRAEGER SCIENTIFIC

New York • Philadelphia • Eastbourne, UK
Toronto • Hong Kong • Tokyo • Sydney

Library of Congress Cataloging in Publication Data

Hardy, Harriet Louise, 1906–
    Challenging man-made disease.

    Bibliography: p. 231
    Includes index.
    1. Hardy, Harriet Louise, 1906–   2. Physicians
— Massachusetts — Biography.   I. Title.
R154.H256A32   1983   610'.92'4 [B]   83-13850
ISBN 0-03-063874-7 (alk. paper)

926.1
H297

Published in 1983 by Praeger Publishers
CBS Educational and Professional Publishing,
a Division of CBS Inc.
521 Fifth Avenue, New York, NY 10175, U.S.A.

Foreword

The story of Dr. Hardy's life is of particular interest today, not alone for the reason that she is a distinguished woman physician in occupational medicine, but for how she developed her career of practice, teaching, and research in an age of technological medicine.

Take her interests first. She developed her special concerns for the health of working men and women in a medical era that was almost exclusively devoted to the hospitalized sick. In those decades of hospital expansion from the 1930s to the 1970s, Dr. Hardy's accomplishments came from working at the margins: not in but outside the medical center—first in school and college health services and then in factory, community, and university settings. That work required special commitment to medicine's more mundane task of prevention rather than to the dramatic cure of hospital medicine.

As this autobiography illustrates, her quest for the improvement of occupational health has many roots. Some might be cultural and familial. Born and raised in the Progressive Era (1900–20), she caught the reform spirit that characterized the period: men, institutions, and social conditions could be improved through political action and scientific research. Her professional search was an effort to understand diseases caused by working conditions and then an attempt to improve those conditions to prevent disease.

She joined her learning with helping action, even when that helping action meant "taking sides." Even today (to the consternation of many practitioners), occupational medicine is not a neutral clinical-science specialty with techniques and knowledge to apply to the workplace or to the workers. For the improvement of health, occupational medicine is politics. Doctors take sides: for the company, for the workers. In this uneven exchange Dr. Hardy always remained with working men and women.

Other roots of her quest were educational. Besides that reform spirit, Dr. Hardy also developed the necessary skills and knowledge in the clinical science we call medicine, first from her medical studies at Cornell Medical School (1928–32), second from residency training at the Philadelphia General Hospital (1932–34), and then from her field work in medical practice as a school (Northfield) and then as a college (Radcliffe) physician. Out of these early practice beginnings in educational environments, she found time to conduct clinical studies of student populations: when did menstruation begin? Do low blood pressure and anemia cause symptoms? Does an elevated white blood cell count (WBC) mean infection? From such school and college studies old myths were exploded — that low blood pressure and mild anemia caused symptoms and that elevated WBCs were always an indication of infections when they could, in fact, be due to menses. Such research in the field of healthy young adults was quite distinct from the laboratory investigations so characteristic of hospital medicine.

Still other roots were the encouragements of her mentors at the Massachusetts General Hospital, Doctors James H. Means and Joseph Aub. For in 1945, at the age of 39, Dr. Hardy moved from clinical work with young adolescent women, taking her first job in occupational medicine with the Massachusetts Division of Occupational Hygiene. There she was assigned to investigate a hepatitis outbreak (which she wrote up) and then those cases of "Salem Sarcoid" that we know today from her distinctive work as beryllium disease. This enterprise joined her clinical skills in the examination of patients, her experience in organizing field work studies, her research interests in solving the problem of a new disease, and her reform spirit in improving the health of workers. Looking back, one might argue that her years as school and college health physician were really occupational medicine in disguise, working as she was in schools — call them learning factories — and dealing with students — call them workers — while contending with teachers — the management. In any event, she had been prepared, if not from graduate school, then from on-the-job experience in practice and in this field.

The story of beryllium disease with the resistances and delays in its recognition by the profession, government, and industry is well known. Putting those brief years of resistance aside, the control of the disease remains a remarkable success story in the annals of occupational medicine and the personal achievement of Dr. Hardy. Following her recognition and description of chronic beryllium disease, substitutes for beryllium were found in 1949. Take this very brief period of five to six years for industrial control of beryllium as a contrast to the control of mine dust diseases. These diseases were noted by Ramazini in the Middle Ages but continued for centuries, even after the invention of the exhaust fan. After her beryllium disease studies, Dr. Hardy's clinical-research and pedagogical interests grew, leading her to an awareness of the hazards of lead, cadmium, asbestosis, and coal mine dusts and into educational fields. Her educational interests are represented in that fine general text coauthored with Dr. Alice Hamilton, *Industrial Toxicology*, and in her lectures to undergraduates and post-graduate courses on her favorite theme: manmade disease. Then from the 1950s there was her special job at the Massachusetts Institute of Technology as director and founder of their Occupational Medical Service. Later came her appointment as the first woman professor at Harvard Medical School and her appointment at Dartmouth Medical School, to mention but a few distinctions.

Having sketched this development of Dr. Hardy's career, what can we say about her attributes that made her career possible? Occupational medicine is working at the margins where creative things can and are done, but it is a lonelier outpost than the medical center, requiring her attribute of stick-to-itiveness.

Her field work, meeting workers in their homes after working hours, she may have also learned in her earlier private practice in Northfield, where patients were waiting for her because they were sick. Nonetheless, she did not give up that special home encounter and the extra work and effort it required to visit workers off-hours at home and at their own convenience.

In the care of patients she demonstrated personal concern, an ancient tradition of medicine's art. As a practitioner and investigator, she worked with disabled patients as their personal doctor, sometimes their consultant, not in one-visit contacts but in long-term care, from which she knew the circumstances of their lives as well as the natural history of their disease. With colleagues she was always direct and honest, for some, perhaps unsettling. Despite her patrician background on both her paternal and maternal sides, she easily related to working people and the issues of concern to them. Finally, she has that attribute of working hard at her own occupation of occupational medicine, for how else would she have done so much useful work! Her autobiography tells that story.

JOHN D. STOECKLE, M.D.
Professor of Medicine
Harvard Medical School
June, 1983

Preface

In unfolding my reasons for choosing a career as a physician and the events that followed, I hope to help others considering a medical career. General readers interpreting current media reports may gain perspective on current advances and worldwide interests in health. My self-study and my relating the details of my life and professional career, I hope, will convey my ideals and ideas.

An initial goal is to stimulate women to study and to *practice* medicine. I am not the first to write of the inborn characteristics of the woman to respond to suffering. In medicine she may concentrate on the needs of a single patient or of a whole army, as did Florence Nightingale. Currently many qualified women physicians seek the protection of a research laboratory, a position as a part-time radiologist, or perhaps a short workweek in medical statistics. These jobs must be done, but it seems to me that the unique human assets of womankind have been in the past in large measure lost to the healing arts and the thoughtful handling of preventable disease; presently this tendency is waning. While I recognize the importance of family life and children, my own experience satisfies me that marriage to medicine can be completely rewarding.

I plan to make the point that medicine, well practiced, need not be as insular and narrow as it has been to date. With too few exceptions, knowledge of history, the arts, and political behavior has been missing from medical education. Lately economic pressures have forced our profession to look out into the world and learn what makes it turn.

Short sermons and caustic criticism have found their way into some passages of my history. These, fortunately, are short, and those who know me will be pleased to read this. Any inadequacies in this exercise I blame on my long illness, while I praise the same pathologic changes in my cranium that forced the free time on me in which to make this attempt at writing. I hope my memoirs will stimulate as well as irritate.

This effort could not have been consummated without the support and empathy of Jane Hardy Stewart, my sister, and Ellen Cumber, my good friend, of Theale, England.

Harriet L. Hardy, M.D.

Concord, Massachusetts
December 20, 1982

Contents

Challenging Man-Made Disease

CHAPTER 1

My Genes and Their Early Nurture

The Family Tree

Darwin's idea of a constantly changing nature has influenced my beliefs about the world and about my own behavior. Thus I begin my story by telling what I know of my genetic makeup and the events that influenced my choice of a career.

In 1935, after spending 15 years gathering data, H. Claude Hardy and Reverend Edwin Noah Hardy published *Hardy and Hardie — Past and Present —* the family history.[1] I am the ninth in line of Hardys to be born in North America and a descendant of Thomas Hardy, who journeyed from England to West Newbury, Massachusetts, in 1618. My genes are a firm mix: on one side is the pious Puritan English and Scottish stock with professional, public service, and farming interests (the Hardys); on the maternal side are the industrious and luxury-loving Dutch (Grandfather Decker) plus the bold-minded, independent, slightly mysterious Welsh (my grandmother, Harriet Jones Decker).

My paternal grandfather, John Henry Hardy, graduated from Dartmouth College and Harvard Law School. At 15 he fought in the Civil War. Later Grandfather taught school to pay his way through Dartmouth College. He served as a circuit court judge in small courts in Massachusetts and was appointed judge of the superior court in Boston. By chance, in 1934 I appeared for the Society for the Prevention of Cruelty to Children in an incest case in Greenfield, Massachusetts. During the hearing I became very angry and complained about the opposing lawyer. At the end of the session, the clerk of the court, an older man, asked if I was related to Judge Hardy. When I told him I was, he observed, "I thought so. He was a peppery old boy and you act just like him."

My paternal grandmother, Anna Jane Conant, I did not know. A long illness, diagnosed as melancholia, ended in her death in 1912. In the light of my experiences, I wonder if she had a brain tumor. Ill health may have been part of my inheritance, although with to-day's medical advances much of that illness might have been preventable.

Judge Hardy and his wife, Anna Jane, of Arlington, Massachusetts, had two sons, John and my father, Horace Dexter, who followed his father, graduating from Dartmouth and Harvard Law School. Father joined three other young lawyers in founding a law firm and was assistant district attorney and a member of the Massachusetts legislature.

John Hardy, my uncle, was a farmer and an outdoorsman who enjoyed hunting and fishing. His wife Dorothy was a reader, with a flair for handcrafts and little interest in housework. Our visits to Uncle John's farm helped awaken our long inheritance of love of the outdoors and the work and pleasure of gardening. This kindly uncle died of pulmonary tuberculosis when he was just over 40.

On the maternal side three Decker brothers, whose family emigrated from Delft, Holland, moved from upstate New York to New Jersey. My grandfather, Charles Martyn Decker, founded some food stores that served as a model for today's chain stores. Grandfather was enterprising and grew prosperous, buying land along a railroad and creating the Decker Realty Company. As his assets grew, he enjoyed a great Victorian-style house in the country of northern New Jersey and the living that it called for.

His 21 grandchildren thrived in his prosperous home with its large kitchen, fine furniture, china, space for play indoors, cooks, and maids to Aunt Rye, the housekeeper to scold or help with play-acting. Outdoors there were meadows for play; Pat, the gardener and coachman who let us jump in the hay or ride the horses; and Tony, the chauffeur who cared so obsessively for Grandfather's blue Fiat with red wheels, which was built like a Victorian carriage, that he scarcely let us near it. During the Great Depression my grandparents' large estate dwindled until, afterward, only fine books, elegant china and furniture, and happy childhood memories were left.

Grandmother Decker was of Welsh ancestry, born Harriet Louise Jones. She was a great reader and loved books. Grandmother was also innovative; she initiated a plan whereby horse-drawn wagons brought traveling libraries to small communities. I never saw her, but I heard tales of her modern and free-thinking characteristics. The first was her boldness in trying to self-induce an abortion by wading in cold water — she considered nine pregnancies enough. Second, one time in church when a clergyman preached on the damnation of unbaptized babies, Grandmother rose in her pew near the pulpit and led her children out of the church, saying, "Any preacher who talks of the damnation of babies is a fool and will not have my support."

My mother, Harriet Louise Decker, was born in 1880 in New Jersey. She attended a young ladies' private day school and later Wellesley College. Once at Wellesley she found studies less appealing to her than were my father and his friends and a lively social life. Returning home after a year, she told Grandmother that she was going to drop her studies. Grandmother replied with surprising firmness that, having started, she would stay four years and graduate, which she did. Harriet Decker had a first-class mind and often said how grateful she was to be forced away from a life of parties, sentimental novels, and boxes of bon-bons. She married Horace Hardy in 1905, and I was born in 1906, my sister, Jane, in 1907.

My father died in 1910 at age 33 of bacterial pneumonia. Through the years I have heard that Daddy Hardy caught pneumonia from me, aged four, and died. Could such a babyhood episode have influenced my career choice? (At this time my mother developed a gross tremor of her right hand, which she never lost.) After Daddy Hardy's death Mother took me and my sister to Maine for a respite. We all slept in one big room. One night I woke long enough to see Mother standing at the washbasin, obviously ill. She fainted and fell, and in so doing her head hit the basin; this brought her to full consciousness, and she managed to walk to bed. Being only five years old and healthy, I soon fell asleep. I never told Mother what I had seen. Could this episode also have influenced my choice of career?

Mother married Charles Maxwell Sears of Boston in 1912, and Jane and I were the flower girls. Daddy had told Mother's friends that he married her because anyone with two such pretty and good daughters could not be all bad. The family was complete by 1913 when my stepbrother, given the difficult name Zenas, was born. Daddy Sears, as we called him, made us all happy. He was a most unusual man. Born in the Boston House of Correction (his Grandfather Robbins was in charge) in 1870, he was educated at Boys' Latin School and studied long enough at Massachusetts Institute of Technology to learn the cotton textile business. He married early, but his first wife died shortly thereafter of tuberculosis. He returned to Boston and lived with his father in a pleasant boarding house in Arlington, the same house to which my mother came to live in 1911 with my sister and me, aged four and five.

Happy years of childhood followed. World War I broke out, and my parents plunged into civic activities. We went to all sorts of dancing and sewing classes but not Sunday school of which Daddy did not approve and kept us at home to teach us himself.

Happier and healthier years followed the dreadful influenza epidemic of 1918. Mother lost a ten-month-old son and a sister. Countrywide, people had been affected by the epidemic, and by that summer relief and rejoicing were reflected in parties and holidays. Mother continued to have sick headaches (probably migraine), and my sister had bronchitis each winter. Brother Zenas grew strong and successful, but until he was in his teens, he was sickly and we had a nurse in our home for long periods. I was ill at times, sometimes severely, with the usual childhood diseases. Obviously, our family needed a resident physician, a role I came to fill.

My sister, only 14 months younger than I, is physically and temperamentally so different that strangers wonder whether we are related. In her youth she was fair, resembling Daddy Sears, although unrelated by blood, while Mother and I were sallow with brown eyes and very black hair. For sister Jane a maternal instinct and her nursing skills became clear as she helped her little brother and patiently bore the role of acting as a patient for me, playing doctor. Although not a strong person, she became a kindergarten teacher. She married in 1948 and gave birth to a healthy boy at the age of 42. Her fortitude, in spite of emphysema, and her patience and generosity are remarkable. Zenas made an interesting place for himself in owning a radio broadcast station in Atlanta, its programs entirely meant for black people. Daddy Sears died in 1946, my mother in 1953.

Early Education

My four years from age 14 to age 18 were spent at a private boarding school, Kent Place, which prepared students for college or served as a "finishing school." Kent Place served me well. It was run by two aging, well-educated gentlewomen, working under the ancient motto "Manners Maketh Man." I developed real interest in ancient and modern European history and English composition and literature. While I managed to reach passing marks, I found nothing exciting about Latin, French, mathematics, or chemistry, all needed for medical school. In the final year, each student was required to hand in each day an original English composition, which could be as short as one sentence or as long as one desired. I believe this exercise led to my pleasure in writing, which has lasted through the years.

In 1924 I entered Wellesley College. I found many attractive extracurricular outlets for my energy—student government affairs (on-campus smoking was under discussion), golf, crew. Then a short talk with the academic dean cast a clear light on the need for me to take my studies seriously. When I arrived at her office, she immediately asked, "Miss Hardy, do you plan to enter medicine?" When I answered that I did, she asked, "When will you begin to study?" I view this taut session as a great favor. I began to study and graduated in 1928 as president of my class and was voted most popular in my class. I realize now how broad was my opportunity to taste the wealth of the world's knowledge and beauty through the study of literature, music, and philosophy, riches I took from Wellesley College.

REFERENCES

1. Hardy, H. C., and Hardy, E. N., Hardy and Hardie—Past and Present, Syracuse, N.Y., Syracuse Typesetters, 1935, privately published.

CHAPTER 2

Medical Education (1928–34)

Cornell Medical School

In the fall of 1928 I entered Cornell Medical School in New York City. Four "hen medics," as we were scornfully called, lived in a third-floor modest apartment, a hand-me-down from older, now graduated medical students. We lived on $4 per week, and, lacking refrigeration, our milk and butter were kept fresh on the ironwork of the fire escape outside the kitchen. At the time our domestic plan seemed simple, easy, and pleasant. My mother came for one of our corned beef and cabbage dinners. After looking around the apartment and sniffing the air, she said to me, "Harriet, don't you want to come home?" This is a good place to include mention of the fact that the family opposed my plan to become a doctor, although once convinced of my determination, I had their backing. I was greatly helped by two older physicians who summered, as we did, in the beautiful village of marble sidewalks and maple trees, Dorset, Vermont. One was the late Dr. David Houston, a contemporary of Sir William Osler in Canada, a surgeon, and a Shakespearian scholar; the other was the late Dr. Richard Pierce, a pathologist and, by the 1920s, the chief coordinator of the distribution of Rockefeller funds for medicine. These two giants took the trouble during their holiday to talk with Mother and my unusual stepfather, urging that I be allowed to go to medical school.

The curriculum of medical education from 1928 to 1932 was very different from the current enthusiasm for electives, microbiology, and laboratory research. Anatomical dissection of a human, required delivery of babies at home, study of public health problems such as sewage treatment and pasteurization, and autopsy room pathologic study are examples from my schedule. Everyone thinks his training is the best, and so I felt about mine. I submit that basic knowledge of the human body, its function, and its reaction to insult by morbid and physiologic change must be part of the student's equipment before he elects this or that specialty. I recall with anger one of today's fourth-year students who said he elected a term course that I gave in occupational lung disease because he knew nothing about the lung. The nature of his questions confirmed his ignorance.

The long hours in laboratory and dissecting room and preexamination nights of cramming hoards of facts into our brains made the life of the medical student odd and tiring. Occasional visits to the country and good theater and music were important antidotes. And most of us women students made time to fall in and out of love with our male colleagues.

In this decade of action to help women as a minority group, remarks have been made to me such as, "Surely you must have been one of the first women to practice medicine in America," which shows ignorance of the facts. A few individuals stand out in history; however, it is true that few females tried to enter medical school until late in the nineteenth century. For the period I know best the average number of women accepted in U.S. medical schools was 15 percent of the suitable applicants.

There was no ill will or unfair treatment of the six women in my class by administrative officers, faculty, or fellow students. We were deprived of only two activities enjoyed by our male colleagues. One, we were left behind when they as a group went to a burlesque, striptease show. Two, although required by the tax-free status of Cornell to study military science, including such important matters as how to dig a latrine and how to hold an umbrella over the colonel's hat, we women were left in New York City when the men went for two weeks' training in an army camp. A few of us went to the dean to protest mildly, little guessing that this action was a slight rumbling of things to come in the late 1960s.

In 1928 I joined for a few miles a torchlight procession of citizens walking along "our" street, East 19th Street, in New York, protesting the fact that Al Smith met severe opposition to his candidacy for president of the United States because he was a practicing Roman Catholic. So I participated in this now-common student behavior of protest. It is well to record that my senior guide, Dr. Alice Hamilton, nearly lost her professorship at Harvard Medical School when she helped Herbert Hoover in his work as a Quaker in the feeding of German children after World War I. She also was a leader of the U.S. citizens who felt keenly that Sacco and Vanzetti did not receive a fair trial before being executed as Communists in 1927.

By the third year of medical school, we were considered equipped to examine patients, since we had been taught the detail of medical history taking and the many mysteries of physical examination during which enlarged hearts and livers were to be discovered. An indelible impression was made on me by a first, surprisingly simple, quiet, and frail Chinese patient whose arms were covered with scars of needle punctures from drug addiction. I asked him to show me his teeth. He slowly got out of bed as he was weak and ill, turned to his bedside table, opened a drawer, and from a dirty handkerchief drew his dentures and handed them to me for inspection. I never asked about teeth again but when required, merely grinned, asked the patient to open his mouth, and produced the ever-ready wooden tongue depressor.

To this year also belongs the experience of visiting the autopsy room for training in the critical discipline of correlating the clinical diagnosis with the postmortem findings. In the United States in recent years, the autopsy rate has gone down; even more alarming to me is the fact that my younger colleagues tell me there is no need for postmortem study because of the excellent noninvasive techniques available for antemortem diagnosis. Quite the contrary. I cannot believe that tiny bits of biopsied tissues, x-ray shadows, computerized laboratory studies, and electrically traced heart action records, with certainty make a diagnosis in all cases. Thus, lacking the pathologic data, assessment of diagnosis and therapy may not be possible.

I can easily recall the smell of the Bellevue Hospital autopsy room in 1931 and my reaction to the cutting and bleeding. My current beau entered with me once, and pride kept me from showing him my distaste for the scene. He had asked me for lunch after the autopsy; I doubt that he ever bought a less expensive lunch, for my meal was a glass of water.

Finally, the fourth year introduced the variety of medical specialties. We had an out-patient apprenticeship with teaching by clinicians, and we were allowed to have "private patients," since we took medical histories and performed physical examinations. I distinguished myself by using a tongue depressor on a child in search of his tonsils so vigorously that he coughed in my face. I contracted scarlet fever and was sent home in a rage to be in bed for four weeks. In 1932 scarlet fever, now long gone, was a serious matter with frequent heart and kidney complications. In the neurotic, hypochondriacal fashion of medical students, who briefly suffer every disease under study, I recall that once back at work for a time I ran as fast as I could once or twice a day, taking my pulse before and after. By this awkward, unscientific experience I intended to discover whether my heart had been damaged! Since it is now more than 40 years since these events took place, it is safe to conclude that there was no heart damage.

Meanwhile, the Great Depression had cracked our comfortable way of life at home. Daddy had launched a new business in 1926: air conditioning installation in Baltimore, Maryland. The concept was needed and new then, now commonplace. After initiating and developing the project and contracting for manpower and equipment, Daddy's assets vanished. The sheriff came to our home, now in Baltimore, to take our fine antique furniture to pay bills. Mother halted this with her inherited money. Events such as these were taking place all over the world, and Daddy had a not unusual reaction. He became a socialist in his political thinking. Eventually, he persuaded the Brookings Institution in Washington, D.C., to support him while he worked out a plan for the collection and distribution of milk to the children of a great city. He took Cleveland, Ohio, for his study. All these attempts at earning money were failures, so he and Mother set about and succeeded in using our summer home in Vermont — saved in Mother's name by the help of a friend — as a guest house. Daddy taught himself to be an elegant cook. Mother, the housekeeper, taught two untrained, irresponsible 15-year-old girls to clean, make beds, and wash dishes. Daddy cooked and washed up, put on a good jacket, and was host, enjoying his own food.

During these years and later, in contrast to the luxurious summers we had spent earlier, after the onslaught of the Great Depression the summers were spent earning. During three summers I served as doctor-in-residence in girls' camps, carrying out a curious mixture of duties. One season my job was to pasteurize raw milk by heating it to the right temperature, then plunging the milk can into the wonderfully cold water of our spring. Twice, I had to act as a practical doctor in treating camp cooks and, by "curing" them, persuaded them to stay at their jobs. On one occasion a small flying insect got deep in the cook's ear, and the buzzing drove him to near panic until I pulled it out. The second crisis was the true emergency of a ruptured appendix, which I fortunately recognized. A rather humiliating part of one summer was teaching campers to make beds correctly as a requirement of first aid. My sister thought this was hilarious since my bed at home never passed inspection. The last summer I worked in a camp, my job was marred by a mumps epidemic, and I was an early victim. Confidently I treated the girls by having the very competent camp nurse bring the sick or wounded to my cabin window where she and I decided necessary treatment.

By my fourth year at Cornell, our family finances were at their lowest ebb, owing to the Great Depression. By chance, a young graduate passed along to me her job as a resident doctor in the Brooklyn Salvation Army Hospital for Foundlings. I was paid $40 per month plus board and room, riches for a student of 1931. I went by subway to medical school every day. Hanging onto a strap from the subway ceiling, I kept abreast of the too exciting daily news and book and theater reviews, as we lurched through the switches and stops, the water of New York Harbor above.

I was much impressed by the excellence of the nurses in the homeopathic Salvation Army hospital. The medical staff served chiefly by phone and took my word for symptom and diagnosis. They prescribed bryonia and aconite for rape or head cold. By such therapy, no one was hurt no matter what the diagnosis. I came to respect the Salvation Army staff, from the colonel in charge to the lowliest scrub woman. All children under seven years left at our door or in a subway station or brought in by police or neighbor were welcomed, washed, fed, and put to bed, often with a warm embrace.

While this schedule with long evening hours of study kept me from most of the social life of medical students, it taught me much of infant care under a variety of handicaps. For example, every newly arrived infant — and these ranged from less than an hour old to a few days old — had to have study of smears from eye and vagina for the presence of gonorrhea. These studies I did in a modest laboratory with no senior to check my findings. The pressure for haste and accuracy arose from the ease with which gonococci could cause irreversible damage in this preantibiotic period. It is grim to realize that only war with its sick soldiers could force the research interest and the financial support needed to discover agents powerful enough to cure this age-old, damaging venereal disease.

Pathos was a real element in the Salvation Army hospital where there was unquestioning faith. For example, a kitchen helper came to see me one evening, upset because her monthly period had stopped. She said, "He seemed kind and then he took me to his room. When he let me go, he gave me a dollar and told me to tell no one." Inexperienced as I was, I told her that her menses would start within a week. A few days later, a crumpled note lay at my place at the dinner table, reading, "It came," a confirmation of my diagnosis of anxiety.

With my mind prepared by genetic gifts and a well-fertilized environment, I began to ask myself questions. The more than 100 children under seven years of age at the shelter being handled in similar fashion as to diet, rest, and training, and coming from unknown hereditary backgrounds, appeared to me to be ideal sampling with which to study the fascinating questions revolving around heredity and environment. I was sure I could spot a future enemy of society or a docile nonentity. I had neither the time nor the knowledge to study these fundamental matters, but as the years go by the original question remains and has cropped up in every form in my future. I shall be ever grateful that New York State law prevented me from adopting an orphan to study and protect, a boy named Clifford. Even for science I doubt that the misery Clifford and I would have caused each other would have been worth the possible scientific findings.

Preparing to graduate from Cornell and the Salvation Army hospital and temporarily very knowing, I invited my mother and stepfather to go on so-called evening rounds with the head nurse and me to see the sickest infants. As we approached the crib of an emaciated few-days-old baby, my mother said in a voice to be heard throughout the ward, "Harriet, aren't you going to call a doctor?" She was not asked a second time.

Philadelphia General Hospital

The next step in training was to persuade a teaching hospital to employ me for a period of apprenticeship variously called internship or residency, depending upon length of service and success in the opinion of the senior staff. I was fortunate in winning a 24-month rotating internship at the Philadelphia General Hospital (PGH), formerly known as Old Blockley, claimed to be the oldest hospital in the United States, whose operation began in the late eighteenth century as an almshouse. At this time an internship at PGH was very desirable; there were a total of 70 positions available, 35 positions being granted every 12 months. Of the 70 there were 10 women. Because of the large number of applicants, successful candidates were chosen by medical school standing, a written examination, and finally an interview with two senior staff members. I had an amusing adventure during my interview because, I believe, of my Puritan background and the parental discipline I received. A group of us were sitting outside the interviewer's door, awaiting our turn. We learned that one question was asked of each candidate: What is a Pott's fracture? I was reasonably sure of the answer — tuberculosis of the bone. However, one of the candidates had a text handy and read aloud the full answer. When it was my turn, I said to the interviewer, without pausing to consider that I might harm my fellow applicants, "It is easy to answer that since someone has just read the description of Pott's fracture from a textbook." Dr. S. laughed and said to his fellow interviewer, "My God, an honest woman — let's take her." And for the next two years whenever we met, Dr. S. would ask me how the honest woman was progressing.

    Then followed a period of such strenuous effort, physically, mentally, and emotionally, as I had never imagined. We were on duty 36 out of 48 hours, free for one month a year during which I worked as a camp doctor to help my younger sister and brother with their education. I lost 45 pounds and my appendix in this period. Three of my 35 classmates developed tuberculosis, and one a peptic ulcer. There was no good reason for this killing pace. More interns might have been appointed. The city of Philadelphia housed and fed us and gave us less than $100 for two years' work. The faculties of the University of Pennsylvania, Jefferson Medical College, and the Women's Medical College used the hospital for teaching in which we house officers participated. In spite of the hectic pace, we learned a great deal of pathophysiology, developed diagnostic acumen, and learned the limits of therapeutics and, more important, the personal frustration of failure to save or relieve suffering patients.

This was a period of world misery due to economic depression. The election of Franklin D. Roosevelt did much to cheer, but poverty did not cease all at once. The Eighteenth Amendment prohibiting sale of alcoholic beverages led to miseries that were reflected in our Emergency Ward population. There were frozen necrotic fingers and toes; there were men drunk from consuming antifreeze, their wife's perfume, sterno for cooking, or other fluids containing methyl alcohol, which is deadly to the vision. Riding ambulance, I visited "flophouses" where for eight cents a man could get a bowl of something called soup, which was contaminated with some type of alcohol, and for the same fee sleep clinging to a rope. Is this sleeping by hanging on a rope the origin of the term *flophouse*? Most of the ambulance drivers were brave and thoughtful men, with some acquired medical knowledge. They warned us of signs of impending disaster to the patient, which we were too inexperienced to notice. They stood guard against mean drunken men when we were called to a flophouse to decide whether a patient with delirium tremens also had pneumonia and should be hospitalized. But by 1933 sera with antibodies against certain pneumonias were available, and the sulfonamide drugs were under trial. Occasionally, the ambulance driver and I helped a policeman to deliver a baby. From experience and good nature these drivers helped to teach us how to assess a home situation as it affected diagnosis and prognosis. Most ambulance drivers also warned of rodents, fleas, and bedbugs nearby and suggested that we sleep enroute to answer a call at a distance. Such training must be rare today. If available, is it in the list of electives? The benefits from ambulance duty are twofold: it provides the opportunity to obtain firsthand knowledge of the home from which the patient comes and to develop skills in swift, accurate observation, leading to wise decision on action to be taken.

The two-year internship at the PGH included two months each of surgery, neurology, psychiatry, dermatology, clinical pathology, gross pathology and autopsy service, pediatrics, infectious disease, tuberculosis, obstetrics, and gynecology and four months of internal medicine. Medical educators of today would consider, with some justification, that such a series of short-term exposures to a variety of fields is quite useless. My answer is that this program made one alert to possible specialties from which to choose. In addition, should circumstances lead one to a general practice, as in my case, the physician would know how and where to seek, as required, more information or would recognize the limits of his skill, thus protecting the patient from harm.

The insight into the human behavior of the sick, dying, troubled, and underprivileged gained by one coming from a comfortable, privileged home as I did was almost overwhelming. I write of a few episodes to illustrate this — examples novel to me and unforgettable. One night on obstetrical duty with a colleague, I was called to help with an 18-year-old girl giving birth out of wedlock to her first child. In a pause between labor pains, she said to me, "Doctor, if this is what it's like being engaged, I'll never get married." What does one do in the face of such abysmal ignorance: laugh or cry? On another occasion in the same room, I arrived in time to cut the umbilical cord wound tightly around a baby's neck. In filling out the birth registration form, I asked for the newborn's name and the mother asked mine. Saying mine was a pretty name, she had me write Harriet Louise Hardy Jones, her seventh child. I asked Mrs. Jones why she allowed herself to have a baby each year. She answered without self-pity, "This is how I get my vacation." At that period a newly delivered mother remained in the hospital for two weeks.

During my two months of service on the infectious disease ward, two crises arose that need never recur because of the availability today of vaccines. The first was a peak occurrence of diphtheria with cases of severe swelling of the throat and tonsils so severe that surgical incision of the trachea (windpipe) and rapid insertion of a proper tube were required to prevent suffocation. The second, more serious crisis was an outbreak among Philadelphia children of the dreaded poliomyelitis for which we had no specific treatment in 1932. To prevent spread of the disease, one ward was isolated for polio cases. Nurses and interns drew lots for places in the polio ward. I drew the job of the polio ward doctor and learned how hard one can work. We had a few artificial respirators, hardly helpful because of the cruel choice of deciding which panting child to "save." I did manual artificial respiration to exhaustion, as did nurses. One desperate effort at more specific treatment was to take a sample of blood from the father and inject it into the sick child's muscles. The idea was that the father had developed immune material, which was carried by his blood, as a result of earlier exposure to polio. I can see and feel today the heat of July 1932 in the room full of anxious sweating fathers who stopped on their way to work to give blood for their children. A number fainted and, as they returned to consciousness, blushed furiously for what seemed to them a shameful lack of manhood. When my term was ended, I went to bed to sleep. I had been aware of backache and headache, which seemed at the time due simply to fatigue. As I returned to work, I felt unusually hot and discovered I had an elevation in temperature. In a few days this passed, to be replaced by slight weakness of the right leg, which persists, causing only a difference in wear on shoes and an occasional unexpected stumble.

Once a month each resident was on call all night to pronounce patients' deaths when telephoned by a nurse-supervisor. During such duty one might document as few as 5 or 10 deaths or more than 20. Such experience gave one the opportunity to study and puzzle over the age-old mystery of physical death. An older colleague dying of a painful cancer put well the thinking of a mentally alert physician near death: "Harriet, I am about to learn the answers to the great questions." These reflections, recalling the number of patient deaths I had witnessed in a large city hospital, lead me to report the strong impression I had gained that the dead human face appears quietly at peace, with an expression suggesting — often with a slight smile — that death had brought knowledge denied the living. I never saw the terrified, horrorstruck faces of the dead reported in books.

The two months of service on the pediatric wards I found more emotionally tiring than night duty pronouncing deaths. The helplessness of the sick children and the far-too-frequent failures of the doctor to cure or even relieve were frustrating. A child with an enormous head (hydrocephalus) was admitted. This was due to a congenital defect causing blockage of the fluid within, and all one could do was a lumbar puncture to draw off excess fluid and hopefully prevent brain damage. In the years since 1934 technical advances in head surgery have changed this picture. A needless childhood death was that of a boy who stepped on a barnyard nail. He was brought to the hospital with the dreaded "lockjaw." Since he had had no tetanus vaccine or antitoxin, all we could do was try to control the muscle spasm with drugs, which finally ended in death. I use these two episodes to describe my experiences. Any resident in any acute hospital in the world may work with equally difficult problems, but outcomes will differ because of advances in surgery and the worldwide use of vaccines.

Psychiatric experiences at PGH dealt with serious psychoses. Fortunately, several older, experienced consultants took the time and care to teach and guide us through this unsettling period. It appeared to me that the patients were caricatures of friends and quite ordinary people whom one might pass on the street. Twice I carried this simplistic notion too far. Patients so sick that they might harm themselves or others were locked in wards into which we were told never to go alone. One evening, anxious to see a patient who had swallowed carbolic acid in a suicidal attempt, I entered alone with my key. It was my good luck that a well-trained orderly looked into the ward and saw a demented patient attacking me from behind with hands just reaching my throat.

A second surprise was waiting for me when I approached a maniacal patient in a bathtub filled with lukewarm water to calm her. She was restrained by a canvas cover. I did not notice her pull her lower jaw down, and in no time she spat a great deal of water over me. In my ignorance I had thought she and I were "friends." And one pathetic, catatonic old woman who was hallucinating called me to her side every day so I could put my ear to hers and hear the Virgin Mary, who the patient knew was sitting in her ear, speaking. This two-month stretch affected me strangely and forcibly. Why did medicine know so little of the chemistry of the brain? How narrow is the gap between the thought leading to action in the so-called normal and in the mad human about whose treatment we know so pitifully little!

In 1934 our therapy consisted of such simple measures as providing the soothing baths mentioned and producing a high fever by intravenous doses of dead typhoid organisms. Since then, electric shock of the brain, a wide variety of drugs, and the skillful use of analytic and nonanalytic techniques to work through the problems of less sick patients (called psychoneurotics) make up today's approach to treatment. As I write and recall the two months caring for psychotic patients, I realize that I lived through a mild depression caused by fatigue plus empathy with the plight of the patients, leading to loss of appetite, failure to initiate, a desire to rest—all symptoms new to me. This experience was a shadow of things to come to me, which I did not recognize and which I suspect most physicians, frustrated by lack of the weapons to cure, endure at some time in training or practice.

A few months before leaving Philadelphia General Hospital, I indulged in a short period of self-study in April 1934. I appear to have decided—from notes made at the time—to become a practitioner of medicine, not a medical scientist. The gratitude of patients, and their requests that they be assigned to my care, was rich food for my ego. I was touched to tears by Father O'Malley's farewell when he said, "South Philadelphia is full of people who pray for you in gratitude." I soon learned that such praise is dangerous, leading to the conviction that one is omniscient.

Slowly a picture of the needs of clinical medicine took shape, and I knew I had chosen the right career. As I grow older, the details of a sophisticated physical examination elude both my skill and my interest, but the treasures from taking a subtle and complete history cannot be exaggerated. The challenge of making a large part of the diagnosis by acute observation and patient conversation remains as my gift. I have learned to make myself welcome practically inside the patient's skin, free to learn or sense what the basis of his complaints is and the complexities of his unique problem. It is experience, and the wish to know the patient's needs, that makes the practice of clinical medicine valuable to the patient and rewarding to the physician. I think many practitioners would agree that the technical tricks of great accuracy available in modern medicine are driving patient and doctor farther and farther away from that intimacy required to serve the sick man's best interests.

CHAPTER 3

First Medical Practice

The Northfield School

What to do next was in the buzz of every conversation. I had intended to become a pediatrician, and the Philadelphia General Hospital (PGH) had agreed to a third year of training to be devoted entirely to this subject. Fortune intervened in three ways. First, our family finances in 1934 were at a very low ebb. Second, a friendly, well-dressed young woman came looking for a woman physician for Northfield Seminary for Girls located in western Massachusetts. Third, Dr. Turnbull, the wise PGH superintendent, told me, "Dr. Hardy, you will be a fool if you do not take the Northfield job."

A trip to Northfield convinced me. The natural beauty of the campus, my beloved Green Mountains of Vermont visible in the west, and the waters of the Connecticut River sparkling below were seductive. The obvious need of the school for medical help and the quality of those who interviewed me convinced me to start in September 1934 with a salary of $1,400 per year plus board and lodging.

My arrival to begin work at Northfield school — 500 girls — and to serve as relief doctor at Mt. Hermon Academy, the related school of 500 boys, was marked by the dramatic fatal shooting of the headmaster of Mt. Hermon. My male colleague at the boys' school was out of town, and my first hours at the seminary were as exciting as the hospital emergency ward, as I tried to answer questions and spread calm without any real knowledge of what had happened.

My job was to establish a small, first-class medical unit to care for students — and faculty if they wished — and make decisions on handling of injuries of workmen or neighbors. We had an infirmary capable of holding 20 patients, a clinic, and a small laboratory, with space to talk privately. Before my arrival two nurses had handled the medical work, calling the Mt. Hermon physician or local doctors if needed. I found that my breezy, self-assured hospital resident manner was not wholly welcome, and perhaps it was my fault that after a trial year the nursing staff departed.

I learned many useful ways of handling minor ills and injuries that were unknown to acute hospital care. For complete recovery, common painful accidents such as a sprained ankle or knee require far more sophisticated (yet simple) therapy directly after the injury than a medical student or hospital intern dreams possible. The adjustment problems of adolescents required new study on my part, and I had conferences with the head of the school and a psychologist who visited once a week. Acute appendicitis was the most serious medical threat, because there were as yet no antibiotics other than sulfonamides and they had limitations. Further, the nearest hospital was 15 miles away, and on a winter night, with slippery roads and the limits of the 1934 automobiles, sophisticated judgment was required when a diagnosis was in question. Repeated white blood cell counts and abdominal examination as careful as my medical chief at Cornell had described, plus conferences with my colleagues at Mt. Hermon, prevented the feared rupture of the appendix, with its true risk to life.

Emergencies new to me made me think how to prepare for and handle such events. A young, innocent faculty member was aggressively raped. A new student drowned in the indoor seminary pool — an event that took place because her family had decided not to tell the school she had epilepsy. Left behind in a dressing room after she had a seizure, she became confused and walked into the pool; she was not missed until dinner. One year a student government officer, disliked by her fellow students because of her harsh disciplinary measures for minor offenses, was so visibly pregnant that I drove the now-silent girl to her home for the sake of peace at the school as well as proper care for her. Working alone in most cases, I was grateful for my rigorous PGH training and my own self-confidence. The common cold, an occasional case of contagious disease like mumps (which our unit could isolate), adolescent skin disease, rarely a case of lobar pneumonia with a long convalescence, plus a variety of lacerations, bruises, and fractures kept the unit active. I shudder to think of the old x-ray equipment housed in the dormitory basement. The Mt. Hermon physician and I took our own x-rays and developed and interpreted them, ignorant of the danger from radiation exposure to patient and ourselves. Today modern radiation protection is required by physicists as a result of development of atomic energy for military use.

At Northfield I made my first feeble attempt at clinical investigation. My idea came from my urge to observe human material — the students — and to ask questions of myself and other medically trained persons who were willing to listen. I tried to ask the right questions of myself and others, then look hard at the evidence, and decide with honesty whether the questions were answered. These concepts had come from my seniors in medical school or hospital training. This attitude has persisted in me through the years from the small medical world of a boarding school to my later professional work in larger spheres. Both brought great satisfaction.

This faint beginning of clinical investigation was directed to the reasons for the wide variation in endocrine function of the 500 adolescent girls I cared for. They were all exposed to the same environment, food, climate, housing, athletic effort, and stress of study. I was fortunate to be able to consult with Dr. Richard Smith, our medical trustee, and a Boston endocrinologist who was studying similar questions in hens. I made no earthshaking discoveries, but by collecting data in an orderly fashion I could say with certainty that students whose homes were farther than 200 miles from the school had less menstrual irregularities and distress than did those living nearby. In addition, from histories given by students (1934–37), I began to see the now well-established fact that menstrual periods and therefore ovulation occurred at a younger age than was reported in textbooks on the subject at that time.

Missing the stimulus of medical study, I spent the summer of 1935, through the courtesy of Dr. Eugene Opie, at Cornell Medical School. My long-held notion was that there was a lack of correlation of clinical course revealed in medical records with autopsy findings in cases of heart disease. By such study I felt that clinical diagnosis and prognosis would be improved. The modest paper was never submitted for publication, but rereading its yellowing pages underlines the tremendous advances made in cardiology by technical wizardry and drugs. A few scraps of value appear in the paper that relate to autopsy findings, and one wonders if the current medical craze for use of electronic devices, catheterization, and radioactive isotopes will provide the whole pathophysiologic picture without autopsy. The decline in autopsy rate is striking today, and the spectrum of diagnostic studies most often chosen is now noninvasive, which often misses underlying cause.

Private Practice

By 1935 I had persuaded the seminary principal that I could carry on the school work and develop a small local medical practice, excluding obstetrics. I needed the money, as did everyone in those days; perhaps I could now make real a rosy dream of childhood by becoming a country doctor, no matter how modest the scale. And so I began. I bought white jackets, office supplies, pills, and an enormous sign picturing a horse and buggy doctor, with my name, bought for $100 from a young hungry-looking salesman, who added the 50 volumes of Dr. Eliot's *Five Foot Shelves* for nothing. My landlady would not let me hang the sign, so it rested in the cellar. For a few dollars I had a wooden board made, which was stuck in the ground and simply painted with my name: H. L. Hardy, M.D. My patients came from school faculty, maintenance staff, and the surrounding community. My fees were modest: 50 cents for an office call, $1 for a house call, and $2 for a call to the local hotel or after midnight. Before long I was too busy to get sufficient rest, and I fell behind in my resolution to keep abreast of medical progress by attention to medical journals and a monthly trip to Boston to visit the grand rounds of the great teaching hospitals.

The joys of such a practice in the country must be experienced to be understood. I had a Model A Ford roadster open to the breezes and sometimes − 20° weather, equipped with a fabric brake lining in which the snow melted by friction and then froze. I carried a hammer to knock out enough ice to allow the car to move. What a properly humiliating position for a dignified, well-trained physician trying to establish a practice!

I acquired a black bag to carry stethoscope and other tools of my trade as well as a variety of drugs carefully chosen as unlikely to harm. Boldly, because of distance to hospital, and patients' fear of implied prognosis and costs, I carried a variety of ampules of concentrated dextrose to do procedures in the home that today would only be done in well-equipped hospitals. I drew abnormal fluids from chest and abdominal cavities and incised local abscesses and bulging eardrums. In certain ways we have come full circle, for modern data suggest that such procedures are most successful when performed away from the hospital where there is exposure to a variety of bacteria not present in the home. Underlying the outcome of my work in the country was the privilege of knowing, by seeing firsthand, the patient's daily environment, both physical and emotional. Since World War II most practitioners insist on handling patients in office or hospital, missing too often, I believe, the clue to the cause of patient complaints — poor food handling, chronic exposure to carbon monoxide from a stove, self-medication, or a sick husband or elderly parent at home.

Life was not dull. I learned to barter and took potatoes or repair of my car as payment for my work. I visited one elderly woman with pneumonia. As I finished my work, her family asked my fee. I said, "One dollar," and was asked to turn my back. Shortly afterward, I was given a $100 bill, which the bank found to be of Civil War vintage. It appeared from under the patient's mattress.

My office practice was the usual routine of preschool examinations and vaccinations, upper respiratory infections, painful "flat" feet, and nonspecific skin lesions. Pityriasis rosea was the exception. An itching rash, preceded by a quarter-sized "herald" spot, covered the body except for face and hands. I was proud to be able to make the diagnosis and assure the patients that the miserable rash would disappear in six weeks to six months.

The most difficult group, and the largest, as all doctors know, are those with no detectable disease but a list of complaints. Serious disease may be masked, or patients' lifelong habits of worry and self-contemplation may create a picture that causes the most patient and skillful physician to have difficulty reaching a wise and helpful course of action. Knowledge of the home life and past history gained by my house calls was invaluable. I read Havelock Ellis, among others, for help in learning and teaching different interpretations of complaints. Best of all was the help I received from my friend, the experienced senior medical consultant to both schools, Dr. Robert McCastline, who had been forced to retire from a busy New York practice by ill health after the influenza epidemic of 1918. The Chief, as I knew him, had never stopped studying history and philosophy, as well as medicine. If I thought I heard a pericardial rub or evidence of pneumonia, Dr. McCastline would pick up his stethoscope and join me to provide both support and vigorous discussion of the findings. We two found time to use Darwin's ideas of natural selection in understanding our patients' maladies and reactions to stress as either genetic faults or educational or social failures.

This was a rich postgraduate training in the handling of both simple day-by-day problems and the more complex care of chronic and acute cases of illness for which there was no specific treatment. I learned to use several of the Chief's vivid dicta, one being, "The well-trained doctor knows what to do for his patient; the especially well-trained doctor knows what *not* to do." A second rule followed Hippocrates: "If you cannot cure your patient, you are bound to relieve his suffering." This last dictum is under a cloud of uncertainty today since fear of patient addiction and libel suits weigh on a practitioner's judgment. My inheritance from the Chief reinforced my own conviction of duty to the patient, which has led me to keep terminally ill patients at home if possible, to order morphine by the clock in cases of malignancy when radiation or chemotherapy fails, and to stop oxygen in suffocating victims who are dying of chronic pulmonary failure.

During these years an old resident with polycythemia vera, who had become a friend, told me that the townspeople were divided as to whether I knew anything. One group, seeing medical books in my waiting room, said I "had to look everything up." The other group thought me wise not to "pretend I knew everything."

A vivid memory is of a young man at the end of the line in my waiting room during a busy afternoon. At last he alone remained. When I asked if he wanted to see me, he shrugged, blushed, and walked bent over into my office. After a long talk he said he had a "bellyache" and could not work. I persuaded him to sit up on the examining table, take off his shirt, and unfasten his belt. At this he looked toward the door and muttered, "I didn't know from your sign 'H. L. Hardy, M.D.,' that you were a lady doctor." By now I knew his trouble—two large inguinal hernias. I persuaded him to agree to surgery, which completely cured him. He apparently spread the word that Dr. Hardy "undresses you." This told me something about the practices of my local colleagues. As the only physician in that county of 52,000 people who could write a pediatric formula and who could and would fit diaphragms for birth control, I received a number of referrals, and my experience broadened.

Some teaching of female anatomy and problems of venereal disease to the seminary girls, talks to groups for the Massachusetts Cancer Society, and work with the county Society for the Prevention of Cruelty to Children (SPCC) rounded out my busy Northfield days. Work with the SPCC was grim, showing me real poverty and malnutrition and incest with visible mental retardation. I persuaded the local medical society to allow me to start a pediatric clinic, a labor that over the years under the leadership of Dr. Merritt Low has become a flourishing first-class operation. Permission to start the clinic was granted with the proviso that the family doctor refer patients to me. There was to be no payment, and the SPCC would underwrite hospital overhead. This was one of the first rounds in my battle with overreactionary, backward-looking factions in organized medicine.

My personal life was at a turning point at this period. Although I had a happy social life, I kept finding reasons for refusing offers of marriage, just as I had done in medical school. I fell asleep one evening in the company of my favorite beau, to my chagrin, and I persuaded my housekeeper to lie for me when I wanted to escape the company of a persistent older man. I believe that I am truly wedded to medicine. I think now of a bright young female MIT student who was thinking of studying medicine. She told me of her ambition while talking to me in my role as premedical adviser at MIT. She suddenly said, "You never married?" When I answered, "No," she continued, "And you never had any babies?" Again a "No" answer led me to realize the difference in our ages and customs. Without the approval of sex practices of current times and because of my Puritan background, I was not faced with other choices. So while I had and have friends of both sexes, my primary allegiance is to medicine. For me at least, this has been utterly satisfying.

By the summer of 1938 I became aware that my stamina was not equal to my appetite for work and more knowledge. This period was the first rumbling of bouts with depression, doubtless due to fatigue. However, periods of unnecessary gloom have followed me through life. In helping me through these mists, Dr. McCastline suggested that I develop an essay on the Value of Illness, an exercise I still use.

Reading at meals and before sleep, with my telephone at hand, cases to see at a distance, patients ill enough to require home visits at night, regular duty for the seminary, some social life, some civic demands — all added up to a total that made itself felt. I was losing weight and appetite, and interruptions of sleep started the misery of insomnia that has plagued me ever since. An occasional week of low or definitely elevated temperature made me wonder if I had brucellosis from drinking raw milk, tuberculosis, or an unresolved pneumonia. I was sending money to my family, since the Great Depression had not passed. Thus my deliberate choices led to my chronic functional illness — I hope that others may learn from this, inwardly digest, and act more wisely.

After convalescence I realized it was time to consider what next step I might safely take in my medical career, a choice I had regretted or lost sight of in this low period. In fact, I think it is not too much to say that this "breakdown" with its fear of self-destruction made me a more sensitive physician. When I returned to Boston after recuperating on the West Coast, I found a job open that I might usefully and safely undertake. It had the grand title of Radcliffe College Physician and Head of the Department of Health Education. This I accepted and started work in the fall of 1939.

CHAPTER 4

Radcliffe (1939–45)

Increasing the Outpatient Facilities

I found that the facilities for medical care of students at Radcliffe College were similar to those at Northfield Seminary. A physician held office hours by day in a small unit in the gymnasium, and the responsibility for care outside these office hours was shared by two resident nurses. It soom became clear that Radcliffe needed a larger outpatient unit. In addition, a small number of beds was needed for acutely ill students: for students in winter when hospitals were crowded; for students returning from hospital life; or for sick students needing observation for a correct diagnosis, either medical or surgical.

With the great help from a trustee, Mrs. Dorothy Hall, a plan evolved for renovation of a beautiful, Radcliffe-owned nineteenth century home, spacious and structurally sound. Mrs. Hall's contribution was invaluable, for she had worked with architects to develop the Dick House at Dartmouth College in memory of her son who had died of poliomyelitis while an undergraduate. In addition to the time she gave to help Radcliffe, she was backing the project financially. The building came to be known as the Radcliffe Health Center, for no one liked the old term *infirmary* with its connotation of the feeble aged with chronic ills. The Health Center served its purpose well until the Harvard Medical Center was later ready to care for Radcliffe's medical problems. Unhappily (it seems to me), the handsome, graceful building that housed the Health Center was pulled down. Its place was taken by a huge pile of concrete, its exterior and interior designed to serve student dramatic activities.

President Ada Comstock reported, fairly, that the position of a full-time physician for Radcliffe was more the result of pressure from parents, alumnae, and trustees than her own choice. The administrative arrangements of Radcliffe with Harvard were odd indeed at that time. There was no Radcliffe faculty; Radcliffe had to arrange with individual Harvard faculty to give identical courses at Radcliffe, the fee to be settled course by course. The Harvard College Medical Department, well manned and with its own infirmary, was closed to Radcliffe students because of their sex. A curious snobbery persisted in Harvard's insistence that employees seeking medical help enter by a door separate from that used by students and faculty and be cared for by different doctors and nurses. I learned that this separation of the sexes and of what could be called social classes rested on the personal dicta of several Harvard presidents. No women were admitted to Harvard Medical or other graduate schools, with the exception of those few who received lowly graduate assistantships in some of the humanities departments and the School of Education. Radcliffe gave both master's and doctoral degrees, which brought some women rather close to Harvard.

The historic fact that began to move Radcliffe into Harvard University was World War II. The Harvard faculty, reduced in numbers, refused to give identical lectures to Radcliffe students, and classes including both sexes were begun by 1942. As most readers will know, Radcliffe gradually merged with Harvard. President Nathan Pusey's appointment in 1953 changed much of the duplication. It is correct to say that by the 1960s Radcliffe was coeducational.

My first duty in the fall of 1939 was to engage physicians, all of them women, to carry out medical history taking and physical examinations on entering students. Basic studies included chest x-ray, hemoglobin determination, and urinalysis. After the initial medical examination I reviewed the records plus the family doctor's opinion, which was sent to Radcliffe as part of the admission requirement, together with any notes from parents. I called students where action was requested or required as, for example, in cases of no smallpox vaccination, asthma requiring regular injections, mild anemia, diabetes, and epilepsy. I helped Radcliffe adopt the policy of admitting qualified students with chronic illness if family and doctor agreed — not a general policy in the early 1940s.

During the students' years at Radcliffe, with the above exceptions, the Radcliffe Medical Department expected students to ask for medical help when necessary. I went to the dormitories to see a sick student if asked by her, her friends, or the resident faculty. I also organized a scheme to have a committee of student government with frequently changing membership to report and receive complaints concerning the Radcliffe Medical Department. Finally, at the end of a student's years at Radcliffe, I offered a 30-minute conference. During this period I reviewed her medical record with her and taught her how to find medical help if she moved to a different community, while giving her the chance to ask questions. I often had the opportunity to talk about subjects such as anxiety about childbirth or breast cancer and fear of venereal disease from public toilets.

I must boast of a diagnostic triumph early in my Radcliffe period. A student came to see me, complaining of blinding headaches and projectile vomiting, signs of pressure within the brain. Promptly, Dr. Jason Mixter, the senior neurosurgeon at the Massachusetts General Hospital, removed a large, benign, orange-sized tumor. The student did well, returning for two academic degrees, and had a successful life as a journalist. During her hospital convalescence, Dr. Mixter tested her brain function soon after the anesthesia had worn off by asking, "M____, can you hear me?" She nodded. He continued, "My grandfather was a doctor, and my father and an uncle. My son and a nephew and their fathers are doctors. Isn't that remarkable?" After a pause, M____ answered, "The family is in a rut!"

After five years of studies of healthy girls aged 12 to 17 at Northfield and five years of examination of equally robust Radcliffe students aged 16 to 21, I came to the not-surprising conclusion that the usual physical examinations were, with rare exceptions, a waste of time, effort, and expense. What was needed to achieve good health for this group came chiefly from the family doctor, a parent, or our initial medical history taking. The medical department, meaning myself and the nurses, learned that minor or occasionally major illnesses occurred when the student was under stress. Such stresses included the rigorous Radcliffe-Harvard academic pace or the emotional strains of this highly charged atmosphere. These together with the pains of maturation produced a number of symptoms mimicking organic disease; sometimes bizarre syndromes exposed the physician to the functional background for the patient's discomfort.

President Ada Comstock agreed with me that prevention and early diagnosis of severe depression and recognition of the onset of a psychosis were worth careful handling. She allowed me to work out consultation with an accredited psychiatrist case by case. To preserve confidentiality, I alone knew which students accepted such help. The college paid the fee in confidence. If serious disease was discovered, varying methods of handling were explored with the student and, depending on the age of the patient, the family. With support from the Health Center and the student's ability and will to take counsel, this plan worked well. A worry was the presence in Cambridge of a number of so-called psychoanalysts, refugees from Vienna who by a sign in their windows advertised their relationship to Jung or Freud but who were in reality without valid training. In retrospect, I suspect that student visits to such pseudotherapists were chiefly learning experiences. It is a relief to report that with the support of our Medical Department and scattered advice from many sources there were no known suicides of Radcliffe students during my five-year tenure.

As at Northfield, I discovered ways to know my male colleagues practicing in the community of Cambridge. I asked for and received a courtesy staff appointment at nearby Mount Auburn Hospital where I admitted Radcliffe students who were too ill for the infirmary but not ill enough to transfer to a Boston hospital. After becoming a member of the county medical society, I found myself appointed to a committee pioneering in a health insurance plan for its members (1943). With the current talk of completely prepaid medical care insurance, the small group of us working 35 years ago with a small insurance company appears as a dot on the horizon.

I also helped the local tuberculosis association with their mobile chest x-ray program, intended for schools, colleges, and industrial groups. This procedure was abandoned after some years because of the hazard posed to those working in these units. In addition, the small x-ray films taken by these units failed to discover any but gross changes in heart and lungs. I personally learned much from the community and from the social life of Radcliffe students. At this time I came to favor outside medical responsibilities for school and college physicians to augment their primary work to help widen what can be a narrow horizon.

One example of my attitude was that after study of the structure of the American Medical Association (AMA), I found it such a narrow-minded, conservative group that I resigned my membership

(1943). I was later invited to give a major paper at one of their meetings, but I was not to be allowed to speak unless I rejoined the group. I, refusing to rejoin, told the committee that invited me that I had spoken to a union the night before, although not a member of *that* group, but this did not impress the AMA and I did not speak.

Grant Study

Eager to make more use of my medical knowledge and background and lonely for meetings with colleagues, I, by happy chance, came to know Dr. Arlie Bock, the Harvard student health director, also a practicing internist who had done valuable medical research. He generously opened two important doors for me, after saying, "By God, if you were only a man, I'd appoint you to my staff!" The first door he opened was to the Massachusetts General Hospital (MGH) in Boston, a distinguished hospital for the teaching and care of the sick. The authorities at Radcliffe allowed me to spend two half days per week in the Medical Outpatient Clinic, where I saw a wide variety of common ills, both acute and chronic, that were easily recognized, plus others of mysterious clinical character that required bed care and great study. These were happy, rewarding days for me, and they brought me into consultation with faculty members of the Harvard Medical School and the staff of the MGH. I think of Wyman Richardson, Fuller Albright, Chester Jones, and Donald King, to mention a few. For ten years I spent half days in the diabetes clinic, with Drs. Hurwitz and Harwood in charge, and learned much about this by-no-means-well-understood disease.

By late 1941 a Massachusetts General Hospital Unit had been called to active military duty. My introduction to my friend J. Howard Means came when he called together those of the staff left behind and remarked, "With the women and cripples, we'll get on." One of the women physicians on the staff (of whom there were less than ten) let us know that she did not appreciate Dr. Means's remark. Most of us thought he was wise in speaking lightly. At that date Harvard Medical School was not admitting women students or staff.

The second door Dr. Bock opened for me was as a visitor, and later a coworker, with the Great Study. This study, supported by W. T. Grant of the former department store of that name, undertook to examine, describe, and investigate all aspects of the so-called normal American male, as reflected in the Harvard undergraduate body. The study was prolonged into the adult lives of the student subjects, all volunteers. Data collected at Harvard were used to study such things as success and failure in college, sickness and health, and marriage and divorce patterns. The Grant Study was unique in the number and variety of indexes recorded. The staff included an internist, a social anthropologist, a physical anthropologist, a psychologist, a physiologist, a psychiatrist, and a supporting staff of statisticians, plus a social worker who visited the subjects once they had graduated. Once a week this staff met to discuss policy and report cases or series that suggested justifiable conclusions.

My reaction as a visitor to the Grant Study was pure pleasure after my own years of study alone of the "normal." I could see that there would be merit in applying some of the tests to volunteers from Radcliffe undergraduate classes, and this was undertaken. Obviously, the results would be biased because of the subjects, but if any or some results were consistent, further trials would be justified. The staff I had for such work included my colleague Harriet Clark and her three assistants, teachers of athletics, all well educated and experienced. Through the Radcliffe student government 100 volunteers were easily enlisted, and the Grant Study staff generously supplied us with advice on details.

On my initiative three common problems were studied, and we made three trials with Grant Study techniques. First, an impressive number of students were taking vitamin and/or iron prescriptions prescribed by the family doctor. Another group was being treated for low blood pressure, although they were free of symptoms. The third group was used to study the problem of accurate white blood cell counts in the correct diagnosis of appendicitis severe enough to require surgery. By a search of the literature, I found the reports showed half the white blood cell counts being elevated in association with menstruation and the other half depressed. By faithfully taking blood counts of healthy Radcliffe students complaining of abdominal pain, we found that any stress — for example, approaching examinations, heavy exercise, or menstrual period — could explain an elevation high enough to push the physician and surgeon to decide to remove what proved to be a normal appendix to be "on the safe side." The studies of blood pressure showed the best athletes to have the lowest levels. The various hemoglobin levels correlated with men-

strual abnormalities, lack of exercise, and foolish diets. Much to my
pleasure, all of this was published in the *New England Journal of
Medicine* with the blessing of the chief of medicine at the MGH, Dr.
Means.[1]

Of the Grant Study results much has been published. The
Radcliffe share was modest, and only two indexes of "the normal"
seemed worth publishing. One described the details and results of
physical fitness testing. It was now wartime, 1943, and there was
national attention to healthy exercise and adequate diet. Neverthe-
less, diet histories from Radcliffe students showed that potato chips
and Coca-Cola were outstanding items. The students felt four glasses
of milk per day supplied a proper diet. As for physical fitness, many
students simply skipped their athletic commitments, and of our volunteers, a number felt unable to go to gym classes, perhaps because
of a recent visit to the hairdresser.

At the time of which I write (1939–45) the Sheldon method
of classifying body types, so-called somatotyping, was in wide use.
We were able to supply Dr. Ernest Hooton, the study's well-
recognized physical anthropologist, and his associates, Dr. Carl Seltzer
and Mrs. Mary Peyton (a graduate student), with 100 photographs
of Radcliffe students. The identity of the students is a secret to this
day; I alone have the identities. The photographs taken nude as "pos-
ture pictures" were shown to our Harvard colleagues. Our discussion at the Faculty Club lunch was nearly broken up by Dr. Hooton's
loud cry, "Harriet, I have never seen so many undressed women together. Isn't it wonderful!" The findings were eventually published.

My final step in somatotyping Radcliffe students was to allow
Dr. William Draper and his associates of Columbia University to use
the 100 photos with similar Grant Study photos to study maleness
and femaleness in the two groups. I found it hard not to laugh when
the young men doing the work came to my office to report that Radcliffe females were more female than Harvard men were male. Draper's resulting article, "The Mosaic of Androgyny,"[2] the basis of this
exercise, is both important and fascinating. In addition, about this
time we were helping Dr. Ira Nathanson in Dr. Joseph Aub's laboratory at the MGH by collecting 24-hour urine samples of healthy,
good-natured Radcliffe students. A now well-established fact, this
work showed females to be excreting measureable amounts of male
hormone at college age.

I used my healthy student population in what proved to be an important point in the development of electroencephalography as a diagnostic tool. Dr. Frederick Gibbs and his associates at the Boston City Hospital asked me to supply them with healthy volunteers. I went to several psychology classes, explained what was wanted, and obtained volunteers. The results of the testing were startling. About half of the tracings were identical with tracings of epileptics. Repeated at another women's college, the results were the same. After history taking and thought, it could be shown that the "abnormal" tracings coincided with the menstrual period and helped explain periods of depression or irritation at monthly intervals.

This reminds me that during my Radcliffe days I had an uncomfortable period, less severe but very like my Northfield anxiety state. I write of these episodes in part to be honest about the ups and downs of a single woman doctor working hard to keep her head above water emotionally and financially and professionally. The Radcliffe "bad" period was triggered by the Coconut Grove nightclub fire (1942) that took the lives of three of our students in the blaze that killed over 400 people. Again I regained my poise and vigor by long solitary walks on Cape Cod with the welcome and protection of friends with whom I stayed for several months and through the wisdom and kindness of my medical advisers and President Comstock. During this period a healing occupation was the close study of birds, an avocation of lifetime pleasure. In addition, my reading, which chiefly consisted of Thoreau's journals and the essays of David Grayson (the pen name of Ray Stannard Baker), provided me with much to ponder in my walks.

After the period of study of "the normal," perhaps best called *clinical investigation*, and ten years of caring for healthy students, ideas of the future course of my career in medicine took shape. I decided that too little was known of the key signals of the onset of illness. Further, if subtle signs of approaching disease could be detected, preventive measures might be found. I submitted my resignation to Radcliffe, to take effect one year later, and went in search of work in the field of what I called *clinical preventive medicine*. I spent nearly a calendar year seeking the job to fulfill my ideas. Because the year was 1944, many male colleagues were still on military duty. In addition, our president, Franklin D. Roosevelt, had created a number of posts for doctors to improve the unemployment and poverty situation and to spend money for health care as one form of social security and welfare benefit. Therefore, I traveled to Washington and received a number of offers; I declined them because they were administrative positions and excluded patient care and decided to settle in Boston with the Department of Labor and Industries.

REFERENCES

1. Hardy, H. L., The clinical significance of data accumulated in the medical care of young women, N. Engl. J. Med., 233:811–816, 1945.
2. Draper, W., The mosaic of androgyny, N. Engl. J. Med., 225:1–9, 1941.

CHAPTER 5

Apprenticeship Learning: Massachusetts DOH

Field Work with Chemists and Engineers

Dr. Joseph Aub, professor of medicine at Harvard Medical School and chief of the Huntington Laboratory for the study of cancer housed at the Massachusetts General Hospital (MGH), was a friendly adviser. In early 1944 he asked about my future plans, and I explained my intention to study the onset of disease under the title of clinical preventive medicine. He appeared dissatisfied with my answer but said only, after asking my age (37), that it was high time I settled into a permanent post. Dr. Aub must have thought about my idea since he soon suggested that I visit Mr. R., director of the Division of Occupational Hygiene (DOH) in the Massachusetts Department of Labor. During a visit there, I learned that the DOH was looking for a full-time physician to work with its chemists and engineers.

The work of the division since its inception in the 1930s had been to investigate by plant visits and appropriate study and measurements any potential industrial hazard in the state of Massachusetts. If risks were discovered, methods of control were recommended. Repeat visits were made where necessary, and certain biological and physical tests might be made routine and performed by the DOH as a check on the success of the controls. Such procedures were essential in the small industries of this state.

My talks with Mr. R. gave me the clue to my career—the study of onset of illness of healthy workers exposed to potential hazards. Very exciting were to be visits to plants with chemical and engineering colleagues that led to the delineation of previously unrecognized disease causes and their controls. Although the salary of $3,600 was $400 less than my stipend at Radcliffe, I hesitated only long enough for Mr. R. to give me permission to spend a day each week at the MGH. I believed then, as I do now, that doctors — especially those working in a specialty — must also, if possible, serve sometime each year, in a general teaching hospital that draws from all educational, national, and economic groups, to keep a broad base of knowledge and to accept the humility of realizing the depths of one's ignorance. Learning about this ignorance comes from questions of students, hospital staff, house officers, and colleagues and, most important, from discovering what fundamental and practical questions or problems still need to be answered.

My job with the DOH was delayed for six months by the strong effort of the state commissioner of health to have the DOH, especially my services and those of a nurse, made a part of the Department of Health. I believed, and experience showed, that state departments of labor were a better agency than departments of health. Various divisions of departments of labor have greater knowledge of working conditions, enforceable regulations already established, union activity, and wages. The Department of Health had never shown any interest in the diseases of industry.

Many pressures made inadequate the laws under which the DOH operated. This division had been instituted by the legislature in the early 1930s because of a scandal in a stove-manufacturing plant. Quartz, harmful to the lung, had been used as sand (silica) in a poorly ventilated workroom, and workers incurred a dust disease easily detected by chest x-ray. Thinking they would gain promotion and praise, several foolish insurance agents from the company that carried the workmen's compensation for the stove company recommended that those workers with abnormal chest x-rays be fired. Obviously, no other company would hire them. Enough workers were fired in this period of the Great Depression to supply newspapers and politicians the excuse for a great outcry. The resulting litigation cost the company not only loss of face with citizens but also a great deal of money for support and medical expenses throughout the workers' lifetimes. Out of this tragedy the DOH was born; however, it was hobbled by the failure of the legislature to provide it any authority or redress in the courts.

In addition, while DOH staff had identifying badges properly signed by the commissioner of labor, right of entry to a plant as
provided by law was often denied. Unfortunately, since the jobs were
political, the commissioner and division heads changed at irregular
intervals, with an expected loss of continuity of policy. There was
no legal backing for liaison with the Industrial Accident Board, whose
members, without required professional training of any kind, administered the pitifully inadequate amounts of money paid to disabled
workers — this often after a delay of years except where an accident
had fortunately been witnessed by other workers. One redeeming feature of the law was that when the courts decided in a worker's favor,
his medical bills were paid. The insurance lobby and the employers'
association of industries must share the responsibility for the wa-
tered-down, politically determined Industrial Accident Board.

In past years union lawyers encouraged workers, who feared
discharge, to refuse chest x-rays and other medical studies as a vio-
lation of their constitutional rights. Today there are improvements
in local, state, and federal laws, but the job is by no means complete.

From February to September 1945 I worked in the Division
of Communicable Diseases of the Department of Health, while the
subject of my transfer to the DOH was being tossed about by mysterious committees and officials. The process was so slow that I visited
a senior member of the State Public Health Committee, Dr. Richard
Smith (a trustee of Northfield School), who helped me reach my post
in the DOH in the first week of September 1945.

This six months of work was not wasted and taught me much
about the problems of a state department that could only make, not
enforce, recommendations to local boards of health. I was assigned
the task of collecting knowledge of infectious hepatitis in Massachusetts: its incidence, diagnosis, prognosis, and treatment, if any. The
war years (1941–45) and experience among the military had shown
infectious hepatitis to be a pandemic disease. The disease, transmit-
ted by transfusion and injection as well as by exposure, is still a constant medical worry.

What I learned of the transmission of infectious hepatitis and
the subtle character of its onset was of permanent value as I practiced the pursuit of clinical preventive medicine in industrial disease.
I chased infectious hepatitis in my ancient-but-dependable Ford (ten
cents per mile and the cost of meals paid for by the state) by means

of physician's reports of the disease, by visits to local boards of health and visiting nurses agencies, and by the miraculous network of neighborly word of mouth. Learning from Boston investigations about gaps in the knowledge of various facets of infectious hepatitis, I brought biologic samples from patients to several Boston research laboratories. Although I had textbook knowledge of epidemiology, I now, by close study of groups of cases, had practical field-work experience, so invaluable in tracing and discovering an unidentified disease-producing agent.

For example, I happened upon a group of young Navy wives, a majority of whom developed jaundice a few days after they attended a fine party that included alcohol. The yellow-skinned young women felt the martinis were responsible. By careful history taking I found the key case, a woman who had had a vague illness ten days before she attended the party; by exposure she had spread the disease. A second, probably rare, experience was finding a doctor in a small country town who had cared for patients with infectious hepatitis during an epidemic in 1911, more than 30 years before. None of these patients developed the disease in the 1940s epidemic, but younger people did — thus immunity is conferred by one attack, although it is now known that the virus is present in a well patient's blood for years.

I collected enough clinical data in 210 cases to report my findings for publication.[1] While polishing the final paragraph of the article, working alone in the empty apartment of a vacationing friend, church bells began to toll. Without knowing the reason, people appeared from their homes. With hardly a word they filed into nearby churches to collect their thoughts and pray as word spread of the destruction at Hiroshima. I was deeply moved that afternoon. In retrospect I realize that the date marked the great change in my medical career from the private position of single doctor-single patient of my country doctor, student health, and medical clinic days to the more public and social field of man-made disease, involving healthy workers and their families and neighbors.

On my first day at the DOH, Mr. R. gave me a six-inch-thick file of papers, with instructions to give my full attention to it, because young women workers in a nearby fluorescent lamp-manufacturing plant were ill of a yet-undiagnosed disease, and of this group, three had died. My predecessor had recorded what was known of the disease before leaving the DOH because of illness. The file was full of technical descriptions of the materials and the operations of the fluorescent lamp-manufacturing industry. In addition, there were letters containing the opinions of those physicians, chemists, engineers, and research workers in the history and then known procedures needed to define a previously unrecognized industrial illness. Part of my plan of attack in these early days was to study all the available literature concerning the materials known to be used. These included manganese, zinc, beryllium, and silica (quartz) as a silicate.

Mr. R. had already collected, in a thorough fashion, U.S. and foreign literature on the potential toxicity of the materials listed. This reading, and my studies of infectious hepatitis and variations in laboratory indexes of healthy young women, made three points clear. First, the European literature described a worker illness much like that in Massachusetts, with an exposure to beryllium compounds and respiratory disease. Second, the widely used U.S. Public Health Service Bulletin no. 181, *The Toxicology of Beryllium*,[2] despite European literature reviewed in the document, ended with the sentence that, based on animal studies, beryllium of itself is harmless. Third, no material used in fluorescent lamp manufacturing could cause occupational disease of similar character if beryllium were harmless. Armed with this much information, I visited a tuberculosis hospital near the plant under study, where some of the sick workers were hospitalized.

The Beryllium Story

I have often been asked to relate the knowledge I have of the events surrounding the recognition in the United States of beryllium and its compounds as toxic materials. Some of my findings are critical of a number of people in government and industry, and the story must be handled with considerable care. Reflecting about this more than 20 years after the events, I know that it was not, and is not, wise or helpful to guard the reputations of those rascals who tried to keep knowledge of worker illness secret; their motive was clearly financial profit. What I write may not all be absolutely true, although to the best of my knowledge none is based on rumor. If we can remain free from slander in a legal sense, the story has merit in teaching lessons involved in our economy of free enterprise, lessons that are applicable to any newly introduced material that carries a hazard not quickly recognized.

My knowledge of the beryllium story began when I started work at the DOH. I gave almost full attention to tracking down a "new" disease that occurred in a few women workers in a plant that was engaged in the manufacture of fluorescent lighting. This disease, recognition of which was just beginning in the United States, is a chronic debilitating lung disease that has deleterious effects on other organs. Its clinical picture will be described later.

Mr. R. was trying hard to persuade the company to look into its own problems and to engage the research services of the Trudeau Sanitarium at Saranac, New York. He was keeping out of the industrial accident law process the cases that were occurring, a practice illegal in Massachusetts. He was hoping thus to engage the loyalty and sympathy of the company and so to get a better answer to the problem. The result of this practice, done in good faith, was to keep reports from physicians and industry by stamping them as "confidential." Not only did Mr. R. lose his job because of this illegal action, but he also was not rewarded by the company for his efforts.

Members of the DOH tried a number of times to gain entry to the plant to make air studies or at least to get a description of the work processes to help elucidate the illness. They were refused. I know of no attempt to use the legislation available at that time to force the company to allow industrial hygiene engineers to study the operations that appeared to be responsible for the illness at the plant. At this time Dr. N., working for an insurance company, for reasons that are not clear worked together with the manager of the insurance company to scatter a number of red herrings across the path of inquiry by insisting that this was a virus disease, sarcoidosis, in epidemic form at the plant, or that some unusual infection had arisen because at high tide seawater had seeped into the basement of the plant. This is an example of the lengths to which these men went to draw attention away from the very significant work exposures. Dr. N. published some of this material in a well-known medical journal, and for a while a certain amount of attention was paid to this theory.

My activities were hardly welcomed by the company because I kept discovering more workers who had developed similar illnesses, chiefly women working in the same areas of the plant. I was aided by Dr. T., who realized that these young women appeared to have miliary tuberculosis, but all tests for tuberculosis were negative. He allowed me to see the patients and their records, as did officials at one of the hospitals where some cases were treated.

When I tried to get information from those in charge at another nearby hospital in the pathology and radiology departments, I ran into trouble. I had become the champion of these sick young women, but I was not allowed to see their chest x-rays. At the hospital I had noticed a plaque that stated that the company where these women worked had bought the x-ray equipment; I made a somewhat rude remark that I understood now why I was not given access to the x-rays. Then I went to the record room, where I had been promised the privilege of looking at some of the records. However, as a result of my remark, the record librarian told me I must first go to the hospital superintendent, and he told me I would no longer be free to see any of that material. By the time I had made a few remarks to him and had returned to Boston, he had consulted the local hospital's lawyers and called the State House to see that I was restrained from revisiting the hospital. I had said to him that I thought this kind of technique might be used in Germany under Hitler but hardly in this country. I was not invited back.

In these early days, following leads from friendly physicians and suggestions from some patients, I spent a good deal of time in my car going from community to community. By April 1946 I had collected 17 cases with three deaths. Dr. Dwight O'Hara of the Massachusetts Medical Society asked me to read a report on the situation at the society's May meeting.

Dr. N. and his associates went to the commissioner of Labor and Industries to persuade him that he be allowed to correct my paper before I read it. There were several stormy sessions at which I told Dr. N. that if I had made any mistakes, as he suggested, I would be solely responsible. I told the commissioner that if there were any attempt to censor the paper by the company, I would not only resign but see to it that wide publicity would be given to my reasons for resignation. I stayed at home for the day following this fuss with a "bad cold," while my patient family listened to me recite the paper.

When I read the paper to the Massachusetts Medical Society,[3] company officials appeared at the session with a court stenographer who sat in front of me, typing my every word. Dr. O'Hara had been warned of this, and he arranged that as soon as I sat down, the next paper would be announced so that there would be no discussion of mine. Several Boston news reporters tried to speak to me; I disappeared into the ladies' room with a woman reporter after me who followed me right into the toilet. She and I reached a compromise arrangement, and she buried my report in a short sentence describing the meetings. I wished no publicity because of the near panic among exposed workers.

Things were never dull after this. Officials of the Atomic Energy Commission (AEC), then known as the Manhattan District, came to see me when the article was published in the fall of 1946. They suggested that if I were right, they were in trouble—and, of course, used to speaking the truth, I said, "Well, you are in trouble," which proved to be true. Because the Massachusetts Institute of Technology (MIT) and the AEC were using beryllium in atomic energy development, some cases of beryllium disease had appeared at MIT and Los Alamos.

I was asked by the AEC to visit the University of Rochester. I suggested that Dr. Robert Grier, who had seen the MIT cases, come along with me. We met with Dr. Harold Hodge and his group, who were charged with the study of potentially toxic materials for the AEC, how hazardous they were, and what safe doses might be. At that meeting Dr. Shilen, in charge of industrial health in Pennsylvania, was present. He had published his conviction that it was only the acid salts of beryllium that caused illness. U.S. Public Health officials who were present, headed by Dr. Neil, were in the embarrassing position of having said that beryllium was not toxic in their Bulletin No. 181 published in 1943. Dr. H. O. Van Ordstrand and Dr. Joseph De Nardi, physicians from companies in Ohio that manufactured and used beryllium, each described in detail cases of sick workers in their care. There followed a long, acrimonious discussion between those who thought beryllium was harmless and those like myself who had become militant in the idea that beryllium was harmful indeed.

I made two trips to the Saranac Laboratories, bringing clinical data of the Massachusetts cases on which there was some autopsy material. I discovered that Dr. N. had not submitted such data to Saranac, as he should have, since the company was retaining Saranac to do this work. I learned during one of these trips that the company had sent a powder of low beryllium content (5 percent or less) for research work; their thinking was that there might be a difference between powders of high and low beryllium content that could be favorable to their cause.

I was very busy traveling to see cases in Connecticut, through the courtesy of Dr. Andrew Jackson, plant physician of the American Brass Company; I traveled to other factories with similar cases and reported our experience to various medical societies. That beryllium was the common denominator of this newly recognized industrial disease became clear because of the comparable character of the chest x-rays, clinical illness, and pathologic findings.

Dr. Leroy Gardner's unexpected and sudden death in late 1946 was a tragedy, as he was in charge of Saranac research. Dr. C. took over his job. In the fall of 1947 a symposium was held at Saranac to present chiefly the data on beryllium toxicity. I was distressed at this time because some of those involved, responding in my judgment to economic pressures, would not tell the truth. I realized, too, that Dr. Gardner's share in unraveling the mystery was not recognized. Before his death he had shown that small animals developed not only malignancy of the bone but also so-called granuloma of the liver and lung, changes like those found in human workers. Dr. C. chose to misinterpret or ignore these findings, and we had several very unpleasant encounters.

A rumor was started at the 1947 Saranac Symposium that Massachusetts was going to outlaw the use of beryllium in the state because of the illness in the company located in this state. This served as a trigger to the beryllium industry to put its house in order.

By this time the AEC had begun to inspect Ohio plants and had stopped using beryllium from a Pennsylvania company. It was difficult to learn all the facts of the situation in Ohio because the plant physician was less than frank about his knowledge of the number of cases of workers who were ill. Many workers left the plant because of shortness of breath and coughing and with abnormal x-rays. In 1948 Dr. C. stated that beryllium was not causing disease in the animals at the Saranac Laboratory, a statement hard to understand. At this meeting I asked if Dr. C. thought that leprosy was not a human disease because laboratory animals did not develop leprosy.

So great was worker anxiety and the litigation that in May 1949 the fluorescent lamp industry agreed that beryllium should no longer be used in manufacture. It is not known whether the plants used up their stockpiles of lamps containing beryllium; the companies refused to mark those lamps that were free of beryllium. I heard, but cannot prove, that those made with beryllium were shipped overseas.

When the United States decided to make the atomic bomb, all users of beryllium were called to Washington and asked to use as little beryllium as possible. At this time the current formula was produced and found to be between 12 and 14 percent beryllium as beryllium oxide, whereas other companies were using beryllium between 2.7 and 4.4 percent. This explains why the former had more cases earlier. Sometime in the 1940s it reduced the quantity of beryllium in its lamps to below 3 percent. At this time a consultant (physician) for the insurance companies went to court to defend this company and said it was not possible for the disease to be produced when the phosphor (powder) was below 3 percent, because beryllium could not get into the air from the phosphor. He said unless beryllium oxide became airborne, there would be no illness, a thesis that remains to be proved. There are cases among workers making powders containing various amounts of beryllium, some less than 3 percent and cases among workers in a variety of other beryllium-using industries.

By late 1949 it was pretty well agreed by most observers that beryllium and all its compounds except beryl, the ore, are hazardous at certain levels. I discovered through my trips to Saranac that two male workers, when they returned from military service, had been reemployed in the beryllium plant and exposed to beryllium even though they had abnormal chest x-rays at the time. I knew their identity, and I went with John Skinner, head of the Massachusetts DOH, to see the commissioner about this. He instructed the assistant commissioner, a safety inspector, Skinner, and myself to meet with the company. The company must have decided that something rough was afoot, so their vice-president in charge of personnel came to the meeting, and we had a showdown. I found then that the New York office did not really know what was going on in Massachusetts. The vice-president announced that there were no cases in the new plant, and I then said, "You lie," in a dramatic fashion, and the illness of the ex-military workers who had been exposed to beryllium before their war duty had to be explained.

I recall a conversation with the manager of the plant's insurance company when we were discussing the needs of one patient in which he asked me if I realized that this patient actually wanted the company to pay for a television set. I became very angry and retorted that if each patient had two television sets as gifts (since this company made them), it would be little enough because its progress and fantastic profits really rested on the health and literally the bodies of some of these workers. We, the patients and doctors, are still suffering from the fact that the insurer begrudges every penny it spends, especially on these poor women who are not desperately ill now but who have had to lead very abnormal lives — resting constantly, lacking companionship with their husbands, obviously suffering a life-shortening disease.

The beryllium problem remains because there often has been a delay in onset of symptoms over 20 years, and not all physicians know how to make the diagnosis of beryllium disease. A U.S. Beryllium Case Registry, funded by the federal government and begun by me at the MGH in 1952, now holds about 900 case records; of these, 408 are dead. In the 1950s and 1960s and to date all parts of industry and the military, including the National Aeronautics and Space Administration, have found uses for beryllium because of its lightness, hardness, and resistance to stress.

I prophesied in 1949 that federal legislation would come. There are now federal agencies — the Occupational Safety and Health Administration (OSHA) and the National Institute of Occupational Safety and Health, begun in 1970 — charged with guarding the well-being of workers and the environment, and OSHA's rulings can be enforced. The operation of this vast government effort is far from ideal. But the worker with and without union protection is currently regarded as more than just a good piece of machinery.

The Saranac Symposium of 1947

I was invited to present a formal report of my clinical experience with the Massachusetts cases of industrial beryllium disease at the Saranac Symposium in 1947. Lake Saranac, in the Adirondack Mountains in New York, was the site of the world-famous sanitarium founded by the late Dr. Edward Trudeau in 1884 for patients with tuberculosis; at that time the only therapy for the disease was fresh air, sunshine, and bed rest. Because tuberculosis was the dreaded, usually fatal complication of industrial chest disease, a research team headed by Dr. Leroy Gardner was established at Saranac in the 1930s. He also initiated a series of symposia. Beginning in 1934 a forum of professionals concerned with dust disease of the chest caused by job exposure met there. These included industrial hygiene engineers, research workers, industrial physicians, pathologists, radiologists, federal and state officials, lawyers working with workmen's compensation, and insurance representatives. Support for these symposia and the research came chiefly from industry, insurance companies that wrote workmen's compensation insurance, and government agencies.

Unhappily, under the claim of trade secrecy or fear of litigation, many of the results of the Saranac studies were never published. For example, while Dr. Gardner received autopsy specimens of cases of occupational disease, the company giving him financial support did not supply accurate work and medical history. For experiments with animals at Saranac, samples of material quite different in quantity or quality from that to which human workers were exposed were used. Knowledge of such behavior by U.S. industry was a shock to me, who, although exposed to a variety of human weaknesses as a medical student and physician, had not realized the possible evils of the free enterprise system. I learned much at Saranac, confirmed by earlier and later experience with industry and insurance companies and especially with legal advisers.

I was now armed, 15 years after graduation from medical school, with good medical training, experience in diagnosis and care of sick people, a taste for clinical investigation, some writing, and two years of apprenticeship in the field of my final choice, to investigate the unexplored possibilities and dark secrets in the field I like best to call man-made disease. My report at this symposium told my experience with beryllium poisoning. The toxic compounds produced dramatic chest x-ray changes and high mortality from intense exposure, although the compounds were not in the form of a dust like coal. This meeting was charged with excitement, for beryllium disease was "new." Trade secrecy and compensation costs added to unwillingness to share knowledge. This symposium was for me both a fiery baptism and a learning session, and it taught me the complexity of industrial competition and unfair compensation awards for the injured worker. Nothing in my home life or education had prepared me for the warlike behavior and disregard for truth I witnessed there.

For example, a physician working for a beryllium-using plant, striving to eliminate beryllium as the cause of the poisoning I had described, stated a novel idea. Beryllium used by industry comes from the ore beryl, found in certain coals and therefore found in coal miners' lungs. The changes found in coal miners' lungs, however, differ entirely from those in victims of beryllium disease. This physician concluded that beryllium could be the cause of coal miners' pneumoconiosis. Confusion followed his paper. However, beryl in coal is harmless, while beryllium compounds and pure beryllium are disease producing. I believe this man deliberately presented his idea to promote confusion. Passage of time and research have shown me to be correct in the cause of beryllium poisoning.

I did meet many top-flight men and a few women in the field of occupational medicine with whom I became friends and who guided me as a learner.

REFERENCES

1. Hardy, H. L., and Feemster, R., Infectious hepatitis in Massachusetts with a review of present knowledge of the disease, N. Engl. J. Med, 235:147, 1946.
2. U.S., Public Health Service, The Toxicology of Beryllium, Bulletin no. 181, Washington, D.C., Government Printing Office, 1943.
3. Hardy, H. L., and Tabershaw, I. R., Delayed chemical pneumonitis occurring in workers exposed to beryllium compounds, J. Ind. Hyg. Toxicol., 28:197, 1946.

CHAPTER 6

A Year at Los Alamos (1948)

The Setting

After driving home from the Saranac Symposium of 1947 quite over-whelmed with the secrecy that industry expected, the evidence of mixed motives, and the blatant use of the work of honest men for profit, I was jolted by an urgent telephone call from New Mexico. The call came from Dr. Louis Hempelmann, head of the Health Division of the Atomic Energy Scientific Laboratory of the University of California located at Los Alamos, New Mexico. He reported that the newly appointed Atomic Energy Commissioner, David Lilienthal, had ordered a health and safety inspection of all AEC laboratories. Professor Philip Drinker of the Harvard School of Public Health, a member of the inspecting team, had found Los Alamos in poor condition with regard to toxic hazards exclusive of radiation. I had been suggested as "an expert" to reside at Los Alamos until the toxic hazards were controlled. The proposal made me breathless and for a short period unable to speak, a state previously unknown to me. I promised to visit Los Alamos and think about the work and the $10,000 salary. Even though at Radcliffe I was paid $4,000 a year and at the Massachusetts Department of Occupational Hygiene, $3,600, there were other things to consider besides money, especially since my work in Boston was well started and satisfying.

The trip to Los Alamos in the Jemez Mountains above the beautiful old Spanish town of Santa Fe moved me very much. The incredible beauty, the helplessness of the mighty men of science about

48

"little" things I knew well such as the dangers of mercury, Louis's personal plea (Dr. Hempelmann explained that on the Pacific side of the Mississippi River persons were to be called by their first names only) — all served to force me to agree to come to Los Alamos for a year if my Boston chiefs granted me a leave of absence, which they did. The National Institutes of Health put aside the funds granted me for work at the Massachusetts General Hospital to be saved until my return. The late 1940s were the years of the cold war. Work done at Los Alamos was still top secret, and bombs were still being manufactured and tested.

My year at Los Alamos (1948) had a dreamlike quality; it was so very different from any previous work, and the natural setting was so remarkable. I lived alone in a so-called Hanford Hut, a small cottage built for wartime, apparently of cardboard but comfortable. Since it withstood occasional great storms, this hut had to be quite strong. My breakfast view was of the great, green-covered Jemez Mountains rising to 13,000 feet above sea level from the 8,000 feet altitude of Los Alamos.

Since I was by no means certain that one with my opinion of the terrors of military might had any business working at Los Alamos, I took great delight in the joyful journey of children and dogs passing by my window, going to school, as a kind of assurance that the evil engineers at Los Alamos would not destroy humanity. Being alone in my cottage was a fruitful experience. I could think over what I had been shown and what I had done in my workdays. I worked in the silence of my Hanford Hut on the galleys of the toxicology text, written and now ready for publication.

My lady-of-all-work brought great humor to ordinary jobs and our conversations. Her name was Lucy, and she, a full-blooded Pueblo Indian, was the wife of the chief of a nearby pueblo. Lucy used sticks to beat the dirt out of my blouses. Her curiosity about my life led her to play my radio, smoke a cigarette from my guest supply, and sip my whiskey. All this she did seated in my one comfortable chair, where I would find her when I returned from my work to pay her. She would calmly say, "I wanted to see what it is that you people do." On the occasion of her annual chest x-ray, Lucy had to wait two hours, for which she asked that I pay her, saying, "It was your idea, not mine." So I paid Lucy.

The year 1948 was a presidential election year: Truman versus Dewey. I asked Lucy for whom she would vote since this was the first year the American Indian was allowed to vote in national elections, a good offshoot of World War II. She answered, "The men will smoke their pipes this evening and will tell us whom to vote for, Dewey or Truman." I reacted vigorously and delivered Lucy a lecture on suffragettes, individual's free choice, and so on. Her answer was, "Dr. Hardy, I have decided to go East with you when you go in order to learn such things."

I enjoyed her company, although my clothes suffered. For instance, I learned from her that during the sixteenth and seventeenth centuries many Roman Catholic missionaries "converted" them and gave them Spanish names at baptism. Lucy also told me her tribe had no written language as late as 1948. I was lucky enough to visit pueblos like Lucy's to see the odd mixture of Roman Catholic ritual and primitive tribal rites. For example, I recall a spring fertility dance during the planting of maize (corn), watched by a statue of the Virgin Mary taken from their adobe church and guarded on either side by two tall and muscular Indian braves armed with shotguns. I learned that World War II brought great changes in the Indians' lives because the draft took Indian males, and those at all able-bodied like my Lucy were given more education. (Oliver LaFarge and Willa Cather have written unforgettably of this part of U.S. history: the three groups with individual cultures — the Indian, the Spanish, and, as we were called, the Anglos — have kept apart for a variety of reasons, intermarried rarely, and until recently held on to old customs and beliefs.)

A short visit from my mother who had visited me after my sister's wedding in the Panama Canal Zone was a disastrous event. She had been bitten by a mosquito carrying falciparum malaria. We were 8,000 feet high, and not one of us on the medical or laboratory staff thought of malaria, although Mother's signs and symptoms were classic. At last, after I had telephoned my brother in the East to prepare for the worst one morning, the medical staff sat down together, trying to make a diagnosis. One physician suggested we go down the list of diseases in the most recent medical text where high fever was a feature (Mother's was 106°F. night and morning); and when the reader reached malaria, we had our answer. With the newest therapy developed for the military, she healed rapidly and I got back to work.

At this time I moved into a charming adobe guest house in the Tesuque Valley just under the Sangre de Cristo mountains, so named because their high-iron content turned them bloodred as the sun went down. The house was on a friend's property; there was an Indian pueblo, Nambe, on one side and a Spanish village, Tesuque, on the other. Peaceful beyond belief and beautiful, 15 miles from Los Alamos, with the noise of water running in irrigation ditches at three o'clock in the morning, and with friendly songbirds and the aroma of piñon pine, my adobe home made the terrible implications of the nearby Los Alamos work seem unreal.

I have been a partial pacifist, more or less vocal, especially in World War II when I joined the Wider Quaker Fellowship, because I was infuriated by the stand-aside attitude of my church (Episcopal). My year in Los Alamos was a severe strain on my pacifist leanings, and old friends did not let me forget my earlier pronouncements. Dr. Norris Bradbury, the director of the Los Alamos Scientific Laboratory, won me over to his view. Norris held with real passion to his vision that at war's end Los Alamos would become an international laboratory studying the peaceful use of atomic energy. Furthermore, as I myself had granted, failure to care for the workers at Los Alamos could hardly be thought a moral act.

Developing a Unit to Control Laboratory Hazards

Against this background, with a bow to pleasant Anglo picnics and parties, I worked very hard while at Los Alamos in my chosen field of clinical preventive medicine. By this time I had come to understand that the ideal of keeping healthy people healthy required more than the physician's skill. The chemist's help was essential in measuring the quality and quantity of a potential hazard. The engineer had to work out air-sampling techniques and the complex steps of protection. This often required great sophistication in design of ventilation. The radiation protection service had to include both electrical engineers to be certain that the instruments for measurement were accurate and physicists to assess and interpret the character and amount of radiation exposure.

My job was to explore the Los Alamos Scientific Laboratory for risks to workers (other than radiation), then to decide their potential for harmful effect, and, finally, to control such risks as needed. The laboratory itself, where the military use of atomic energy was at the state of completion, was a group of wooden buildings, war-time barracks in the early years, later of poured concrete, surrounded by a high, wire fence and guarded at intervals by blue-uniformed men, fully armed. No one could pass the entering gate without a special badge. On the badge was one's photo and a few capital letters referring to the areas one might enter. These badges were a kind of status symbol, and differing letters occasionally caused childish squabbles. My badge allowed me to enter most, but not all, areas. With my usual bravado I went to find a mercury hazard in a very remote and secret laboratory. The professor there was unimpressed with the risk, so I launched on a mercury-poisoning lecture and failed to hear the five o'clock whistle indicating that the site was to be cleared. A security guard came for me with his machine gun pointed at me and a dead-serious look on his face. I left promptly and thereafter paid attention to whistles.

In fact, working with secrecy of areas and of reports was an occupational hazard. For example, a document marked "Top Secret" was brought to me—its title, "A New Method for Analysis of Urine for Mercury." Mercury has been in industry and research laboratories for many years, so why was there such secrecy? Angrily I went to see the lawyer in charge of classifying documents. He explained to me that we did not want the Russians to know we were using mercury as a coolant. In view of worldwide work with mercury, this explanation seemed to me foolish indeed. In fact, I was an irritant to the classifying staff during my Los Alamos stay because more than once I knew that some of the material marked "Secret" was already in the open literature, and more of it should and could be open without giving aid and comfort to the enemy.

The work of the Los Alamos Scientific Laboratory was apportioned into various divisions. Dr. Hempelmann was head of the division in which I worked, the Health Division. Subgroups referred to as H_1, H_2, and H_3 included staff concerned with administration, radiation health, and worker health (mine, H_2). As the need arose, other groups were formed, as, for example, safety research. Our group, H_2, handled preemployment medical reports from doctors in the village nearby. In time I learned that some reports were filled out and signed by the local veterinarian or barber, so that many follow-up medical examinations, blood counts, and chest x-rays were needed. Carpentry, plumbing, painting, and other maintenance work drew on outside civilian contractors with little or no health program.

These workers, often at considerable risk, had to have at least a medical and work history and the minimum laboratory study of blood count and chest x-ray. On the surface this program sounds dull enough. However, since the population was comprised of university professors who refused chest x-rays until the usual 2.0 r per exposure was reduced to 0.2 r, Spanish Americans frightened in ignorance of finger pricks for a blood count, and American Indians so unafraid through ignorance that they ignored instruction and might be exposed to a hazard unnecessarily, the work of H Division was far from boring.

In addition to the reaction of our human charges, there was the fact that a number of materials of unknown potential harm required a well-equipped division for biological research. I was in constant argument with my colleagues about the fact that their studies were chiefly made with animals. At hand were human workers whose indixes of organ function coupled with accurate exposure data might yield the information needed to forestall irreversible damage. In fairness, I must report that safe standards developed by Los Alamos animal studies have apparently prevented to date the damage expected from plutonium exposure. A safeguard Dr. Hemplemann described to me soon after my arrival, as we toured the laboratories, was the fact that so sensitive were the instruments used to study low-level radiation that many human workers were automatically protected.

Diagnosis and treatment of a variety of radiation injuries have gradually evolved from experience in the manufacture and the original use of the atomic bomb dropped on Hiroshima in 1945. There are lessons to be drawn from the sequence of events following the earlier discovery by the Curies of the properties of radium and its daughter products and Becquerel's demonstration and use of x-rays. Sickness and death of workers in industry, of investigators, and of patients due to use of radiation energy occurred long before medical recognition. In addition, an unfortunately long period elapsed before recognition was put to use for prevention of radiation damage. A third fact arises, in my experience, from the lack of communication, with rare exceptions, between the physician and the physicist. I place the "blame" on doctors who since primitive days have chosen to act alone. This ancient custom is rapidly changing, and it is ironic to realize that this valuable action is directly due to the events of World War II.

My special knowledge and authority were useful in attention

to old and new nonradioactive hazard material in use at Los Alamos. An example will make this clear. Very soon after I began active duty, a worker came to the nurse of H_2, complaining of bleeding gums and a skin rash. In taking his job history I found that he and three other men were engaged in cleaning dirty mercury, an element widely used. Next I visited the job site, and even though I have no engineering skill, I knew from my Massachusetts Department of Occupational Hygiene experience that the mercury hazard was great in this dirty, shedlike building. The three other men who had worked there also showed various signs of mercury poisoning. To protect these men and others, I ordered the work stopped and the shed closed while it was being cleaned. Loud complaints from those using mercury reached Dr. Bradbury, the director. His reply was that I was the expert in this field, hired at great expense, and my orders were to be obeyed. There is a great lesson to be learned from Dr. Bradbury's behavior, which occurred at the beginning of my job, that had been visualized by Professor Drinker of Harvard and outlined by him in his report to the Atomic Energy Commission in Washington. The point I have made and will make again is that unless there is definite commitment of executive authority, government agency, industry, or academic institution, occupational medicine and hazard control cannot thrive. When I entered this field, Dr. Aub said to me, "Harriet, if you work for industry, make certain before you start that you report to the president and that he intends to back your proposals."

Dr. Bradbury's backing made my path at Los Alamos smooth. I visited all the laboratories, the hospital outside the guarded wire wall, the physicians caring for all staff, workers, and their families as well as our Santa Fe consultants. I came to enjoy and depend on the counsel of our chief medical adviser, the late Dr. Eric Hausner, Czechoslovakian by birth. He shared my enthusiasm for clinical investigation and the upgrading of bedside skills.

The work of H_2, charged with the detection and control of laboratory hazards other than radiation, required the special skills of industrial hygiene. This field is manned by chemical engineers who know how to sample and assay the workroom for potential risks, their quality and quantity, and to design protection when needed.

Briefly, there are four methods available for worker protection. First and most ideal is the substitution of a harmless material for the harmful one if the demands of the work can be met. Second, if substitution is not possible, physical isolation of the dangerous work may suffice. If this does not serve, the third-most-used method is the design of ventilation suited to the problem. Finally, if none of these three does what is required, personal protection must be used; this is often referred to as *the mark of engineer defeat*. The face mask may not fit, and so the harmful dust or chemical may be inhaled in quantity. The filtering device on the mask may be wrong for the kind of hazardous material in the worker's breathing zone or may be dirty and clogged, preventing its functioning properly, if at all. If the job requires great physical effort such as in underground mining, the mask may prevent the man from getting enough air to do muscular work. For great risks for short periods of work, whole body or head protection with an independent air supply like that used by men exploring space, is required. So-called dry boxes were used at Los Alamos, with workers having tongs and special gloves to manipulate the radioactive material inside each box, which was vented separately with filters and proper monitoring equipment to control contamination of neighboring areas. Most of these techniques have been adopted in the postwar world by industry, research laboratories, educational institutions, and government agencies. As technology changes, these basic control measures are refined to meet understandable anxiety and potentially serious man-made hazards.

Travel — Expanding the Los Alamos Story

A rich dividend of the Los Alamos year was recognition of the need and permission to travel to various parts of the United States to help with the diagnosis of beryllium disease, which was appearing in several atomic energy laboratories. An occasional trip was made to the AEC headquarters to report to a Boston friend and colleague, Dr. Shields Warren, medical director of all atomic energy development laboratories, and his deputies, Dr. Charles Dunham and Dr. Charles Hardie. We dealt with questions of litigation and the formulation of safe working standards for beryllium, put forward by a small committee of which I was chairman.

Similar safe work standards cover a long list of substances in the United States and have had a rough, controversial course, influenced by industrial and financial interest in the cost of protection. In addition, failure to acquire and study data correlated with human industrial illness and overenthusiasm for short-term, heavy exposures in various experimental animal testing have made standard setting in the United States an almost useless exercise. Standards have been dictated by engineering concepts and costs and with rare help from the medical profession simply because U.S. medical schools are not committed to teach what is known of occupational disease and to stimulate excellence in research.

My committee on beryllium toxicity is an example of how poorly the present system works. Because an acute disease in man and animals occurs at a relatively constant level of beryllium in air, the committee decided to use a figure less than half this but *failed* to include the length of time a man might safely handle this amount. In contrast, a figure of one-twelfth the acute dosage was chosen as average for the 40-hour workweek, and for safety of neighborhood air the figure was 0.03 mg averaged over 30 days. Ridiculous! No biological system waits to average toxic material!

The plan suggested by Dr. Harold Hodge at the first meeting was to make null the figures at our current meeting and make a new set based on fresh data each year from those working in industry or research laboratories on this subject. The first figures were to be for the use of AEC laboratories only. However, our original figures were quickly circulated and used in courts, thus acquiring a "legal" status. After ten years of useless meetings, I, as chairman, disbanded the committee after writing organizations in the field and government agencies to say that they must take up the task of making a single safe figure. One of my Washington superiors of the AEC, hearing of the abolition of the committee, said, "Why, Harriet, no one ever disbands a committee once formed!"

I enjoyed my U.S. travels enormously, and I learned much more of the work needed in my field. Perhaps of even more lasting value, I learned the variety in character and achievements of my fellow countrymen and some of the soft spots in our national fabric. Having lived on the East Coast from birth, I was greatly impressed, very like "a foreigner," with the cities of the West, especially San Francisco with its apparently contented Chinese population and its culture; the bustle and success of Portland, Oregon, impressed me, too. Quite different were the populations of the desert communities where retired or chronically ill young artists worked near native Indian pueblos and Spanish villages. Indians and Spanish lived separately, speaking their own languages, following their ancient customs. There were Roman Catholic churches of varying sizes, made of adobe, with enclosed cemeteries clinging to their sides in natural settings of large old lake beds or on a mountainside with a few brave piñon pines adding their green in contrast to the white adobe. The native Indians appeared to me to be impressively independent. The Spanish talked among each other like a gaggle of pigeons, giving me the impression that life was happy — because of their trust in the church and their simple natures.

When possible, I traveled by train to see more of the Wheat Belt, the prairies, the Rocky Mountains, the Indian pueblos, and the great industrial areas of Ohio, Indiana, and Illinois, the latter all ugly and dirty with their stacks pouring out the fumes of their trades. Inside, the train was not unlike a giant house party, as it crossed the country, a three-day trip. My route was most often covered by the Atchison, Topeka, and Santa Fe Railroad, and when I first began to travel in 1948, it was the line favored by the famous of Hollywood. The train housed a hairdressing shop, a barber shop, a massage "parlor," a gift shop, and a great domed car where one could watch the sky and doze as the landscape slipped away. Famous-named personalities such as John Wayne, Claudette Colbert, and Bob Hope might appear at the cocktail hour and be merry with us ordinary mortals. Talking with one movie star, I could not help noticing that she had a headache, and I offered her a favorite pill I used for sinus infection, since she reported this to be the cause of her malaise. When next I saw her, she asked for a prescription, as my yellow capsules had helped her. She then said, "I wonder why my husband never gave me those pills — he is a nose and throat specialist!"

A moving experience came in a talk I had one evening with a woman who shared a table in the dining car of the very grand Super Chief. We talked of many things. She told me she earned her living designing hats and was now enroute to Hollywood to work with Miss Colbert, who would not make a picture without her help. In a flash of confidence she then told me she was a Negress and had suffered many insults because of her race. After reciting details of a number of her trials, she ended with a pathetic smile, saying, "How would you like to leave home each morning wondering what form the insult would take this day?" I have often wondered if changes in the United States in the past 30 years have made her life more pleasant.

Finally, travel seemed to me to be the chance to catch up with my half-formed idea for the development of my work in Los Alamos and Boston. I wrote medical papers in draft, outlined lectures, and answered mail, often while seated on the uncomfortable shiny benches of railroad stations. My Los Alamos secretary, who was also named Lucy, said often as a hint to me, "Dr. Hardy, I don't know whether I like it better when you are away or when you are here. When away, you mail work, not always intelligible. When you are here, you find new work for all of us."

Los Alamos Takes Shape

The work at Los Alamos took shape with the appointment of an experienced industrial hygiene engineer whose skills could assess what work appeared harmful to humans. I toured the many laboratories, guided by some knowledgeable staff member, and learned a great deal about the sophisticated protection of those who must work with high levels of radioactivity. Advanced technology had produced manmade materials whose properties, apart from their ionizing radiation effect, were unknown. It was during my year there that the Bikini bomb tests took place. We treated some of the physicists and pilots who participated in these tests. They were flown back to us because of burns suffered when they disregarded safety measures and removed their gloves and protective clothing in their haste to examine testing equipment and samples of unusual short-lived isotopes brought back from the tests. Because of such new possible risks and potential hazards due to those elements and their compounds, known but little used by industry or educational institutions, a well-manned section of the Los Alamos Health Division was charged with biological research. I made it part of my job to learn what this group was doing, to the limits of my comprehension of physics, electronics, and biochemistry, subjects either not taught at all during my college years or learned by me long ago. It is amazing and reassuring to discover, however, how much one can learn by observation and by asking small and large questions of the researcher.

One spectacular achievement of H_4 (biology-radiation

research) was the building and utilization of a so-called whole body counter, a machine to measure radiation exposure to the whole body. The need for such an instrument arose from several causes. First, there is a natural background of radioactivity — having nothing to do with military or peaceful use of atomic energy — that varies in different parts of the world according to proximity to the sun. In addition, owing to man's folly, alas, there are measureable amounts of radiant energy arising from tests or military devices, except for those conducted deep underground. Some of the increment is to be found in us all, more in workers and military personnel and in those given known amounts for medical reasons.

High-explosive research was part of the work at Los Alamos. Loud reports from nearby canyons persuaded some of the recently hired secretaries and me at first to rush to the window to look for "the cloud," thinking that Hiroshima-type bombs were being tested. Certainly the shaking of the flimsy barracks that we worked in and the rattling of the windows were convincing evidence.

As a matter of fact, the chemicals used in such explosives might be inhaled or could penetrate unbroken skin and offer an unknown hazard. From industrial and previous wartime experience, it was known that certain members of this group of chemical compounds irritate the urinary tract and, depending on intensity and duration of exposure, produce malignancy of the bladder in workers. Using this knowledge, H_4 worked on the problem of detecting what chemical compound resulted in the body from the material reaching the blood by inhalation and skin penetration. H_2 worked at regular medical checkups of those exposed, seeking to discover early evidence of toxic effect. The industrial hygiene group learned how to measure the chemical risk and determine protective controls, and proper clothing and gloves were tested to be certain that the hazardous material could not penetrate the skin.

Because of the explosive risk, the hazard from high-voltage electrical equipment, and the chance of serious injury from inadequately guarded machinery, another Health Division group was assembled to study and design controls for all problems falling under the heading of safety.

My experience with beryllium poisoning was of value to the AEC. This disease mimics other better-known illness and defies diagnosis unless one knows of its reality and how to elicit a history of significant beryllium exposure. I found a single case at Los Alamos and one in my travels, both isolated cases, and a series among other laboratories in Cambridge, Massachusetts; Ames, Iowa; Chicago; Berkeley; and Columbus, Ohio (at Batelle Institute). I was still learning the varying clinical pictures that may be produced by such different exposures as from machining beryllium to make a variety of alloys. There might be high-level, short-term exposure received intermittently or low-level exposure of longer duration. My experience during the Los Alamos year taught me that — depending on the above-outlined factors — there were to be found cases of beryllium poisoning of varying character: acute, subacute, repeated acute (because of reexposure), acute developing chronic illness with or without further beryllium exposure, and chronic with delay period ranging from no delay to five or more years. With this knowledge my travels took me to see cases or possible cases and to lecture to AEC staff, at medical schools, and at medical meetings.

    A new disease attracts attention. Until I learned the mischief that the press can do to one's patients and one's work, I talked freely to reporters. A few headlines appeared, like that in the New York *Times*, saying that the A-bomb causes a new disease. And some years ago when I was asked to guess how many cases were missed, the Washington *Post* said that I had said about 2,500 new cases of beryllium poisoning. This item appeared in a British journal as being 2,500 new *deaths* due to beryllium poisoning. I had been asked how many unrecognized beryllium cases I thought existed. I replied (a mistake), making a guess, that there were one-third more cases than the 800 reported in the Beryllium Case Registry. From this reply the reporter somehow reached the 2,500 figure. I wrote the editor, threatening a libel suit, and received a cablegram of apology within hours.

Minister without Portfolio

As my year at Los Alamos went on, I served as self-appointed minister without portfolio. My self-chosen charge was to try to make the professional relationships among those of us in the Health Division behind the security barbed wire and the staff of the local hospital more mutually worthwile. Los Alamos had grown from a small staff

picked by Robert Oppenheimer and was housed in the empty buildings of a boy's school on a mesa (plateau), surrounded by canyons
backed by the Jemez Mountains — an easy location to secure. By 1948
there were about 12,000 residents, with a variety of needs, and the
number was steadily increasing. Of necessity there was a small hospital in the town staffed by competent physicians and surgeons; it
had been originally manned by the medical staff of the military engineers assigned to the work of the then-called Manhattan District,
the manufacture and delivery of an atomic bomb. In 1946/47 a civilian commission, the AEC, took charge. I mention this detail because there was a distinctly "town and government" feeling in the
air, with wasteful hostility.

Senior consultant to the Los Alamos Scientific Laboratory was
Dr. Franklin MacLean, a distinguished physiologist known the world
over for his work on the metabolism of bone as well as for his administrative skill at the University of Chicago and for the Rockefeller
Foundation in China. Franklin and I became great friends. A new
hospital was being built, and the hope entertained by Franklin,
myself, and Eric Hausner, our internist consultant in Sante Fe, was
the joining for mutual benefit of the Health Division and the hospital staff. We had great visions of new insights leading to unique research as well as refreshment for those doing the essential job of caring
for sick people. Dr. J. Howard Means and Dr. Chester Jones, experienced clinical professors at Harvard Medical School who also worked
at the Massachusetts General Hospital in Boston, were invited to come
and hear our plans. Unhappily, all of this activity appeared to be
futile, lost in the individualistic views of colleagues. Perhaps this statement is too gloomy, for some enduring bridges were built by common research interests. For me there were real dividends, although
I was in residence for only the year 1948 and made occasional consulting visits at intervals through the 1960s. I became a regular visitor
in the Chicago home of Franklin and Helen MacLean. Helen was
a physician, first an obstetrician and later a leading psychoanalyst
of the Alexander School. Their home was open to students, transi-
ents like myself stuck in Chicago on medical consultations, and many
Asian friends, as both MacLeans had worked in China. The MacLeans
read widely, and their hospitable, literate home provided me with
a real rest from Los Alamos, much as I enjoyed that world. I served

as eyes and ears for Franklin as he continued his Chicago work, and by giving Franklin the detail of daily trials and animus at Los Alamos, he served as a safety valve for me.

Eric Hausner, the chief medical consultant, and his beautiful European wife Suzette entertained me with lively unique meals as part of my support. Eric and I had clinical counsels together with great joy. Eric was more deeply depressed than I by the failure of the Los Alamos hospital staff to see their role broaden to include clinical research as well as care. Dorothy McKibben, an ex-tuberculosis patient, one of the earliest staff and now widowed, had a curious assignment. In the early days of research at Los Alamos, her job was to move staff from all over the United States to the laboratories on "the hill," as Los Alamos was referred to, in complete secrecy. After the awful detonations at Hiroshima and Nagasaki, Dorothy's work was less demanding, and she enjoyed taking me and many friends to the tiny villages over the back roads to picnic and wander around the adobe churches. She taught me the meaning of hand-carved wooden holy figures for home and church — the Santos and the Bultos. My year at Los Alamos included parties in the huge homes of rich Anglos, as the Indians called them. In August a great pleasure was a holiday with my old friend M. P. S., in my second-engine Ford, to the Grand Tetons, to Aspen, and to Denver via the Continental Divide where one must shift into low gear while apparently going downhill. To one of my talkative nature, it was a healthy experience to be awed and silent, to feel completely dwarfed and deprived of glib explanation.

Taking Stock of the Los Alamos Experience

As 1948 came to an end, I realized that in 12 months at Los Alamos I had added an important increment to my experience both professionally and personally. Working with those charged with the prevention of radiation damage, I came to learn enough of their vocabulary and techniques of measuring early evidence of harmful effect to fulfill my criteria for the practice of clinical preventive medicine. What knowledge I had acquired at Los Alamos made me better prepared for the next step, which had not yet come into view. Living near, and working with, two cultures different from my own, the

Pueblo Indian and the Spanish, helped to broaden my views and forced me to ask questions of my so-called Anglo way of life in the American Southwest. The Indian and Spanish workers were quite unpredictable in their reactions to the dangers of work at Los Alamos. Some were frightened — and so, unable to understand the explanations and regulations, they could not be allowed to continue. Others, equally ignorant, had to be closely watched, as they sensed no danger and wandered into areas posted as highly dangerous. Many were killed by motor accidents, as they bought powerful cars with their wages and drove at great speed up and down the curving narrow roads that bordered the deep canyons.

One cannot learn enough in one year to draw great conclusions. However, I can write that my experience with healthy young men and women at Radcliffe and Harvard College made assessment of minor changes from the norm simpler. Further, my clinical experience with beryllium poisoning stretched my knowledge of internal medicine and led to requests for my consultant help in many parts of the United States: California, Iowa, Connecticut, Illinois, Rhode Island, Pennsylvania, New York, and Washington come to mind, as I recall individual patients and their physicians. In fact, in 1948 my travels took me to all but 2 of the then 48 states. It was a busy year, as I had formal papers to prepare for presentation or for publication. The subjects covered both experience gained working for the state of Massachusetts, at the Massachusetts General Hospital, and at Los Alamos. My list of publications shows me that in 1948/49 I discussed beryllium poisoning, of course; the harmful effects of benzene, the solvent; mercury; and cold wave solution damage to hairdressers' skin — illustrating the broadening effect of occupational medicine.

The public — and my personal — reaction to the use of atomic energy by the military to destroy communities and to kill or sicken civilians was a mix of anger, secret relief at the end of war, and foretelling of doom. Perhaps the most serious trauma was suffered by the scientists. Many of them did not visualize the devastation, and others had believed that the initial atomic bomb was to be used on a reef or small island in the Pacific. This latter group felt that our enemies, seeing the power of the atomic bomb, would sue for peace at once without damage to people.

There is nothing new in these thoughts. They lead, however,

into the picture I shall always carry in my mind of a meeting held at Harvard by scientists to consider how to protest past and future use of atomic energy now that the twentieth century Pandora's box was open. The meeting took place after V-J day. An eminent physician adviser to the military addressed us first. He said the Japanese were suing for peace before the atomic bomb was used. He was asked, "Then, why was it used?" The doctor in a gloomy voice said, "Because so much money had been spent in its manufacture."* The reader will recall that the public was told that if the life of one of our soldiers was saved, the Hiroshima episode was worthwhile. As I write, I still feel my share of the guilt as well as shame and fear for the future use of one of nature's secrets now in the hands of man.

---

*The meeting I described was held in early September 1945. Its purpose was to form an organization, the Association of Atomic Scientists, and to publish a journal. More recently, the Union of Concerned Scientists has been formed. These two groups valiantly fight the use and control of atomic and nuclear energy.

CHAPTER 7

Junior Author with Dr. Alice Hamilton (1946–48)

Shortly after my first paper on beryllium poisoning was published, I received a letter of congratulation from the late Dr. Alice Hamilton. Dr. Alice was the pioneer in the field of industrial disease in the United States. The dean of Harvard Medical School in 1918, Dr. David Edsall, had persuaded her to become the first woman professor at Harvard, and to Harvard's shame she was never promoted beyond the post of assistant professor, although her work, largely original, was recognized throughout the industrialized world. Her autobiography, *Exploring the Dangerous Trades*,[1] is recommended not only as an important social and political history of this country but also as an unusually interesting and stimulating personal saga.

Following an exchange of letters, Dr. Alice — as I was privileged to call her — suggested we have lunch together at a Boston hotel. I had seen her only once before, when she had addressed a medical club to which I belonged at Wellesley College. Because I had a car at the time, I had been chosen to meet her and return her to the railway station. During these brief trips we managed to discuss a number of the world's problems. Some 20-odd years later we met in Boston, and with little introductory conversation, Dr. Alice invited me to be the junior author with her in updating her 1934 textbook, *Industrial Toxicology*.[2] I protested that I had been in the field less than two years and so was incompetent to carry out such a task. Dr. Alice chose not to hear me. (I learned later that she had deliberately turned her deaf ear toward me.) She swiftly divided between us the subjects to be covered in the new edition. Unable to persuade her to recognize my amateur status, I brought forward the problem of my work at the DOH and the MGH. We parted with my promise that I would consult my employers — all of whom said much the same as Dr. Aub, "Oh, yes, Harriet, you must do as Dr. Hamilton asks. It will be good for you."

So I became a junior author, with permission to take time off from my regular work. Aside from the satisfaction of the work itself and the association with Dr. Alice, I cannot overestimate the value of long hours in the library learning the past and present history of occupational disease I was to describe, the gaps in knowledge, and the hints of clues for further investigation. My share was shipped to Dr. Alice in late 1947, to be published in 1948 by Hoeber. Dr. Alice and her sister Margaret compiled the bibliography and the index. A printer's strike delayed the production of the galley until 1949. Dr. Hamilton, having won the Lasker Award for excellent work in the field of public health, with its handsome purse, went abroad with her sister, leaving the galley in my innocent and ignorant hands. Proofreading, I discovered, is a whole separate skill, differing from anything I had done before.

This learning experience proved useful in my future career, although little financial reward was to come from it. As junior author I received five cents for each copy sold, and Dr. Alice received fifteen cents.

The text appeared in 1949[3] with an edition of 2,500 copies, and it was completely sold out. A few devastating criticisms appeared in medical journals. The chief criticism was that the text made no mention of dust disease of the lungs, not even silicosis. When I asked Dr. Alice about this omission, she said, "I know Becquerel, the first man to take chest x-rays, but as I have never seen a chest x-ray, I thought it dishonest to discuss in print disease relying on x-ray." The book included reports of cancer of the lung under the subject of the supposed causative agent, and my chapter on beryllium disease had much to say about chest x-ray changes as a diagnostic point. In my view, Dr. Alice's failure to describe dust disease in this edition of *Industrial Toxicology* made an important point. She was a well-trained chemist, and her pioneer experience in the United States had been chiefly with reaction to toxic exposures to metals and chemicals. Much mischief in the field of industrial medicine has been, and is being, caused by those who, untrained, offer damaging opinions on reports of disease outside the limits of their knowledge.

In 1974 with the help of younger colleagues — Asher J. Finkel, Clarence C. Maloof, John D. Stoeckle, and Lloyd B. Tepper — we updated certain sections, especially those dealing with chemicals and radiation.[4] In addition, I wrote original chapters on particular metals and occupational lung disease, material not covered in the 1949 edition. This, the third edition of Hamilton and Hardy, sold over 7,000 copies in the United States and abroad, and a fourth edition is in print. Its popularity must be due to the vital interest, now worldwide, in environmental disease. It is fair to say, however, that Dr. Hamilton set an early example of what a person with medical training, an observant eye, and social political sensitivity might accomplish.

The success of the 1974 edition of Hamilton and Hardy led to my decision to ask Dr. Finkel, who had contributed to the third edition, to edit and update a fourth edition, which appeared in the fall of 1982.[5] My disabilities by this date included a tremor in my right hand and odd deficits of central nervous system function (due to my 1972 head surgery). As a result, I read galleys, offering suggestions to Dr. Finkel as I continued my great interest in occupational medicine by reading its literature and by talking with those active in the field.

REFERENCES

1. Hamilton, A., Exploring the Dangerous Trades, Boston, Little, Brown, 1943.
2. Hamilton, A., Industrial Toxicology, 1st ed., New York, Harper, 1934.
3. Hamilton, A., and Hardy, H. L., Industrial Toxicology, 2d ed., New York, Hoeber, 1949.
4. Hamilton, A., and Hardy, H. L., Industrial Toxicology, 3d ed., Acton, Mass., Publishing Sciences Group, 1974.
5. Hamilton, A., and Hardy, H. L., Industrial Toxicology, 4th ed., A. J. Finkel, ed., Littleton, Mass., John Wright•PSG, 1982.

CHAPTER 8

Reviving Industrial Medicine at The Massachusetts General Hospital

Getting Started — Lead Effects

Returning from Los Alamos to work at the Division of Occupational Hygiene (DOH) and the Massachusetts General Hospital (MGH) in April 1949, I began a lively period of work. My salary — the magnificient sum of $3,600 from the DOH and $1,500 from the hospital — did nothing to deter my enthusiasm. I gave lectures at the Harvard School of Public Health. Gradually, I collected series of cases of sick workers coming to the MGH as both clinic and bed patients. Using what I learned at the DOH — from study of the literature (chiefly foreign), frequent visits with Dr. Alice, and help from interested residents and staff — I felt able to seek funds to support the cost of special studies, the fees of indigent patients, and, perhaps later, a fellow to learn from and to assist me. By this time I had two aims: first, to teach my colleagues to recognize industrial illness and, second, to investigate by clinical study the variations, occasionally unique, of the body's response to toxic insult.

The MGH has a history of interest in industrial disease, begun by Dr. David Edsall, when he was chief of the Department of Medicine. In 1911, when he became dean of Harvard Medical School, he had at the MGH inaugurated what he named the "Industrial Medicine Clinic." Some work in this field continued until shortly before my active interest in 1945. Dr. Joseph Aub and his colleagues — Dr. Donald Hunter from London; L. T. Fairhall, a chemist; and P. Reznikoff, a hematologist — undertook an ongoing, careful study of toxic lead effects during the 1920s. The clinical material was used in Boston teaching hospitals by Dr. Aub.[1] With Dr. Hamilton also teaching at Harvard Medical School at that time, the stature of lead poisoning as a complex clinical entity gave the field of my choice a real boost for me. However, Harvard Medical School was not as committed to the teaching of occupational disease as it was to the teaching of infectious disease. The lead project was dependent on funds from the lead industry and the enthusiasm of able men who gradually found other interests; while it continued, it did not command great attention or attract many clinicians.

I applied to Dr. J. Howard Means, chief of medicine at the MGH at that time, for permission to start a one-half day per week clinic for the diagnosis and care of worker illnesses. The great social service worker, Ida Cannon, sister of the physiologist Dr. Walter Cannon and colleague of Dr. Richard Cabot, had been actively interested in the human side of industrial illness. Miss Cannon, although about to retire, gave generously of her time to answer the many questions I had. Little was at hand except Dr. David Edsall's famed table of diagnostic criteria of the chief occupational diseases, a copy of which was hanging rarely noticed in each office in the medical clinic.

The greatest asset — in fact, the critical factor — in the success of this venture was the support of a small steering committee of senior staff, including Dr. Nathaniel Faxon, the hospital director; Dr. Aub; Dr. Guy Lane, chief of Dermatology; Dr. Oliver Cope and Dr. William McDermott, both surgeons and active teachers; Dr. David Rutstein, chief of the Department of Preventive Medicine; Dr. Donald King, chief of the Chest Service; and Dr. Means. We often met for lunch, and I persuaded them to act as my Advisory Committee whenever I had questions about administration or ideas of expanding my little empire. My idea was to revive the knowledge available and to stimulate the investigation of the unknown and thereby to initiate appropriate clinical investigation.

Adequate financial support was supplied through the good offices of the late Mary Switzer, one of President Roosevelt's early appointees to high office in what has since become the Department of Health, Education and Welfare. Miss Switzer was a graduate and a trustee of Radcliffe. I was granted a lengthy appointment in her

Washington office after which she telephoned Dr. David Price, then a high official in the newly forming National Institutes of Health (NIH), and gave me a grand introduction to him, which helped mightily when I explained my mission.

I applied for and received money to develop my work at the MGH under the gloriously vague title of "The Study of the Pathogenesis of Certain Occupational Diseases." Since I needed other patients in addition to those suffering beryllium poisoning, I wrote, with hospital approval, to the chiefs of all the hospital departments, informing them of the reestablished Industrial Medical Clinic and the funds granted with which to study hospitalized patients and asking for the referral of cases. I took care to explain that I was not working to acquire patients for myself and that I did not plan to ask payment for my consulting services. Special laboratory studies and x-ray examinations were paid for by my research grant. By this letter, my presence in the outpatient clinics (medical and diabetic), and lunch in the doctors' cafeteria, I gradually acquired a reasonably active consultation practice.

Perhaps the most satisfying outcome of my experiences in general practice, in the care of "normals," in the Department of Labor, with the AEC, in travel to other countries, and in writing with Dr. Hamilton, was that my work flourished as I began to use the funds granted me by the NIH. I call this "clinical investigation," not "research," because the research worker can usually control the variables in his experiment. Quite different is work such as mine in which there are many unknowns. For instance, the worker may not know of his toxic exposure, since the material is usually marked only by number and the exact formula is kept secret for trade competition. The sick worker may be a heavy smoker or drinker, have had other jobs with hazardous exposure, or have had dangerous hobbies at home. Very often a sick worker fails to tell the doctor details, and the doctor in turn fails to ask the proper questions, thus overlooking critical clues, since many occupational diseases are delayed in onset for months or years. If the knowledge of the total number of workers at risk and the intensity and duration as well as the quality of exposure are well established, much may be learned by the epidemiologist, the expert who studies disease among the *demos*, the people.

A series of short stories of these years will make this, the favorite slice of my medical career, more vivid. I was asked to see a hairdresser who was thought to have "thesaurosis," a lung disease produced in animals dosed with certain hair sprays. This reaction, according to the literature, had been diagnosed in a single human case, 1 of at least 1,000 hairdressers studied. Our possible case at the hospital caused a stir among the residents, and the patient's bed was surrounded with white coats as I arrived. There was much chagrin among the senior staff when I learned from the patient that she had worked in a beryllium company that was known to have caused other cases of beryllium disease. This was a good teaching case and made the point that the occupational history must include all jobs, from early after-school tasks to later-life hobbies.

The combination of work with the DOH and the MGH from 1945 to 1947 proved exciting. The only hardship was that there were only 24 hours in each day. In part by nature and in part because of my collapse after the hurricane of 1938, my vigor demanded rest. Professionally happily launched in Boston, my family reasonably content, my own social life satisfying, my health quite dependable if I took vacations, it became clear that my career choice had evolved in such a fashion that my wish to study onset of disease with a view to prevention was being realized.

I was invited to speak before the Royal Society of Medicine in England in 1950 and at the time had an opportunity to travel in the United Kingdom and on the Continent. When I returned to Boston in late 1950, two fair-sized projects showed signs of growing productively. The Industrial Medical Clinic at the MGH brought only a few patients for diagnostic assessment, but there was much contact with lawyers, members of the Industrial Accident Board, unions, politicians, practitioners in surrounding small towns, and such government units as the Veterans Administration, and this made the work known. This list is intended to show that legal, social, and political issues were and are a part of the world of work-related illness.

Much of the knowledge needed by the doctor to handle such issues was foreign to my medical education. Unhappily in the 1950s of which I write, patients and their families suffered as a result. By the 1970s there were real improvements, but much remains to be done. In my view, premedical, medical, and hospital training must take a more active part in providing the doctor with knowledge of the working of our industrial society.

Beryllium Case Registry

In addition to the Industrial Medical Clinic, the AEC provided us with funds to start and to develop a Beryllium Case Registry of all cases of beryllium disease in the United States.[2] The aim of the registry was to discover the character of the illness, which proved to be potentially bodywide and involved many organs, biochemical changes, and complications such as kidney stones.

Chronic beryllium poisoning in the Massachusetts fluorescent lamp-manufacturing industry was first identified and reported by me in 1946 (see Chapter 5). I visited the homes of a few sick workers whose addresses were given to me by a doctor at a nearby tuberculosis sanitarium where the patients were taken for diagnosis. Dramatic weight loss, cough, and shortness of breath occurred, but no evidence of tuberculosis was documented. Through the courtesy and interest of local physicians and word-of-mouth reports among the patients, a number came to the MGH for help. There was no treatment by 1949 except bed rest and oxygen until the family of steroid drugs became available and safe to use.

Our studies taught us that the earliest-studied cases were heavily exposed and all in the same work area. The plan I designed at the hospital was aimed at describing the character of the beryllium illness and its diagnostic criteria using chest x-ray, lung function tests, and biochemical assay. When a reliable method became available, bits of tissue — skin, muscle, liver, lung, bone, salivary glands, and lymph nodes — were studied both to help in diagnosis and to increase knowledge of the behavior of beryllium, that is, where it was stored and what paths it took until excreted by the body. The tissues we collected were reviewed by Dr. David Freiman, a colleague interested in sarcoidosis, the disease most like chronic beryllium disease. There gradually emerged a pathological (abnormal) picture unique with few exceptions for toxic beryllium effect. When 30-odd cases were so studied, I concluded and reported to medical societies that *chronic* beryllium disease was an industrial illness with bodywide effects varying in severity with the beryllium exposure. That this is a serious malady was shown by the work of the Beryllium Case Registry. No case has recovered completely, although with steroids as treatment many patients have had periods of health adequate for sedentary jobs or light housekeeping. The mortality rate has been high. There is from

25 to 30 percent mortality among previously healthy people, all but a few below 40 years of age. There comes to my mind as I write the bravery of L. H., among others, who agreed to take ACTH experimentally and suffered the side effect of suicidal impulses almost tragic. Yet he trusted us as safer drugs became available. He allowed us to try endless lung function tests. Today some 30 years after the onset of his disease, although breathless on effort, he works daily as a supervisor. There were a number of heroes, male and female, who submitted to our early stumbling attempts to understand beryllium disease, its course, prevention, and cure.

Two interesting observations were recorded, first by me in 1947 and later confirmed by others. First, close neighbors or relatives might develop beryllium disease as a result of handling dirty work clothes brought home for laundering (instead of being left at the plant as is now the practice). Another group of cases existed called "neighborhood cases" because their homes were close to a plant that had no control device to limit the amount of unwanted beryllium that poured into the neighborhood air. The second point of interest made me guess that beryllium upset the body's handling of an essential element, calcium. During World War II two out of three work shifts were manned by women, and when the war ended many of the beryllium-exposed women became pregnant. Pregnancy led to childbirth without trouble. However, at the time of lactation the mothers with a beryllium body burden began to lose weight, to cough, and to become short of breath. When a careful medical history was taken of ill *male* workers, beryllium exposed, I discovered that what I chose to call *trigger factors* — combat flying, surgery, other toxic work exposures, or reexposure to beryllium in spite of abnormal chest x-rays assumed due to other causes — proved beryllium poisoning is related to exposure not gender.

Long-term study of my MGH beryllium cases showed that kidney stones, salivary gland and lung stones, and increasing severe lung damage with right heart failure as a result were usual complications leading to complete disability and death. Beryllium is excreted slowly and can do harm over a period of years for reasons not clearly understood. A month-long study in Ward 4, an endowed research ward at the MGH, of a very ill woman and her less-than-a-year-old baby showed beryllium present in her urine a year after exposure as well as in the baby's. This child, like others we surveyed, showed no evi-

dence of toxic effect. Children of other mothers — sick and well —
are free from harm as far as we know. The exception is a small but
important number of children living in homes near beryllium plants
or those where two or more adults brought dirty work clothes home
for washing.

    I summarize for the reader what is certain. European litera-
ture (1929–40) and reports from Ohio and Pennsylvania (1943) describe an acute chemical pneumonia due to a heavy dose of certain
beryllium compounds that results in complete recovery or death in
most early cases, depending on the size of dose. There are also so-
called subacute cases caused by lower or intermittent exposure. On
further exposure to beryllium (or in a few instances, without such),
these cases may slowly become the much more serious chronic beryllium disease. Tragically, in 1943 the U.S. Public Health Service reported beryllium harmless[3] and repeated the error in a report in
1972,[4] relying heavily on animal studies for conclusions. Some experimental animals develop malignancies after being dosed with
beryllium. The species of animal differ, and the dose and kind of
beryllium compound used also differ from one experiment to another.
The question is, Are humans who are exposed to beryllium in danger
from some form of cancer? In my opinion there are not enough data
yet to answer firmly yes or no. Industry is troubled by possible liability cost, as are officials in government positions, for the U.S. government now allows itself to be sued. Since delay from beryllium exposure to the onset of illness may be as long as 25 years in a few cases,
and since there are a variety of reasons, some not laudable such as
the discharge of a worker who is ill, the number of those persons at
risk in the beryllium industry is unknown. Unhappily, even the Social
Security banks and their computers are not wholly adequate to give
the answer to these questions because erroneous information has been
entered at some time. Time alone can solve completely the problem
of safe amounts of exposure to beryllium and the many-as-yet-un-
answered questions in the behavior of this industrial disease.

    While beryllium has not been used in the manufacture of neon
and fluorescent lighting since 1949 in the United States, Table 1 shows
how wide the distribution of toxic beryllium compounds in industrial processes can be. There are nearly 900 cases of beryllium disease in the Beryllium Case Registry, and slowly the number increases.
Since 1947 I have been scrapping with industry, insurance carriers,

Table 1

Uses of Beryllium, 1977

Beryllium mining	Chemical plants
Beryllium extraction	Salvage of fluorescent and neon
Beryllium metallurgy	lamps
Beryllium alloy manufacture and users (with Ca, Al, steel, Ni, Mg, Pt)	Beryllium ceramics manufacture (crucibles, spark plugs, bricks, thermal coatings, rocket motor
Beryllium phosphorus manufacture	parts)
Fluorescent lamp manufacture*	X-ray tube window manufacture
Neon sign manufacture and repair	Nuclear reactor manufacture
Gas mantle manufacture	Atomic energy development
Plastic manufacture	(research)
Solid rocket fuel development	Electronic tube manufacture
Aircraft and rocket structures (research)	Guidance system manufacture (gyroscopes, housings)

*Until 1949 in the United States.

Source: Hamilton, A., and Hardy, H. L., Industrial Toxicology, 3d ed., Acton, Mass., Publishing Sciences Group, 1974, p. 44. Reprinted with permission.

federal government officials, and lawyers. In 1966 at a meeting of representatives of the above-listed groups, the idea suddenly appealed to me that someone else should enjoy this battle. I found a willing colleague and gained the approval of the AEC, the funding agency, for the transfer of the Beryllium Case Registry to its office in Washington. When industry learned of the plan, it raised such a fuss that for two years the cartons holding the registry files were kept under the desk of an official of a government agency. In 1968 an official was sent to see me with a box of candy in his hand, like a schoolboy going to see his teacher. He wanted me to take the registry again, for there were no plans for its continuance by the government, in part owing to industry's wish to control it and government agency trouble about funding. The AEC was no longer responsible for health and safety in the beryllium industry.

Having had a minor stroke in January 1968, I decided not to accept it again but persuaded my colleague, Dr. Homayoun Kazemi, chief of the Pulmonary Unit at the MGH, to take the registry under his wing. Knowledge of beryllium toxicity grows, and a number of fellows of the unit have had a taste of occupational medicine, a matter of great satisfaction to me. An important goal of the registry was to accumulate as much data as possible to establish beryllium exposure, its intensity and duration, and the beryllium compound involved. The planning and development of the registry proved to be a difficult, long-term job. By publicity from talks, formal papers, and notices in medical journals, new cases with differing histories came to light. A good-sized roster of contributing physicians was collected through the courtesy of a number of doctors (at one time 300). Chest x-rays and pathological material were accumulated. Our funds provided for a fellow who worked on our files, helped study cases in the hospital, and made field trips to communities where groups of patients and physicians were willing to collaborate with the registry efforts. Most insurance companies and employers were not pleased with our enthusiasm for the discovery of the increasing number of cases. This increase was seen because many cases became clinically active only after a period of delay lasting as long as ten or more years. The fellow attached to the registry made the work more feasible and released my excitement to enlist others to enjoy the challenge of occupational medicine. Dr. Arthur Rosenbloom, our first fellow, died tragically of a tumor of the heart six months after starting work. Dr. Warren Weil was a fellow for two years before going into general practice. Dr. Lloyd Tepper, a fellow for several years, chose a full-time career in industrial medicine. He and I collaborated in writing a monograph and several articles, and he contributed several chapters to the third edition of the Hamilton and Hardy text, *Industrial Toxicology*.[5]

There were problems of competition for space at the hospital and threat of withdrawal of financial support as government agencies felt less need for and interest in the work of the registry. The greatest threat to the life of the registry arose from industrial management. The cost of compensation and the possibility of government prohibition of beryllium use by the military encouraged beryllium users to tireless pursuit of tactics to discredit the registry and my role. It is hard to report but true that some doctors, a few government officials, and a group of those trained as engineers (called industrial hygienists), working alone as industrial consultants or for insurance companies, testified in court or wrote deceptive reports. Finding my way from the cloisters of college and medical education through this maze of techniques used in our free, competitive industrial society taught me much of the "real" world.

In 1952, using the clinical material accumulated by the modest start of the revised second Industrial Medical Clinic, I described my findings in a paper read at the National Industrial Lead Association meeting, later published.[6] I had now begun my missionary activity designed to attract other physicians to this field. I listed diagnoses and my view of their occupational causes. Several of my conclusions were challenged. However, helping Dr. Hamilton develop her text (with the help of Drs. Aub, Hunter, and Mallory), reading the older literature, and encountering problems while gaining correct identification of beryllium disease all gave me confidence to suggest that many cases of industrial disease go unrecognized.

Later, when I still held my clinical post at the MGH but was spending most of my time at the Massachusetts Institute of Technology Occupational Medical Service, our two groups studied as a team many other problems, with me as "the boss" responsible for the caliber of the work, its funding, and its initiation. The problems we chose for study arose from requests or questions from staff and family physicians, lawyers, medical students, union leaders, doctors I met at professional meetings, and, perhaps most fruitfully, patients under my care. To underline the variety and interest of my experience, I list certain projects: exposure to pesticides; investigation of cyanide salts; early use of ACTH for beryllium poisoning; two cases of malignancy in asbestos workers (1952); chemical trials with EDTA for treatment of lead poisoning; cataracts associated with ultra-high-frequency radiation; differential diagnosis between beryllium poisoning and sarcoidosis; repeated exposure to carbon tetrachloride; the amount of arsenic in hair, liver, and urine of nonworkers; increased uric acid in blood of patients with beryllium disease; and compensation experience of patients with chronic beryllium poisoning. This incomplete listing serves to illustrate that occupational medicine is a viable specialty for internists that medical schools must recognize.

REFERENCES

1. Aub, N. C., Minot, A. S., Fairhall, L. T., and Reznikoff, P., Recent investigations of absorption and excretion of lead in the organism, JAMA, 83:588, 1924.

2. Tepper, L. B., Hardy, H. L., and Chamberlin, R. I, Toxicity of Beryllium Compounds, A Monograph, Amsterdam, Elsevier, 1961.
3. U.S. Public Health Service, The Toxicology of Beryllium, Bull no. 181, Washington, D.C., Government Printing Office, 1943.
4. Tabershaw, I. R., ed., The Toxicology of Beryllium, Washington, D.C., U.S. Public Health Service, Pub. no. 2173, 1972 (revision).
5. Hamilton, A., and Hardy, H. L., Industrial Toxicology, 3rd ed., Acton, Mass., Publishing Sciences Group, 1974.
6. Foreman, H., Hardy, H. L., Shipman, T. L., and Belknap, E. L., Use of calcium EDTA in cases of lead intoxication, Arch. Ind. Hyg. Occup. Med., 7:148, 1953.

CHAPTER 9

Occupational Medical Service: The Massachusetts Institute of Technology

OMS Assignments

When I returned from Los Alamos at the end of 1948, Dr. Dana Farnsworth, medical director of Massachusetts Institute of Technology (MIT), asked me to serve as his consultant for the government-sponsored research laboratories working on beryllium and its compounds. Dr. Aub and his associate, Dr. Robert Grier, had discovered a series of nine cases of beryllium poisoning in one of the MIT research projects, described in Chapter 8. Dr. Robert Grier and Dr. M. B. Hoagland had shown in the laboratory that beryllium upsets certain enzyme systems. During the period of this research (1943–48), government agencies still insisted that beryllium was harmless despite European literature and U.S. reports of illness in beryllium workers in Massachusetts, Pennsylvania, and Ohio.

In view of my commitments to the Massachusetts DOH and my nicely growing progeny at the MGH, I wondered if it was wise to accept MIT's offer. Once again my senior medical advisers – Dr. Cope, Dr. Means, and chiefly Dr. Aub – urged me to accept. The advice proved excellent: I gained wonderful experience in fields new to me and a most congenial atmosphere of collaboration, with scope in which to test my own wildest ideas of the toxicity of this or that material.

Since I was hired to prevent work-related illness in the MIT population, it became necessary to develop an arm of the medical department, named, first, the Occupational Medical Service (OMS) and, later, as its duties expanded, the Environmental Medical Service. Dr. Farnsworth is responsible for this rather unusual development. After I had worked six months on the beryllium hazard, he called me to his office and said, "Harriet, I believe you should start at the Massachusetts Avenue entrance [the main entrance] and work your way through the institute, making surveys of every department and research laboratory as you go, while looking for unnecessary and potentially harmful risks."

Some of my interesting assignments had nothing to do with toxic exposures. When I was first appointed, there were few women students, in contrast to the present number of nearly 1,500. I helped the dean as his adviser on women's affairs. This meant that disgruntled women planning to become engineers came to complain to me that faculty ignored them, surely true in some cases. When Dr. Farnsworth left MIT to become medical director of Harvard University, my MGH chief of medicine, Dr. Means, took his place—in semiretirement. He and I worked hard to improve medical record-keeping, a rather dull but essential job. I also worked on the character and technique of preemployment medical examinations. Special thought was given to the problem of records being used in compensation cases. Medical histories of entering students, sent from family doctors, were referred to me for review.

An assignment I enjoyed during this period was serving as premedical adviser. In 1960, my first year in this role, instead of the 12 students my predecessor had promised, there were 50 who had to be interviewed, faculty references collected, and a letter from me compiled on each. By 1966 I had to call for help since the number had risen to over 100 applicants per year. I learned a lot from my talks with these premedical students. MIT's funds allowed me to visit medical schools, especially those who had always refused MIT students despite their good records. I discovered that some of these schools did not know the breadth of MIT's required curriculum, thought that MIT was still a technical school for engineers, and did not know that the quantity of humanities studies required exceeded those of Harvard.

We had all sorts of questions arise. One day I received a telephone call from a frightened postgraduate student who said, "I am alone in the laboratory. I was using laser beams to make new chemical compounds. Now I smell almonds, and I know that means cyanide. What shall I do?" I replied as calmly as possible, "Since you are talking to me, you are alive. Why not walk over to my office and I will examine you." This he did, and I found nothing wrong.

The variety of materials and energies used at MIT required an array of tests, literature study, and help from faculty members as each hazard became clear or a funding government agency asked for elucidation. The underlying working philosophy was that those doing the experiment — student, technician, faculty member — were responsible for possible hazards. OMS members were advisory, but I (perhaps this was the mother-guardian role) held that when a job was shown to be dangerous, the worker next higher in seniority would be told, with recommendations as to precautions. If recommendations were not followed, the appropriate OMS staff member, often myself, went up the ladder of seniority, rarely ending in the president's office.

As at Los Alamos, support for the OMS work came early in my MIT life, given me by the president at the time, James Killian. The beryllium work continued to be hazardous because engineering controls had not been installed. A formula I had used at Los Alamos led me to go to President Killian's office to explain the problem, saying, "I can no longer be responsible for those in Building Z lacking proper controls. I recommend that you close the operation, and I prophesy that the needed ventilation will be in place in a few days." President Killian sighed and looked out of the open window for air and inspiration. It was a very hot day, and his rolled-up shirt sleeves and stacks of paper on his desk showed me a busy, uncomfortable president. Finally he said, "Dr. Hardy, I will think about what you have said." The work was stopped, and within a week the protection controls were in place.

The OMS was hard at work. The faculty committees formed to advise the OMS helped with the difficult problems, including those of the "bad boys" unwilling to take our work seriously. Committees, formed as needed, included Radiation Health, Nuclear Reactor Safeguard, Laboratory Hazards, Animal Care, Experimental Use of Human Subjects, and Biological Hazards.

The construction of a research nuclear reactor taught me of new worlds. In 1956 Professor Manson Benedict asked me to be responsible for the health of those working there. So the OMS developed a group with proper training — to be located within the reactor shell and on duty whenever it was operating and to measure not only levels of radiation during operation but also air and water pollution by the reactor. Since this giant and novel device was on a crowded city street with factories and dwellings nearby, MIT authorities thought it wise to have individual meetings not only with their own corporation, faculty, and students but also with the Cambridge City Council, the governor of Massachusetts, civil defense officers, and the state police. So I joined a retired general (who in 1957 became an MIT vice-president) and an admiral (who was vice-president in charge of research) to meet the groups of notables and to tell our story. The city council came to MIT in a body to sit around a great mahogany table, where we were joined by then President Julius Stratton. The story was told again, and the city council, once past their awe of the reactor, asked intelligent questions. Asked about possible sabotage, the admiral chose to answer, saying, "If a man wheeled a wheelbarrow loaded with explosives inside the reactor and ignited them, the reactor shell might quake, but I doubt that any harm would come to the neighborhood." He spoke from his knowledge that it was built on piles sunk deep in the soft earth because of our proximity to the Charles River. My contribution to the Reactor Safeguard Committee was to insist on the presence of one MIT vice-president, a senior faculty member from nearby Harvard, a biophysicist, and skilled individuals from outside MIT as needed.

I realized I lacked the knowledge to sound an alarm. My experience had taught me that no individual can judge whether perchance a potential risk exists in his own experiment. Each investigator is anxious to go ahead with his work. For example, the chemical 2-nitropropane was proposed for use in sealing gaskets. I recalled investigating illness at a small plant making 2-nitropropane when I worked with the DOH, and therefore I asked what steps had been taken to learn of its toxicity. I was told that an undergraduate student had looked through the literature and found no report of harmful effects. Still not satisfied, I consulted our senior chemist, who answered promptly that 2-nitropropane had explosive properties. Thus, if it had been used, rupture of the gaskets would have meant leaking of radioactive gases. I have spun out this story because this was historically one of the first reactors, and it was developed among an inexperienced population of students and faculty who were to learn on and from it how to use it. Those in authority at MIT behaved intelligently and with vision. In my advise to the committee, I used lessons learned at Los Alamos to make clear my convictions that pre-planning of a risky operation with members of various skills work-ing peacefully with each other will prevent accidents. I believe that there is no work so dangerous that it cannot be undertaken if those in charge are willing to take adequate advance steps and are provided with adequate funding. At this writing the only biological damage that has occurred at the MIT reactor has been skin burns suffered by senior scientists who chose to take a chance with the risk of harm-ful effects well known to them.

The Beryllium Struggle Goes On

At this period (1961–71) my life was perhaps too full for me to di-gest all my experiences. The OMS as a protective, warning unit found more and more graduates and faculty at risky work, and its staff, including myself, had made friends and engendered respect for our professional stance so that most of our recommendations were fav-orably accepted. Worker-patients continued to come to the outpa-tient clinic for diagnosis and treatment. Calls for consultation brought me and my fellow workers both simple and complex questions re-quiring good relations with research, pathology, radiology, and pul-monary faculty as well as much library search.

The Beryllium Case Registry grew, and there were almost al-ways victims of beryllium poisoning in the hospital for diagnosis, treatment, and study of the new disease that had been identified in the United States less than 20 years previously. In my "spare time," I and my colleagues wrote papers publishing our findings. I accepted invitations to speak here and there, to teach, and with grant support, to travel.

Part of the beryllium story reflects both my quick temper and the chaos in the beryllium industry in the 1950s. Two young men from a company manufacturing explosives came to my office seek-ing knowledge of beryllium toxicity. They would not tell me what the beryllium was to be used for. I gave my facts and showed them chest x-rays. They seemed mildly impressed and mentioned that the president of the company that would supply the beryllium had told them that there were no cases in his plant. This president was my

Enemy No. 1 just then because he had published an article in a business magazine stating that: beryllium toxicity is a myth. Turning to my visitors and rapidly losing my temper, I asked if they had wives and children — both did. I then pulled from my desk preserved samples of autopsy specimens that came from workers made ill in that plant. The young men became silent.

In a short time I received a letter from the angered beryllium company president, stating that there were a few cases of chemical pneumonia due to the acids used but no cases of beryllium disease. A final sentence implied that if I did not stop accusing the beryllium industry of causing illness among the workers, the president would feel justified in bringing a libel suit against me personally. Having made my angry statements under MIT's wing, I was impressed enough to pay a visit to the senior lawyer for the institute, a wise and experienced man who knew the beryllium background. He smiled while I talked. I wondered what he found so funny and, following his gaze, saw he had noticed a worn place in my jacket lining. Said he, "Harriet, you are not a subject for libel."

A sad story I recall came from a visit from a third-year medical student who had chosen occupational medicine as his summer elective. He told me tearfully of the government official who with anger squelched him when he protested against continued beryllium exposure and disease. The government official stated that society had the right to cause illness and even death to ensure industrial progress. The young student's answer was that men were sent home without even a chest x-ray or advice to see their own physician, and he felt this was to avoid any litigation for compensation, should they become ill.

A different but equally educational episode took place in my office. Two senior officers, one from each of the two large beryllium-manufacturing companies, visited me to learn the latest information on beryllium toxicity. Feeling cross at their hypocrisy, I began an angry answer when the telephone stopped me. An officer in the air force was calling to ask if I thought he should evacuate a village ten miles from a test site before the air force fired a rocket engine using beryllium as fuel. The two executives, thinking such work highly secret, wrote this all in their notebooks as I repeated aloud my answer. They realized that I was using all the influence I could muster through Congress, MIT colleagues, friends in government agencies, and personal visits to various Washington offices to halt the use of beryllium as a rocket fuel.

The beryllium industry had to recognize what the hazards might be, so I explained my opposition to beryllium-fired missiles: first, huge amounts were to be used; second, finely divided particles, easily inhaled, were required; and finally, as on the occasion of U.S. atomic bomb tests in the air, there was no way to recover the beryllium or to determine its distribution on earth.

The session with these men did not break up before a second phone call interrupted. This was the advocate general of the air force. He said, "Dr. Hardy, suppose a beryllium-powered device was to explode while men were in a small building nearby, monitoring the work. And, suppose something went wrong. Would the men acquire beryllium poisoning?" Of course, no accurate answer was possible. I asked if the men were hospitalized for study and care, and the answer was no. Throughout these phone calls the officials sat writing, quite hypnotized. An air force physician later came to my home to discuss missile firing. He reported that the exposed men were sent home without a medical examination, chest x-ray, or recommendation for future medical follow-up. Again, the fear of litigation acted to corrupt the physician's clear duty.

Other Problems Referred to the OMS

My tale would become out of proportion if I wrote in detail of all that happened to me, of what I learned, and of the wonderfully keen and loyal staff in the 21 years I served MIT. A sample of the problems referred to the OMS will have to suffice.

An early problem came in hot weather when a leak in a pipe carrying mercury overexposed the workers trying to mend the leak. Because of its physical characteristics, mercury vapor becomes airborne even at room temperature, and when it is heated, the amount increases greatly. Experience at Los Alamos taught me that many people are unaware of this or are unimpressed by the toxicity of mercury. All four workers showed laboratory signs of intoxication by the vapor, affecting their kidneys. We found excess amounts of mercury being excreted. A hectic period of argument with the senior physicist led, after I showed him the literature and the data that the OMS had collected on his workers, to mutual respect. The workers' findings became normal after a month of no exposure to mercury.

One group conceived the idea that study of the behavior of sonar bats from Trinidad might yield important clues in radar detection. A Trinidad bat flying above the water could choose between two fish swimming together to decide which one it wanted for food. When tested with controls, it was shown that the bats could make their choices with uncanny accuracy. So bats were brought to MIT — but, unfortunately, they carry rabies. The Pasteur treatment for rabies is long and painful; therefore, when I was consulted, I studied a preventive vaccine using duck embryo. All but one of the staff working with the bats accepted injections of vaccine. The staff became too friendly with the bats, naming them and feeding them from their fingers. The expected happened — the man who refused vaccine (he said he was allergic) was bitten by one. Since therapy was as hazardous or perhaps even more hazardous than vaccine to those with allergy, prayer and watchful waiting were the successful form of treatment. But for a time I became an expert on rabies.

For a variety of tests, MIT had an experimental wind tunnel that generated velocities that simulated high-altitude flying. Protective devices for men's ears had to be found to block out noise. We had other problems there, too. Accidentally a huge measuring instrument full of mercury was placed at the mouth of the tunnel and it broke. Because of the force of the wind, the mercury was smashed to atom size and spattered all over the walls of the tunnel. The OMS was asked how to clean the tunnel, a matter that seemed impossible. But Fred Viles of our staff pointed out that flowers of sulfur, a powder, would combine with the mercury, and the compound that formed could be safely washed off. Thus the tunnel was treated and ready to be used once more.

It was my job to know where there were potential hazards and to plan precautions and follow-up medical examinations as required. A real problem was posed by persons who persisted in using their mouths to suck small quantities of a radioisotope (tritium) into a glass pipette for accurate measurement or transfer. Sudden distraction or Monday morning inattention might lead to the swallowing of the radioisotope solution. Characteristics of the isotope could result in its retention in the body, perhaps at critical sites in liver or gonads. The OMS talked at length to the faculty concerned and showed modern instruments capable of doing the job mechanically. Since some professors refused to change their method, I decided we must conceive ways of protecting the technicians, students, and faculty as far as possible. Based on advice from our biophysicist, Dr. Martin Lubin, our plans were designed for women of child-bearing age. The feminist movement took it hard that women should be excluded from laboratories of professors who persisted in using mouth pipetting, but I called all persons in this category to my office; I described the problem, took a full medical and occupational history of each, and arranged for biologic samples to detect whether tritium was already present in the body. In addition, the OMS had developed and simplified the use of the whole body counter: an individual sat in what appeared to be a barber's chair, which was equipped with delicate instrumentation to monitor the presence of any radioactive material. The final step for the worker was a lecture on possible harm to genetic material or to young fetuses from even small doses of ionizing radiation. The arrangement was made that the individual should notify her supervisor if she became pregnant, following which she would be temporarily shifted to nonradioactive work. Because of rapid changes in this population, we have only negative evidence of the value of the program. However, such informal teaching on a one-to-one basis helped the OMS relationship with graduate students and faculty involved. We were, of course, laughed at by some faculty, much as the danger of research on DNA has been a subject of scorn in some quarters and hysterical reaction in others. But there is not enough knowledge for anyone in novel basic biologic research to come down flatly on either side.

The nutrition department at MIT, interested in all aspects of food and its preservation, is important. More and more it must work with animals and human volunteers to increase knowledge of nutrition, good and bad, in normal and deprived populations of the world. An incident involving normal MIT students demonstrates the need for a sense of responsibility by senior faculty. A recently appointed young faculty member took heart-action measurements before and after volunteers had to run to near exhaustion. Next he gave them diets lacking in an essential element and then had them run. When heart tracings were done after the exercise, they were abnormal. The designer of this research was asked to resign and leave the institute.

From this same department, late one Friday, a safety officer telephoned to say he had been asked to clean up a spill of pure botulinum toxin, the agent causing the dreaded food-poisoning disease: botulism. The facts were that a student had been asked to carry a rack of test tubes from the safety area to the high-temperature equipment designed to destroy active botulinum toxin. The girl had slipped and fallen, the fall breaking all the test tubes. The senior professor in charge of the laboratory had departed for his home, leaving others to clean up the spill. As he left, he said to the group that alcohol would neutralize the toxin. The professor stated that all people who worked in canning factories who might be exposed to botulinum made a practice of drinking alcohol steadily, and none became ill. The OMS quickly sent men with completely protective clothing, including respirators with outside air supply. I manned the phone and worked through medical texts to refresh my memory of signs and symptoms of botulism. I made phone calls to the MGH and state and federal offices for information as to where and how to get botulism antitoxin. The only antitoxin I could locate was held in a Canadian hospital, and authorities there promptly sent me the antidote with instructions on proper dosage. This potentially awesome accident (there were a number of workers in the laboratory at the time) had a happy ending. The young woman who dropped the test tubes was the only one to develop signs and symptoms; unhappily they were those in the textbooks associated with botulism. Her young hopsital doctor and I, at home, spent a poor night exchanging alarms at intervals. The best call came from the hospital. The patient reported that she and a male colleague thought it best to follow the professor's "cure." She, unused to drinking alcohol, took several gin martinis and half a bottle of red wine. Small wonder she had a tremor and what appeared to be crossed eyes. In a matter of hours, all the symptoms disappeared.

The team approach to assess and protect the myriad of operations of a lively, growing teaching institute was used. To try to be ready for any and all questions, our group met over lunch weekly to discuss our activities. I built up a library, a good collection of slides and x-rays plus appropriate books and journals on toxicology and industrial medicine. This OMS room was so valuable to us and to many others in the institute that much of the time we were forced to keep it locked.

I and my colleagues at MIT and the MGH developed techniques to study in some detail the clinical and biochemical manifestations of well-known and novel worker risks. As a result of my months at the DOH and at Los Alamos, I acquired what most physicians lack: respect for and recognition of the professional help of chemists, engineers, and physicists in discovering the quality and quantity of a harmful agent and how to reduce it to reasonably safe working levels.

MIT — A Move Forward

By the mid-1950s a satisfying career had evolved. In retrospect I could see that my first jobs in institutions for women alone, while of interest to me in learning "normal" variations and carrying out a small amount of clinical investigation, were steps on the way but not enough to hold my interest nor to use my developing skills. My first-class education plus my small-town country practice provided me with a rich background of thought and action. My move to Cambridge and Radcliffe led to greater clinical experience and a postgraduate course in many facets of medicine by my attendance at the teaching grand rounds of the MGH. Because of World War II and the absence of men physicians, I was assigned a modest amount of teaching at Harvard Medical School.

In 1945 came the move to the DOH where my energies, imagination, and ideas of social responsibility were, I then thought, completely engaged. The work as junior author with Dr. Alice Hamilton in the writing of the second edition of *Industrial Toxicology*[1] led to hours in the library and concise writing of summaries of my work at the DOH for inclusion. The excitement and responsibility of my year at Los Alamos increased my knowledge of the basic harmful effects of radiant energy and provided me with further experience in the recognition of toxic chemicals and metals as used in atomic energy development.

When government funding made clinical investigations at the MGH a reality and the project was approved by senior staff friends, my cup was full. Beginning in 1950, when I joined the MIT Medical Department to prevent, if possible, damage to the population in this great institution, my cup was indeed overflowing!

Being self-confident and clear in my notion of the character of preventive medicine, as well as unafraid to ask questions that showed my ignorance, the 21 years at MIT taught me a great deal.

They forced me to study and showed me how broad indeed are the horizons of the universe physically, mentally, and spiritually. I learned new vocabularies to understand my friends in metallurgy, reactor technology, and modern biology. Partly because I am endlessly curious about everything and everybody, I found it easy — with rare exceptions — to make friends with each patient and with fellow workers of every rank. For those I held in contempt, such as harmful practitioners of medicine and law, I did little to hide my true feelings.

Of great value to my self-esteem was the remark made by Dr. Dana Farnsworth, my first boss there, after he had supported my recommendations in a difficult situation: "Harriet, the reason you can work successfully at MIT with its male population is the fact that you always leave a man room to get out if the changes you propose are too much for him."

REFERENCE

1. Hamilton, A., and Hardy, H. L., Industrial Toxicology, 2d ed., New York, Hoeber, 1949.

CHAPTER 10

Clinical Investigation
of Occupational Disease

Causative Agents

Knowledge of dust diseases of the respiratory tract dates to the years when men started digging in the earth for materials of value. Some of these are harmful like the best-studied dust, silica (SiO_2), called quartz and found everywhere in the earth's crust. Table 2 shows the most common uses of silica. If inhaled as finely divided particles about the size of a red blood cell (5 μ in diameter) invisible to the naked eye, its disease-producing power cannot be exaggerated, especially if tuberculosis is a complication or the amount of silica inhaled is great. Through the ages Nature has developed a variety of so-called silicates, combinations of metals with silica, resulting in "new" dusts of various chemical composition with differing powers to cause disease. My late colleague Dr. Henry Schroeder[1] and others have pointed out that in general the body has developed defenses and methods of disposal or storage for elements found in air, water, and soil before the industrial era. On the other hand, materials recently dug out of the earth present new problems for existing biological defense. For example, tin, barium, aluminum dusts, and coal from low quartz ores are harmful only when inhaled in great quantity over a long period so that the normal anatomy of the respiratory system is crowded or destroyed, leading to heart failure or overwhelming infection the body is unable to handle.

My experience at the Massachusetts General Hospital (MGH) stimulated my interest in occupational lung disease due to mineral

Table 2

Uses of Silica—Partial Listing

Abrasives manufacture	Refractory manufacture
Ceramics manufacture	Road construction
Foundry work	Sandpaper manufacture
Furnace and kiln lining	Sandstone grinding
Granite cutting	Silver polishing
Mining	Street sweeping
Pottery making	Tunnel work

Source: Hamilton, A., and Hardy, H. L., Industrial Toxicology, 3d ed., Acton, Mass., Publishing Sciences Group,
1974, p. 429. Reprinted with permission.

dust, chemicals, and vegetable dust. The workers who came from
referrals of staff, unions, and lawyers, unhappily, did not respond
well to antibiotics or modern antituberculosis drugs if they suffered
both silicosis and tuberculosis. All dust diseases are named a form
of pneumoconiosis, which when translated means "reaction to dust
in the lungs." Table 3 is a simple but incomplete classification of occupational lung disease for the layman, with examples chosen from
hospital and Division of Occupational Hygiene (DOH) experiences.
Thus, our patients were called "silicotics" — those suffering from silicosis with or without tuberculosis or bacterial pneumonia.

Two points in the long history of the silica hazard are worth
including. First, Agricola (40–93 A.D.) noted and recorded that the
women in the Carpathian Mountains each had had seven husbands
because of silica and tuberculosis in this area, which caused deaths
at an early age. The second is the aforementioned report of the Massachusetts stove factory, which used considerable silica in the 1930s.
Because workers had abnormal chest x-rays and on the advice of the
insurance company were discharged, a public outcry arose and led
to the formation of the Division of Occupational Hygiene (DOH)
within the Massachusetts Department of Labor.

A few cases we studied at the MGH will help these chest diseases of industrial workers seem more real. A 35-year-old Italian
foundry worker who came to me from Ohio had very abnormal chest
x-ray changes but no complaints. Compensation authorities had de-

clared him 100 percent disabled for life. He said a friend had come to our hospital and was cured because all the dust was removed from his lung, and I was to do the same for him! This patient, Tony, was bright but uneducated, and his use of English was limited. I put him to bed and submitted him to a battery of heart and lung function tests. For treatment Tony received low levels of oxygen four times a day, 15 minutes each time, given with as much display of elaborate

Table 3

Partial List of Disease-Causing Dusts, Bacteria, and Chemicals Used in Industry

---

I. Due to dusts (pneumoconiosis)
  A. Benign (harmless)
    1. Tin, aluminum, some forms of iron
    2. Coal, with 2 percent or less quartz in the ore
  B. Scar-producing (harmful)
    1. Silica (quartz) with or without infection
    2. Talc (not all forms)
    3. Asbestos
    4. Coal with more than 2 percent quartz in the ore
II. Due to chemicals
  A. Acute pneumonia
    1. Acids and alkalis, nitrous fumes
    2. Cadmium oxide
    3. Beryllium and its compounds
  B. Chronic lung and/or bodywide disease
    1. Beryllium
    2. Cadmium
  C. Malignancies
    1. Chromium
    2. Arsenic
    3. Hematite
    4. Asbestos
III. Due to vegetable dusts
  A. Cotton, flax, jute
  B. Silo dust—fresh green grass
IV. Due to bacteria
  A. Anthrax

---

apparatus as possible. Patient questioning brought out the fact that Tony had been working with iron alone. Because of the intensity and duration of exposure, small round opacities in both lungs showed on chest x-ray. All tests were normal. After a week of bed rest and re-assurance, Tony and I ran up two flights of stairs together. I took both his and my pulse and breathing rates before and after the exer-cise. Tony's reaction to the exercise was far healthier than mine, and I pronounced him "cured," avoiding the question as to whether all the dust was gone. I wrote his personal doctor and begged that a job be found for him without a required preemployment chest x-ray. His diagnosis was siderosis, harmless iron deposits of which the body could not rid itself, with the result that many employers would not hire him because of his abnormal x-rays and possible employer liability even though he had normal heart and lung function findings. Alas, I never heard from Tony, so I do not know the end of his story. Of course my treatment was a placebo. I was criticized by some of my colleagues, but I felt comfortable knowing that I was treating Tony with his modest understanding rather than his chest x-ray changes, which were harmless and would perhaps disappear in time if iron exposure were stopped.

Less fortunate were workers I studied who had inhaled both iron and quartz, which led to heart and lung failure. Reports since the mid-1950s suggest that men who mine certain iron ore may have a higher risk of cancer of the lung. Most mines contain cancer-pro-ducing radioactive gases, which makes it hard to assess iron ore as the single cause.

Asbestos

Asbestos is a harmful silicate with at least four industrially used forms, which are mined in various parts of the world. Asbestos from each region has a differing chemical composition and a variety of damag-ing biological effects in man and experimental animals. The media in industrialized Western countries have publicized the ill effects of asbestos quite out of proportion to the risk, especially that in city streets, schools, hospitals, and drinking water. The reader has doubt-less seen or read much about asbestos, particularly since Dr. Irving Selikoff began writing and speaking of his experience among insula-tion workers in New Jersey in the early 1960s.[2]

The asbestos story is very old. Dr. Donald Hunter of London writes that Charlemagne had a tablecloth of asbestos that was cleaned by fire. Also, Hunter reports that the wicks of the candles used by the Vestal Virgins were made of asbestos, the first use of the name.[3] In 1900 Dr. G. S. Christie, also in London, described the postmortem findings, the first on record, in a worker dying of asbestosis. Similar reports followed, punctuated in 1933 by Dr. E. R. A. Merewether of the English Factory Inspectorate who recorded that one-third of the men dying of asbestos also had malignancy of the lung found at autopsy. In the 1930s two U.S. radiologists, H. K. Pancoast and E. P. Pendergrass, reported chest x-ray changes of asbestos workers as differing from silicosis.[4] In 1948 K. M. Lynch published a U.S. study of pathology,[5] and I and two hospital residents, K. Isselbacher and H. Klaus, in 1952, published a full pre- and post-mortem study of a worker who died of lung failure.[6] A malignancy was found. Before long a second case under our care showed similar abnormalities. A note on the second case included the query, Since men were heavy smokers, might not the cancer be due to a combination of cigarette smoking and inhalation of asbestos fibers?

Two other disease reactions to asbestos are described. A fatal malignancy associated with inhalation of a single form (crocidolite) of asbestos invaded the chest wall (pleura) and/or the abdominal wall.[7] From Finland first and later from other countries came reports of calcification of membranes easily seen on x-ray. Some observers concluded that there is an increase in cancer as an end result.

Industrial uses of asbestos (Table 4) give evidence of the widespread contamination of workers and the environment. I feel that the facts to date do not support the many claims of asbestos effect on those with slight exposure. Without a doubt, workers in or near dusty operations using asbestos may in a significant percentage develop asbestosis, and in the case of cigarette smokers an important number will be found to have lung cancer as well. Dr. M. L. Newhouse of London has found that asbestos may cause disease in neighborhoods of factories or in the families of workers who bring fibers into their homes on their clothes or hair. This story of asbestos damage is now internationally known, and unanswered questions of differences in fibers from various areas and their harmful effect and the problem of safe working and neighborhood levels are engaging the skills of a number of research groups.

Two of my asbestos patients and their care illustrate the hu-

Table 4

Uses of Asbestos—Partial Listing

Heat insulation	Air filtration
Brake linings	Paint filler
Electrical wire insulation	Shingles, asbestos boards
Pipe and furnace fitting	Pump packing
Asbestos textiles—clothing, blankets	Fireproofing steel beams in the construction industry
Vinyl asbestos tile	Laboratory hood construction

Source: Hamilton, A., and Hardy, H. L., Industrial Toxicology, 3d ed., Acton, Mass., Publishing Sciences Group, 1974, p. 421. Reprinted with permission.

man problem just beginning to appear after World War II, now very much on the minds of doctors, patients, families, lawyers, and social workers. For example, Mr. R. had for many years been at the job of weaving asbestos cloth into products to be used as brake linings. He was a heavy cigarette smoker. During the years prior to his hospital admission, he had begun to cough and noticed gradually increasing shortness of breath, at first only with exercise but eventually even at rest. When seen in the hospital, he had evidence of serious heart and lung disease. He was a willing volunteer, and we tried a variety of tests and therapy. The tests confirmed that he had serious and progressive pulmonary abnormalities and secondary heart abnormalities associated with his work history of asbestos exposure. At last he was moved to the intensive care unit and treated with oxygen alone. As some days passed, he appeared to be suffocating as lung scarring (fibrosis) made it impossible for his failing heart to pump oxygen to the body. One morning, witnessing his extreme suffering, I ordered the nurses to stop the barely supporting oxygen and administer a drug to allay his misery. Within hours, after his priest and his friends had visited him, he died. I was blamed by the nurses and young doctors for "acting like God." I suggested that if Mr. R. had not been a patient in the MGH God would have acted far sooner to release the patient's agony. Mr. R.'s death took place in 1951, and I have a hunch that knowledge of Nazi behavior in the 1940s influenced the young staff's reaction to my decision. I also know from my own hospital training that when one is healthy and young, defeat in "curing" patients cannot be tolerated. However, the injunction to the physician in the Hippocratic Oath is to relieve suffering if cure is not possible. Dr. Cicely Saunders, medical director of the London-based St. Christopher's Hospice, comes to mind. She has written wisely on the care of the dying and has attracted worldwide attention. Privileged to visit St. Christopher's Hospice for the dying in 1977 and to talk with Dr. Saunders, I found that she is using doses of both pain-killing and hypnotic drugs sufficient to keep terminally ill patients comfortable.

In contrast, a brief account of Mr. P's fatal illness while under my care at MGH covers what I believe is a fairly common and blameworthy course of events. Mr. P.'s job for the previous ten years had been to line boilers and sidewalls and install plumbing in ships and submarines. His work kept him below decks, and so he received heavy doses of dust since it is difficult to ventilate these areas. The amount of dust that Mr. P. inhaled was increased by wartime demands for long hours at work. When he complained of pain on breathing, his doctor gave him commonly used analgesics and finally small doses of codeine. The patient did not get relief and so was sent to a psychiatric hospital because of fear of drug addiction. A chest surgeon consultant had him moved to the MGH, and at the weekly chest disease conference his story and lung x-rays were reviewed. It was 1957 and I had recently returned from South Africa where I had been shown a series of x-rays and postmortem specimens with abnormalities thought to be asbestos related. I asked the resident physician to describe Mr. P.'s occupational history. The resident, as was true too often, had not asked and so did not know. To arouse attention I told the group that Mr. P. had a 100 percent fatal tumor of the pleura, a thin layer of cells covering the lung. Mr. P.'s tumor of the pleura, called a mesothelioma, I prophesied might involve a similar thin layer called the peritoneum covering the gut and lining the abdominal wall. Small wonder that Mr. P. suffered constant pain, since breathing was impaired by growing tumors — their size acted to collapse the lung, which was also scarred with the effect of asbestos, and to press painfully on abdominal organs.

I ordered drugs to relieve his pain. Unhappily, the nurses were busy, and the patient did not get the drugs regularly. Mr. P. was deaf as well as stoical by nature, so he complained little. At last the nurses and I understood his wishes, and then he was given the drug every few hours. Finally he was comfortable enough to go home. Shortly he returned to the hospital to die, overwhelmed by enlarging tumors of chest and abdominal walls. The course of Mr. P.'s excruciating pain was explained by the autopsy finding that tumor cells had grown into the spaces between his ribs. Thus each breath must have hurt him in a fashion very like that endured by those tortured on the rack. Mr. P.'s case illustrates the failure of hospital staff to carry out the command to relieve suffering. Often the motive, not a carefully considered one in cases of terminal illness, is the thought that addiction may follow.

International interest from 1960 to the present shows asbestos-related diseases, including malignancy, may arise wherever asbestos is mined or used. Much current research is directed both toward finding a treatment for asbestos-caused tumors and toward correlating diseases with the dose inhaled and each type of asbestos fiber, its size, and chemical and geological character.

I would plead that every reader look at all reports in the lay press and on television with great skepticism. My reasons are shown by the following examples. A state health commissioner is using funds that he has to underwrite an antismoking campaign. Deception is a mistake no matter how noble the cause. Because a plant situated on a U.S. Great Lake dumped waste asbestos into the lake, which serves as public water supply to a nearby city, fishing was forbidden and the livelihood of an important number of people denied. The evidence that water containing asbestos fibers is harmful and may cause cancer has yet to be assembled.

Coal

During a trip I made to South Wales in 1950, I had a chance to visit the Pneumoconiosis Research Unit, a British research group. Supporting pathologists and research workers were staff of the Welsh National Medical School in Cardiff. In addition, I visited a coal-mining town where a chest x-ray survey was in progress. This plus the increase in U.S. literature on the subject led me to choose coal miners' chest disease for clinical study at the MGH while receiving support from the National Institutes of Health. Studies of other dust diseases of the lungs, especially where fibrogenic dusts occur when silica is present in the ore, persuaded me that U.S. authors were mistaken in concluding that the coal miners' disease of South Wales and that of the southeastern United States were identical and thus would behave the same way in the lung. Welsh coal is said to contain less than 2 percent silica; on the average 8 percent silica is reported to be present in United States coal. The terminology in various countries and in different groups in one country makes understanding of this subject unnecessarily difficult. The useful term *mixed dust pneumoconiosis* of Drs. A. I. G. McLaughlin and H. E. Harding corresponds to the long-popular U.S. term *anthracosilicosis* (coal plus silica). The use of each industry with *pneumoconiosis* — for example, coal, tin, or asbestos pneumoconiosis — is satisfactory. I would precede such terms with the word *disabling* if in fact this is the case.

The reader may think that this 6 percent difference in the amount of silica in the coal is of little importance. The facts are that coal without silica is inert. Inhaled, it is collected in basketlike fashion in a network throughout the lung and in the lung defenses known as lymph nodes. The harm that coal can inflict depends upon the quantity of small-sized dust inhaled, which in turn depends on the number of years of work in the mine, the amount of work in certain especially dusty operations, and the lack of controlling devices in the mine such as adequate ventilation and water sprays. Another factor is the blasting. In the past, and in small mines to this day, miners were paid by the amount of coal brought to the surface per day. Because of this, miners did not wait for blasting fumes to clear before entering the mine and thus inhaled fumes harmful to the lung. Frequent infection, sometimes tuberculosis (seen more often in the past), cigarette smoking, and malnutrition in bad economic years combined to cause poor general health, bronchitis, and pneumonia. Curiously, coal miners suffer less lung cancer than do their neighbors. The miners believed that their constant spitting while at work and their chewing of tobacco — in fact, even the coal itself — afforded various degrees of protection.

If a greater and greater amount of respirable coal reached the small airways (bronchi and bronchioles), serious damage to the respiratory anatomy occurred both with and without infection. The familiar diseases of bronchitis and emphysema followed. Plugging of blood vessels might cause death of lung tissue. An additional infection might destroy or replace with scar tissue so much functioning lung that the afflicted miner became an invalid. In the period before antituberculous drugs were available, few miners with tuberculosis lived long enough to reach a bed-and-chair existence.

How were we at the Massachusetts General Hospital to find disabled coal miners willing to come to Boston and stay in a hospital bed while we tried to study the respiratory disease itself, its effect on heart and lung function and psychological well-being, and its difference, if any, from the disease of South Wales coal miners? It was my good fortune that my associate Dr. John Stoeckle agreed in the mid-1950s that the subject was worth the time and effort needed to study it.[8] In the years prior to our interest, Josephine Roche, assistant to John L. Lewis of United Mine Workers fame, persuaded him to start a welfare fund to defray certain medical costs. The late Dr. (Admiral) Stark Draper pioneered the use of this fund, unique among U.S. unions. Dr. Lorin Kerr, an old and valued friend of mine and an officer in the U.S. Public Health Service, replaced Dr. Draper. Lorin and I had lively differences of opinion on the mechanics of disability of coal miners. His article on the subject started our "controversy" on Welsh versus U.S. coal miners' disease. The United Mine Workers Fund under Dr. Draper built clinics in key communities in West Virginia, Ohio, and Pennsylvania, among other states, and found physicians to staff them. Needless to say, the American Medical Association (AMA) was shocked by the implication that "their" doctors were not caring for the miners and their families properly. The United Mine Workers invited an investigation by the AMA. Such a low level of medical practice was discovered that no more was heard from the AMA.

John Stoeckle and I used our favorite prophecy that careful and complete study of a small number of patients with the same disease over as long a period as possible would yield knowledge of a larger population at similar risk. With encouragement from Lorin, we planned the precise studies and enlisted the help of Massachusetts General Hospital colleagues. These were the experts: a surgeon, a pathologist, a radiologist, a pulmonary physiologist, and a psychiatrist. I thought that mine owners would be pleased to know of our study because its conclusions might clear the confusion surrounding the humane and legal problems of compensation claims. A colleague and friend was medical director of a huge steel company that owned a number of coal mines. My colleague arranged a luncheon meeting for me so that I might outline our Boston plan to a vice-president of this steel company, that is, to bring 30 to 40 disabled coal miners to the MGH for a month of study. I recall that it was a good meal, eaten in the elegance of the high officials' private dining room, which was atop a tall building in Pittsburgh overlooking the two great rivers coming together. Easy to see in the distance were the thick red clouds coming from the steel company's furnaces. Except for the view and the food, I might have used my time to better advantage. When I finished my proposal, the vice-president said, "You had better ask John L. Lewis. He takes four dollars a ton from us for medical costs."

That evening I had dinner at the home of Lorin Kerr's chief internist, Leslie Falk, a Rhodes scholar and now professor and chief of the Department of Community Medicine at Meharry Medical College. Dr. Falk and I worked out the details of a trip we would take together (his wife didn't seem to mind) for three days. Visiting the largest clinics, I met and talked with the staff and, with their consent, found disabled men that were willing to come to Boston. Not only did I talk at length with each volunteer coal miner, describing the studies we planned, but I also made detailed notes of their work histories. In addition, I used a portable instrument I had brought with me to roughly assess their degree of lung damage independent of their subjective complaints. Dr. Stoeckle took a similar trip to enlist volunteers and meet their physicians. By visiting the United Mine Workers' clinics and hospitals and the small mining communities, meeting the men on their own ground, John and I gained a wealth of knowledge not to be learned from a man in a hospital bed. We tried for a larger number but finally settled on 35 men, all of them disabled and all on so-called black lung compensation. This term I deplore as emotive and not based on the facts of dust disease of U.S. coal miners.

The volunteer coal miners came to the MGH in pairs, and all but two submitted to our studies cheerfully. Their stoicism and their special sense of humor made these disabled men favorites of other patients, nurses, orderlies, dieticians, and doctors. In a few cases, our surgical consultant cut between the ribs to obtain a bit of lung for study by the pathologist. After careful clinical study our cardiac consultant submitted several volunteers to cardiac catheterization. With proper rubber tubing and special x-ray devices, it was learned how much harm had been suffered by the right side of the heart, where blood pours in from the lung burdened with coal dust. Of interest were the reports of our psychiatrist, Dr. J. C. Nemiah. He was surprised to find very little depression in spite of the men's knowledge of mining risk and loss of friends or relatives by accident. Dr. Nemiah considered their stoicism and lack of fear of their jobs a positive hindrance to public health efforts to find cases at an early stage and to encourage regular chest x-rays or treatment. John and I found, with few exceptions, this group to be happy in spite of shortness of breath. They told us of fishing and hunting jaunts made independently without asking the boss. One could guess that from the point of view of the mine owner seeking efficiency and high production, the coal miners we came to know were maddening.

What did we learn in addition to the carefree and stoical character of our volunteers? As I had expected, the chest x-rays varied so greatly from one miner to another that they offered little toward diagnosis or assessment of future course and prognosis. Our findings did not support the value of the many classifications of x-ray so popular with some investigators here and abroad. Two of the men were motormen. Their job was to cover the tracks on which the coal-filled cars ran with finely divided sand to control the speed of the cars and to help with friction on the upgrade. By biopsying lung tissue, these two men were shown to have silicosis plus infection, pulmonary tuberculosis, with small patches of the black pigment of coal. Thus, these motormen did not have black lung (for which they were compensated) but silicotuberculosis, which proved fatal. We learned several reasons other than cigarette smoking for the bronchitis, emphysema, and poor capacity of their lungs to diffuse the essential gas — oxygen — in the lung and to remove the unwanted gas — carbon dioxide — from the lung. The reasoning was as follows.

Much blasting into coal-bearing rocks created nitrous fumes, damaging to all parts of the lung and making the respiratory tract more vulnerable to infection. In most U.S. mining operations, long cables carrying electricity are used to bring coal-filled cars to the surface. Such cables are covered with insulation that, because of friction in motion, often catches fire. The fumes from such fires are extremely irritating, making the worker cough violently, vomit, and complain of chest pain. In severe cases caused by prolonged exposure to cable-fire fumes, especially in confined spaces, the worker may be forced to rest for as long as a week or be hospitalized for treatment with oxygen and antibiotics. There is little mention in the medical literature of these complicating factors, which are useful in explaining chest x-rays and biopsy material showing little or no coal burden after 30 years of exposure. Certainly a heavy lung burden of coal added to other insults makes the disability of U.S. coal miners easy to understand. Through the years, methods of dust control by ventilating, wetting the dust, wearing individually fitted face masks, and rotating jobs have been used in varying degrees. In our MGH group our findings reflected many methods of both mining and control. Our work was published in 1962 in the *Journal of Chronic Disease*.[8] It attracted little attention, much to our disappointment. We had hoped that clinicians might be interested and also some coal-mining committees and ex-miners with a broader view. At this time when Dr. Cochrane in Wales had begun to classify chest x-rays, sophisticated lung function studies were considered more important in the United States.

In 1969 I became a member of the United Mine Workers Medical Advisory Committee, which met in Washington occasionally. There I heard much of changing mining techniques and the economics involved. Mine was the chief voice raised in favor of long-term clinical studies, better data on exposure, and less work on litigation, best left to lawyers. The most striking impression was made by reports of advancing technology that could lead to silicosis in young men, for example, the wonders of putting coal into solution (a slurry) for easy transport.

Other Factors in Disabling Occupational Chest Disease

The important subject of chronic bronchitis and emphysema, complicated in many cases by secondary involvement of those parts of the blood supply affected by lung disease, may be discussed here as a subject linked with coal miners' illnesses and other occupational chest diseases. The U.S. coal miners we studied all had bronchitis (cough, excess sputum, frequent "colds," and shortness of breath). Judgment of the cause has been overshadowed by the common belief that cigarette smoking was the single or major cause of bronchitis. Our studies led us to agree that smoking was certainly a factor. But added to smoking were the hazards of working with finely divided dusts (coal, asbestos, talc, silica) or with chemicals (nitrous fumes of blasting, irritants such as acids and alkalis).

My travels to South Wales, England, Germany, Belgium, and the International Labour Organization in Geneva showed me that students of occupational chest disease were struck by the frequent occurrence of bronchitis. The disease is closely associated with industrialization and crowding in cities, with poverty and poor nutrition, and also — it is true — with smoking habits. As I visited the great English cities — London, Manchester, Sheffield, Newcastle upon Tyne — my host would invariably say as he put his chest x-ray in the viewing box, "Let me show you the Sheffield chest, the Manchester chest." Unless the patient had a heavy load of dust arising from his job, the x-ray showed the dark, overdistended lung of emphysema. Drs. Lynne Reid of London and J. C. Leopold of Cardiff, among other pathologists, have worked out the anatomical abnormalities of airways and lung that follow the battering by dust, the direct action of certain chemicals, and infection. Study of their work and the Swedish work with radioactive materials makes it not surprising to find that cough and shortness of breath are very frequent and disabling complaints.

There are a vast number of agents in and out of industry that lead to some variation of cases that I have seen in Boston and in travel, some asthmatic in character. In Manchester I learned of two unique causes that led to acute or long-lasting asthmatics. One followed handling of sacks used to ship castor beans. The asthmatic breathing was so violent that the worker was hospitalized. After recovery, a foolhardy investigation using workers reproduced this frightening effect by presenting a few affected and brave workers with small doses of castor bean dust. In my view this is unforgiveable "research," and had I had any authority, I would have forbidden it. Anyone who has witnessed or treated a full-blown case of so-called anaphylaxis, the most violent of the family of allergic reactions, will understand my sentiments. Many vegetable dusts, a family of industrially useful chemicals called the *isocyanates*, and certain detergents are on the list of harmful materials that at certain doses behave as does castor bean dust. And I have had experience with patients affected by all these plus by dust from grain silos. Such experience has led many investigators to study experimentally exposed animals in the hopes of unraveling the mysteries of disturbance in the human immune system that cause allergic responses.

A unique form of chest disease called byssinosis (from the Greek word for flax) was shown to me while I was in Manchester, the great industrial city in the county of Lancashire in North England. The great cotton mills are in Lancashire County and in Manchester and its suburbs. In the past when business was slack, there were idle periods that caused great poverty and malnutrition, which made respiratory diseases, especially tuberculosis, common. In some, but not all, of the operations the workers developed byssinosis. I was told that the same has been and is true in Holland, Spain, Italy, Sweden, Egypt, and India. From my study of the cases I saw in Manchester, I believe that U.S. workers do not suffer the byssinosis described by R. F. Schilling and the late Dr. A. Bouhuys. Brian Harvey, the industrial hygiene engineer in Manchester associated with Professor Ronald Lane at the medical school, guided me around a typical cotton mill. From this trip and talks with other knowledgeable people, I concluded that the operations and social conditions differ in the United States, which explains differences in opinion. The byssinosis of Manchester reported in medical literature as caused by hemp and jute as well as by cotton and flax, has medical distinction. As Schilling reports, in Stage One a worker previously unexposed to cotton notices "chest tightness" early in the workweek. This complaint disappears over the weekend but recurs the following Monday. Stage Two is reached when the chest tightness lasts all week but is relieved by a holiday. Stage Three finds the worker short of breath, with a dry cough, the nonspecific dark chest x-ray of emphysema, and frequent respiratory infection. At Stage Three the disease is irreversible, and the disabled worker eventually dies of heart failure.

Because of a report of oval, brown-staining foreign bodies in cotton workers' lung, without known connection with the disease, certain U.S. union leaders refer to byssinosis as "brown lung" for compensation purposes. In 1966 I was a speaker at a New York meeting of union leaders who were attending to learn more about industrial disease. A physician discussing byssinosis referred to it as "brown lung." When I rose to protest the term as nonscientific, the cotton workers' union leader stood up and spoke to me sharply, "Dr. Hardy, the coal miners have their 'black lung' legislation, and we are going to get our 'brown lung' compensation."

Cyanide

My apprenticeship with the Massacusetts Division of Occupational Hygiene (DOH) included experience with cyanide salts in solution used in plating operations. There are a number of small plants in Massachusetts engaged in such work; curiously there is little damage to men with such exposure, although where hydrogen cyanide gas for fumigation is used in a poorly ventilated space, the danger is very great.

Because some of the men had been at the same work for years, it was decided that a survey of cyanide-plating operations was in order. In preparation I studied old and new reports of the biological behavior of cyanide salts and found three pertinent points. One, unless cyanide salts are taken rapidly, the body converts them to relatively harmless thiocyanate. Second is the fact that cyanide as a sulfur compound, thiocyanate, occurs widely in nature, including seafood, the cabbage family, and certain tobaccos. The third fact of interest is that thiocyanate had been used as a drug for the control of high blood pressure. However, thiocyanate is used as a drug less and less because of harmful side effects at medically useful doses. Nonspecific central nervous system signs and symptoms and thyroid enlargement were the significant undesirable effects of thiocyanate used as a drug. While this survey did not uncover these toxic findings among cyanide workers, I found and reported in the medical literature both cyanide-caused thyroid enlargement and cases of disabled cyanide workers suffering disability mimicking a stroke.[9] The DOH chemist could not help in assessing excess exposure to cyanide by urinanalysis because diet and smoking habits obscured the job-related thiocyanate — this we learned from sampling the urine of the DOH employees free of cyanide exposure.

I learned from this little exercise several simple truths to be borne in mind in studying industrial illness. One is the obvious, often forgotten fact that sick workers are not at their jobs. Thus, I found cases of thiocyanate effect in cyanide platers in the MGH thyroid and neurological clinics, not in the plants. Another bit of knowledge from cyanide study is that the same biological pathways are used by differing materials, food and tobacco, for example. Thus the urine levels of thiocyanate gave no clue to the amount of exposure to cyanide. Workroom air measurements and history of duration of exposure are relied upon to guard exposed workers. The clinician with knowledge of industrial hazard can detect early signs of disease and, by stopping exposure, interrupt its development — certainly the ideal goal.

Cadmium

An illustration of an unexpected pressure that served to obstruct the correct handling of job-related disease is provided by my experience with cadmium while at the DOH. This episode took place in 1946 while my knowledge of occupational illness was limited so that my general medical experience had to be used. An engineer and I were sent to a small factory working to coat large locomotive wheels with cadmium. The wheels were dipped in a large bath of heated metal to provide resistance to weather and wear. There were complaints of illness in one area of this plant, and minor respiratory illness such as cough, chest pain, and some intestinal complaints led to our visit. It was a family business, so the directors were also workers and were rarely absent from the plant.

I was well acquainted with the past medical literature on the toxicity of cadmium since I had developed a chapter on this subject in the second edition of *Industrial Toxicology*.[10] Cadmium had been used in medical school teaching to study the mechanism of vomiting, with cats as experimental subjects. Human experience showed vomiting to be caused by zinc- and cadmium-lined ice trays and thermos bottles. Unexplained outbreaks of violent attacks of vomiting among military troops and certain groups in big cities were thought to be due to bacteria until someone suggested that cadmium used in thermos bottles was the cause. Further, in Europe storage batteries for motors were made with cadmium rather than with lead as in the United States. Reports of signs and symptoms of respiratory illness and curious x-ray changes of the bones came from French storage battery plants in the years of World War II. Through the years, evidence of damage to kidneys and fundamental biochemical systems has accumulated, and, more recently, back pain in older, postmenopausal Japanese women has been documented as well as malignancy of the prostate in men — all these harmful effects following various doses of cadmium exposure from workroom and/or environmental pollution.

In this small Massachusetts plant, the cadmium solution in a bath was heated, and the huge wheels were lowered by a giant crane. Fumes of reddish color rose to the breathing zone of workers grappling to be certain that the wheels were evenly coated. The engineer accompanying me explained that the fumes were freshly generated cadmium oxide, well known to be biologically harmful. While my colleague took measurement of the fumes, I talked with each of the eight workers most exposed and with the crane operator, for one could see the fumes rising toward the crane during the process. I wrote in detail each medical history and each work history from the earliest job. Workers felt generally sick and weak as the day went on but recovered after going home. The crane operator, who ate lunch in his cab, was being treated for stomach ulcers. All men complained of cough and chest pain when the fumes were visible; "dopiness"; weakness; and in the case of the crane operator, who had dust in his cab and on his lunch, abdominal pain, nausea, and lack of appetite. The amount of cadmium in the air where the men worked was above the safe level, and the metal was found in each worker's urine sample, the crane operator having the highest level. This confirmed the exposure since cadmium is not normally found in urine.

My next step was to spend a few days in the medical school library. I found reports of all the symptoms of my group of workers, but the exposures had been to accidental or experimental *single high exposures*. Thinking about my workers, I wondered whether repeated lower cadmium exposures might over a longer period of time produce similar complaints. The literature described bone changes seen on x-ray in French cadmium workers and lowered hemoglobin in exposed men and animals. After talking with my "boss," I went back to the plant where I hoped to persuade those in charge to allow me to take hemoglobin levels and chest and bone x-rays, since there was an agreement with the Department of Public Health and that the tests would be done without cost. And because the plant I am referring to was a small family business, it was possible to call a directors' meeting to hear my request. When I met with the company directors, who were brothers or cousins, I explained what I knew, including the fact that cadmium fumes had been considered for use as a war gas because they are so quickly damaging to the lungs. After an impressively intelligent and short discussion, permission was granted. The next day, one of the executives telephoned me to say that the consultant of the large smelting company that sold cadmium to "my" plant said that there was no such thing as chronic cadmium poisoning. The permission for further investigaton was withdrawn. This same consultant was an editor of the best-known journal in the field of industrial disease at that time and a professor of the subject in a university. I had a phone call from this industrial consultant-professor a few days later, asking for a paper describing my experience with cadmium. My temper became red hot, and with anger I answered, "There was nothing to report — you saw to that." After what seemed to me to be a useless back-and-forth discussion, I agreed to write what little I had learned. So with my engineer boss as coauthor to describe the job, a short article with the title "Chronic Cadmium Poisoning" was published in 1947.[11]

The study of cadmium poisoning records my realization of the vast difference between acute and chronic industrial disease, a concept quite familiar to physicians working with infection. I caught hold of the professor-editor's phrase, "There is no such thing as chronic cadmium poisoning," and I have thought of it ever since while working with beryllium, lead, ionizing radiation, benzene, carbon tetrachloride, and dusts. The concept that I find most helpful is expressed by the following variables: the size of the insulting dose, the *rate* at which it enters the body, and the duration of exposure. All of these variables and their effects depend upon the character of the insult and the health of the worker. For example, aged cadmium is thought to be harmless. Freshly generated cadmium fumes are damaging or lethal, depending upon the size of the dose. These matters are much discussed in the United States in setting standards for safe levels of exposure to toxic material such as cadmium. But not enough thought has gone into the influence of the variables I have listed. In other words, the host (the worker) will react in a variety of ways to the differing insults he meets at home and at work, so the rigidity of the legislated time weighted average (TWA) is a biologically impossible standard. Can a fetus recognize that his mother is inhaling a safe amount of cadmium or beryllium, for example? For beryllium, the neighborhood air TWA is 0.03 μg per cubic meter of air averaged over a month. What if the embryo gets the whole month's allowable dose in three seconds?

Chronic cadmium toxicity has now become a matter of world-wide interest, and all writing on the subject begins with reference to the short piece published by H. L. Hardy and J. B. Skinner in 1947.[11] I spin out this cadmium story for several reasons. It was a real shock to me to realize that a senior faculty member would stifle investigation in favor of industrial gain. In retrospect, I can see that serendipity and common denominators (medical complaints plus documented toxic exposure) plus study of old and current literature can serve to uncover unrecognized causes of industrial disease. The cadmium experience serves to illustrate that in my case the nurture of medical education plus investigation with clinical studies of the so-called normal helped me to point out a "new disease" in 1947, now a matter of worldwide interest.

Benzol (Benzene)

While study of beryllium workers had my first attention, I was learning the behavior of other toxic materials and the methods by which the DOH attacked their recognition and control. The identification of the chemical or dust in use was often impossible since containers of chemicals carried only numbers or trade names to guard (as we and the workers were told) the secrecy necessary for trade competition. Studying the operation, for example, in the manufacture of rubber heels, raincoats, and rubber shoes, the DOH knew that benzol (not to be confused with benzine, which is used for cigarette-lighter fuel) was used. Benzol, by its effect on the blood-forming organs, had been responsible for many deaths as a result of fatal anemia or leukemia. The staff, by measuring the amount in workroom air and studying urine samples, was able to learn how much a worker absorbed after inhalation. If there was a plant doctor, I paid him a visit and gently quizzed him on benzol poisoning. The ignorance of my fellow physicians struck me many times. The likely outcome of a history of uncontrolled benzol exposure is so serious that if our technical staff reported exposure above the so-called maximum allowable concentration (MAC), I tried to get complete blood counts with the help of the manager, union steward, and doctor, or occasionally by myself.

A few case histories illustrate the basis for fear of benzol. I was asked by Dr. Earle Chapman of the Department of Medicine at the Massachusetts General Hospital to see the case of an artist who was suffering from leukemia (malignancy of the white blood cells), a disease also caused by ionizing radiation (for example, among Hiroshima victims and radiologists). Painstakingly detailed history taking revealed that to support herself she had, as a student, cleaned old paintings and frames. She had used a variety of solvents (a large family of liquids that dissolve grease). Dr. Chapman's patient thought that she knew the smell of the dangerous liquid, also called benzene. When I brought her several unmarked bottles with numbers as a code, she could not correctly identify the harmful benzol. After her death I visited the Boston Museum of Fine Arts to ask a senior member if his staff knew of the lethality of benzol. He reported that all of them knew its aroma and were careful in its use. After I pressed the matter, he agreed to call his staff to test their recognition of benzol. Our senior chemist prepared six bottles with wide mouths, each labeled erroneously. When we passed the bottles around for a sniff test, not one individual could identify all of these, and several made the mistake often made by doctors and laymen alike of calling a sample of *benzine* (cigarette-lighter kerosene) *benzene* (benzol). The former is dangerous as a fire or explosion hazard; the latter, depending on dose or duration of exposure, can cause an anemia or a fatal leukemia.

Following these leads, Dr. Hervey Elkins of the DOH and I gathered data on benzene in the air and in the blood of workers in a shoe factory where this chemical was in use.[12] The safe level of benzene in workroom air at this time (1948) was given as 65 ppm (parts per million) of air. I found a number of cases of mild anemia, and one worker, seen in a Boston hospital, was thought to have leukemia. At the next annual meeting of industrial doctors, chemists, and engineers, Dr. Elkins and I prepared and read a paper suggesting that the safe level be reduced to 35 ppm.

So widespread is the use of benzene (see Table 5) and so serious is its potential for biological damage that the current limit is 5 ppm — some authorities suggest using less. In striking contrast is Dr. Alice Hamilton's report of the late 1920s that responsible companies used 1,000 ppm, which was reduced because of 50 percent mortality. Most American observers (in contrast with European) have been slow to accept the fact that benzene can cause leukemia.

Table 5

Uses of Benzol—Partial Listing

Constituent of aviation and motor fuel
Degreasing agent
Starting chemical for materials in the chemical industry
Rotogravure printing
Extraction of oils and fats
Sealing of cans
Manufacture of
  Rubber
  Plastics
  Paints and lacquers
  Linoleum
  Artificial manure
  Glue and adhesives
  Floor waxes and polishes
  Straw hats
  Shoes
  Cameras
  Cardboard boxes

Source: Adapted from Browning, E., Toxicity and Metabolism of Industrial Solvents, New York, Elsevier, 1965, p. 5.

When I was in Milan, Italy, studying the work of the Clinica del Lavoro, a facility formed in the eighteenth century by Ramazzini for the study of industrial medicine as well as for the care of patients and for teaching and research, I was shown three cases of benzene-induced leukemia. I persuaded the chief, Dr. Enrico Vigliani, to write of his experience, and his article, published in 1964,[13] spurred interest and a flurry of reports from the United States.

In this period of interest in the toxicity of benzene, a point of importance, not original with me, surfaced in the work histories of two patients with blood abnormalities. I refer to the notion that since the body has a limited number of ways of reacting to insults, a series of toxic exposures may produce disease and have a fatal result even though each one of the insults may have been received at or near safe levels. One patient was a man who worked with industrial x-rays and later with TNT, the explosive known to depress blood-forming organs, and finally with benzene as a cleansing agent. The other, another woman painter, used unknown amounts of benzene and, owing to an abnormal pregnancy, suffered repeated blood loss, which was a serious drain on the already damaged blood-forming organs. Both of these patients died.

As a result of worldwide knowledge of the treachery of low-level amounts of benzol inhaled over a period of time, there have been national and international efforts to substitute a harmless or less harmful chemical for the useful but dangerous benzol. Exposure to benzol, unfortunately, continues in most parts of the industrialized world and in academic and medical laboratories. Dr. Alice Hamilton's 1934 edition of *Industrial Toxicology* gives some notion of the haphazard fashion in which knowledge of benzol has been collected.[14] Atypical blood cells prophetic of leukemia were mentioned by Tracy Mallory in 1939, but it was not until the publications of 1948 (Hardy and Elkins) and 1964 (Vigliani and Saita) that malignant disease clearly associated with benzol exposure was established.

Carbon Tetrachloride

A widely used liquid solvent is carbon tetrachloride (Table 6). It was once used as a drug to rid the body of various parasites, but it was abandoned when it was learned that carbon tetrachloride was able to kill a man after as small a dose as a teaspoonful and that a smaller

Table 6

Uses of Carbon Tetrachloride—Partial Listing

Dry cleaning
Fire extinguishers (used less and less)
Fumigant for grain
Manufacture of the refrigerant Freon 12 and of DDT
Extraction of oils and fats
Degreaser of machine parts
Solvent in rubber and paint industries

Source: Adapted from Browning, E., Toxicity and Metabolism of Industrial Solvents, New York, Elsevier, 1965, p. 174.

dose could damage the heart muscle. Many industrial workers have been poisoned by inhaling fumes of this substance, easily airborne. Kidney and liver are the organs usually attacked. If the liver is already damaged by infection, hepatitis, or excessive intake of alcohol, the hazard from carbon tetrachloride exposure is greatly increased.

The dramatic danger from its inhalation is shown by an experience I had while finding the autopsy records of one worker and the history of a fellow worker thought to be still alive. These two men worked at cleaning rust from the pipes inside huge boilers that were to be installed in a large factory in whose backyard the boilers stood. The workers were given a pail of carbon tetrachloride and appropriately shaped brushes and mops. One man was taller than his co-worker and worked at the upper pipes; as a result he had access to more fresh air. The shorter man actually stood *in* the lower pipes to do his job. Both complained of nausea and dizziness at the end of the day's work but went to the nearest bar. One drank gin, the other beer. Both returned the next day to the same job. As the lunch hour came, both felt so ill that they went to the bar for gin or beer and then went to their respective boarding houses. The short man, the gin drinker, was found dead in bed the next day. The tall man with access to fresh air, the beer drinker, was desperately ill for several weeks but recovered. This true story illustrates the extreme toxicity of carbon tetrachloride, as well as the slight edge the tall worker had because of access to air. The different percentage of alcohol between gin and beer may have caused the well-established lethal potential of carbon tetrachloride and alcohol in combination.

Anthrax

An ancient scourge of man and animal is a disease called anthrax or malignant pustule. Anthrax is caused by an anaerobic organism, that is, one that thrives in the absence of air. These organisms can live for unknown periods in soil that is dry and warm, and grazing animals are exposed to them. By this grazing or by exposure to another animal, the anthrax bacilli travel and lodge readily in the hair and hide of goats, pigs, camels, llamas, and some cattle and horses. After being subjected to a number of different processes, animal hair is used for shaving brushes, cold weather clothing, and carpets, for example. After tanning, the hides are made into shoes, carpets, purses, and a variety of clothing. It is difficult to clean the material completely, and, therefore, the anthrax bacilli are able to survive the many industrial operations of manufacture.

Anthrax as a human disease, prior to the availability of penicillin, was rarely cured. The original appearance of anthrax was marked by an ugly, nonhealing abscesslike lesion on an exposed part of the body — face, arm, hand, or leg. An abrasion or cut allowed the anthrax to enter the body. The organism multiplied under the surface of the skin and was able to gain access to the bloodstream. Meningitis might follow or, if anthrax had been inhaled, a lethal pneumonia.

I was assigned the task of making a survey of Massachusetts industries working with hides and hair when I was with the DOH. The immediate reason for the survey was the occurrence of two cases of anthrax in a carpet factory. One of the safety inspectors guided me on this survey since he had legal authority to force employers to provide decent washing facilities. Some of the shops, storage houses, and tanneries were incredibly messy, dirty, and bad smelling, and workers were pitiable in their sloppy workroom, their skins often being dyed the color of the material being tanned and dried. One employer supplied his workers with no running water or toilets. Workers had to run across the street to a bar for such facilities. When we asked to see his washing facilities, required by law, he said, "Why, those men are just pigs. They wouldn't use soap and water if I supplied it." He was given an order by my safety inspector, but I sensed that this was not his first order and his men would continue as "pigs."

The continued occurrence of anthrax in the United States, even in dry, clean jobs such as carpet weaving, resulted from the lack of inspection and treatment of hides and hair coming into the country. A period of treatment with steam will kill all but a very few well-covered anthrax bacilli. Such handling is a law in Great Britain. In addition, it is true that most doctors know how to diagnose anthrax and the magic effect of penicillin therapy. However, I learned from some hospitalized workers with anthrax that they had pointed out the "malignant pustule" to the doctor helping with diagnosis. Of course, this is not true in big plants, which have their own physicians. Today most contagious disease hospitals treat meningitis of uncertain etiology with penicillin, so the mortality rate of anthrax is now low. An interesting page in the history of anthrax is the fact that workers' wives did sometimes contract anthrax from dirty work clothes. Now in most plants workers are provided with clothes to be kept at the work place, and a shower before leaving is required.

Lead

Of all my experience studying industrial disease, next to beryllium poisoning I found the toxic effects of lead the most interesting. Since the days of the Roman Empire, lead has been used by man. It has had such a variety of uses that a complete list would be tiresome to read. For example, lead has been used to sweeten wine and to bring about abortion, and one author, S. C. Gilfillan, has published his opinion that the Fall of Rome was caused by the drinking of leaded wine.[15] He contended that the lead in the wine prevented conception or produced stillborn or malformed babies.

During my years at the DOH, I spent many days visiting storage battery plants and some foundries. Of interest was a visit to a large ship that was to be scrapped after war duty. A great amount of red lead paint had been applied to prevent rusting, and this was to be removed by chipping or by using machinery, both of which raised a great deal of finely divided, easily inhaled dust. Because the work required considerable mechanical paint removal and was done in warm weather, the workers found it difficult or impossible to wear a proper face mask. Fear of drowning by falling from the ship made face masks unpopular. This taught me that in many jobs face masks are useless and give a misleading sense of safety.

I saw so many cases of industrial lead poisoning with many changes and subtleties due to toxic lead effect that I learned much firsthand. Not unusual was the occurrence of acute abdominal pain, leading to exploratory surgery at which no pathologic change was found. As a consultant to other hospitals and at the MGH, I saw other cases who had escaped abdominal surgery for removal of appendix or gallbladder because an anxious medical student had found the stippled cells in the preoperative routine blood count and ran to save the patient and ignorant surgeon from a mistake. I was usually asked to see the patient to confirm the diagnosis. This I did chiefly by taking a careful history of jobs and hobbies and doing tests for excess of lead and other substances not normally found in blood and urine. A teaching case I used was that of a woman physician thought to be suffering from acute gallbladder disease. Enroute to the operating room, a young medical student reached the surgeon in time to report not only stippled cells but also a history of her use of a sanding machine to remove indoor paint in a very old house. The patient was as upset as the hospital staff, for she knew of lead poisoning in her role as a member of the State Department of Public Health. A good sport, she allowed me to bring her before an amphitheater full of medical students to elicit her history.

Another fascinating lead problem was found in a steeplejack, deeply jaundiced and quite ill when he entered the MGH. His local physician had diagnosed him as having infectious hepatitis. At the MGH we found that he was suffering not from infectious hepatitis but from acute lead poisoning. He had sanded the old paint from a steeple, and so that he would not fall from great heights, he worked very close to the leaded dust. So great was the dose of lead entering his body quickly that the red cells were destroyed, their pigment turning his skin the yellow color of jaundice. His past history showed other lead exposure. The steeplejack healed himself by excreting the lead but not before we discovered that such a flooding of the body with toxic lead caused abnormal changes in muscle and nerves and that these could be reversed as the body burden of lead decreased.

Because of the effect of lead on red blood cells, many cases of mild poisoning are missed, especially in children where the anemia is thought to be a result of poor diet. In adults having lead poisoning without an obvious cause for an anemia such as a bleeding peptic ulcer, I learned that lead anemia correlated well with high exposure or with lower levels of exposure of long duration.

A thorny case was that of Mr. Szemba, who worked pulling wire through a heated lead bath, so-called annealing. He also had a few cows on an ancient farm. His fellow workers had small amounts of lead in urine, while Mr. S. had twice as much lead in his urine as they did. Suddenly the answer came to me: his water pipes at home and to the watering trough for the cows were made of lead. Thus, Mr. S. inhaled half his daily dose of lead at work and drank the other half at home. He was ill because the total exceeded his body's ability to excrete or store his daily dose of lead. I had a wonderful case of teaching the fact that the body may be thought of as a "teacup" that can handle a certain quantity of lead but only that much — if this limit is exceeded by a triggerlike infection, for example, or surgery, intoxication results because the "teacup" overflows.

The resident doctors provided me with an unusual example of these ideas by asking me to see a bartender with bilateral wrist drop. Until recently, this disease had been seen chiefly in older housepainters using lead-based paint. The lead causes changes in the nerves supplying the muscles used most and paralysis follows. In adults, especially in those working with their hands, the nerves and muscles allowing extension of fingers, wrists, and shoulders become useless, whereas in children the front and lower leg become useless, since they are the most used in running and playing. Our bartender told of drinking gin and ginger ale while on duty, so alcohol seemed a likely factor. However, urine and blood showed excessive amounts of lead. I urged the residents to visit the bar where the patient worked to see for themselves and to bring back samples of the liquors and ginger ales there. Meanwhile, I learned from the sick man that he earned extra money by scraping off old paint and applying fresh leaded paint to boats kept in his shed, which was shut tight for warmth. So our bartender inhaled lead in boat work and drank lead while working at the bar. Thus his "teacup" (body resources) was overfull. The wrist drop disappeared while he was in the hospital and receiving Versenate (see below) by vein. After leaving the hospital, not believing us and needing money, the patient returned to his former jobs. We were proved correct because within a few months the wrist drop recurred. This event turned the patient into a missionary fighting lead poisoning. He willingly allowed me to present him and his case to the medical students.

By 1946 I had begun to realize what a heavy hand lay on my work because of excess organization in government agencies and the all-too-obvious greed of employers. One example was presented in the lead industry by a local storage battery plant. For a period of a few years, the levels of lead in its workroom air were excessive by Massachusetts DOH records, and this state agency has no power to force change. The amount in the workers' urine was also excessive, and a majority of those exposed had a mild to moderately severe anemia with many abnormal red cells appearing in the smear. The owner of the plant had to hire a series of doctors because as each new physician learned to diagnose lead poisoning and asked about preventive measures, he was fired. I learned of this by making plant visits with the engineer who had recommended and designed proper control ventilation a number of times. Further, I helped several newly appointed doctors prepare blood smears and count stippled cells. Several workers were sick enough to be hospitalized with disabling abdominal cramps, so-called lead colic. The owner had decided to pay for the cost of workmen's compensation and medical bills rather than to undertake the engineering correction of the hazard, not a unique story. When this employer was brought into court, the judge dismissed the case when the employer complained that worker protection with ventilation was so expensive that if he were to be forced to make changes, he would have to close his business and the workers would be unemployed. This plea worked well for the employers, since the Department of Labor inspectors from experience already felt that they were made to look foolish when their cases were dismissed by the courts. By law Massachusetts employers of more than five workers must carry workmen's compensation insurance. The plant I have just described had such a bad record that the authorities assigned a different insurance carrier each year to handle its claims. Probably what saved the workers in this plant from the severe toxic effects of lead such as muscle paralysis was the fact that most of them worked only short periods before discovering the hazardous conditions and then left.

An exciting period in my experience at the DOH and the MGH was in the search for better treatment of lead intoxication. Through the work of my adviser and senior professor of medicine, Dr. Aub, among others, it had become known that lead follows calcium into various organs and then into bones.[16] For a long period milk was used to prevent lead poisoning, and injection of a calcium compound into a vein was used for acute toxicity. The best form of treatment was and is, however, to remove the worker or patient from exposure. But owing to the wide use of lead, a lack of lead-free jobs in small industries, union seniority rules, and its use in some paints for homes, cribs, and toys, this has not always been possible. My DOH colleague J. Clarence Maloof helped me follow a clue from the literature for treatment by trying to chelate lead. The word *chelate* comes from the Greek word for "claw," a pincerlike organ of a crab. A chelating agent will combine with, or "grab with its chemical claw," lead and thereby make it nontoxic as well as available for excretion in the urine. We first tried a chelate in 1951. There was a measurable but unimpressive increase in lead excretion. By 1953 a powerful chelating agent was introduced by Dr. Henry Beeson to dissolve kidney stones. Certain cancers produced excessive levels of calcium in the blood, and high doses of this new drug were tried for this complication. Dr. Aub and others suggested its use at lower doses in well-studied cases of lead poisoning. It worked dramatically in spite of its formidable name, calcium disodium ethylenediaminotetraacetate, a name later mercifully shortened to EDTA or Versenate by the drug house developing the chemical for treatment. In 1953 I invited those interested in lead poisoning to a day-long conference at the MGH. I reported our small but carefully studied series treated with EDTA, in collaboration with Elkins and Ruotolo of the DOH and Drs. W. H. Baker and J. Quimby of the MGH.[17] Amazingly, with the use of Versenate, colic, red blood cell changes, and wrist drop were reversed, and quantities as large as 40 times the pretreatment level of lead were excreted in the urine. We learned about the need for periods of rest between short periods of treatment and that the drug must be given by vein, not by mouth.

My interest in lead toxicity continued, and other ideas of exploring low-level lead effect brought me a five-year grant from the National Institutes of Health. Ideas were stimulated by working with Clair Patterson, a geologist from California. Dr. Patterson and I agreed with the concept best stated by my friend the late Dr. Henry Schroeder in 1969. The three of us sensed that since lead was deep in the earth during the early years of man's evolution on earth, pollution of soil, air, cooking utensils, drinking water, and food might even at low levels cause damage that would be overlooked, especially to children and lifelong lead workers as well as to small animals and foods growing in leaded soils. The greatest point of interest was harm to the brain in young and growing tissue, especially that of the embryo.

My work with Dr. Alice Hamilton led me to study old literature that described a wide array of central nervous system changes in former lead workers long free of lead exposure. It occurred to me, among others, that by discovering how much lead would be excreted after a small dose of Versenate, a reasonable estimate of stored lead could be made. Two noble women, dieticians, and one doctor agreed to be normal subjects to find a baseline. They lived in Boston, which meant that the contamination of urban air would be included. The results produced identical levels, half the level certain to be found in lead poisoning. Toxicity studies had been done by Dr. Harry Foreman at Los Alamos, so we were not asking the volunteers to take unknown risks.[18] At about the same time, similar studies were being done in Prague and Glasgow that showed that if the amount of lead excreted exceeded a certain level, one could conclude that the patient was carrying an excess body burden of lead. Further, if there were signs and symptoms, they might be due to lead plus some other factor such as surgery, which, by changing body chemistry, would release previously harmless lead stored within the body. Thus we had a safe tool for diagnosis.

About this time (1965) C. C. Patterson attempted to publish his paper on environmental lead pollution. It quickly became clear that the lead industry was angry. Only by heroic means did Dr. Katherine Boucot, the editor of the *Archives of Environmental Health* persuade the editorial board to publish this paper.[19] Several industry-supported research workers and plant doctors who read the now-famous Patterson paper threatened dire consequences if it were published, as did Patterson if it were not. My share at this stage was to work on the draft of the publication with the author one hot August day under the shade of our apple trees, with a cool drink in hand. I tried to get some of his wild rhetorical questions removed, with mild success. Since the U.S. government was soundly scolded by both sides (industry and the medical profession), a meeting was called while Patterson was at the South Pole to, so I was told, calm industry's fears of restrictive legislation. A few clinicians like myself were asked to a government-sponsored meeting, supposedly to talk informally. Fortunately, I had prepared carefully and formally a paper, published in 1966 under the title of "What Is the Status of Knowledge of Lead Effect on Identifiable Groups in the Population?"[20] I decided it was a good piece of work when a professor of occupational medicine wrote me, "I wish I had thought of the contents of your paper before you did."

The meeting was held in a huge room in Washington. It was no "shirt-sleeve" session, for there were two tables of press and more than 100 senior officials of the lead industry. The few of us who were invited to talk took little space in the front rows of seats. The discussion was noisy, angry, and sometimes incoherent because of emotion. After lunch there were more talks by government staff trying to make the atmosphere less tense, and the meeting broke up. A few of us were asked to stay for the press conference, a very cold-blooded affair. I almost felt sorry for one of my industrially hooked, very senior colleagues. The press asked him what his salary was and who paid it and what money supported his laboratory. Unhappily, all his funds came from one large industry. This meeting was, I think, a small-stage warning of the restrictions to come in control of environmental lead pollution in the United States. Patterson had won; Harriet was not far behind in addressing medical ignorance and needless worker illness. Returning to MIT, I had to ask protection from my many phone calls, which was well provided by Bob Byers, head of MIT public relations. My favorite letter of many received was one from the president of a New York brewery, threatening a libel suit. I had reported a measurable amount of lead (0.1 mg/liter) in beer. I was pleased to supply the source of this statement since it came from a brewer's journal! The suit was dropped.

At about this time, I interested some of my colleagues — Drs. Howell, Maloof, and Rabe, Richard Chamberlin and George Boylen — in pooling our data on environmental lead poisoning in Cambridge and Boston.[21] Important help was provided by Dr. Edward Rabe, pediatric neurologist at Boston Floating Hospital, in allowing us to study his cases of lead harming the brain, as well as by fellows at Boston City Hospital, local mental hospitals, and teachers of so-called slow learners. After much planning, a number of houses were studied to obtain crib and window sill paint, putty, and toys as well as street-air samples where children played and soil from a variety of sites to correlate with traffic densities. I received an education in administration and tact while dealing with scared politicians, civic groups, lawyers, legislators, and reporters. The basis for this work and the grant was and is my enthusiasm for new or improved methods for detecting what harm, if any, is caused by repeated small doses of an ancient poison well studied at high doses.

Since Rachel Carson's book, *Silent Spring*,[22] was published, and since the United States has formed new enforcement agencies since 1970 with new tools to work with, our studies have become a shadow of things to come. At the time we made our surveys, there was novelty in our study of lead in snow deep in the woods; of lead in soil at various distances from a lead source; of lead in cow's milk, dried or fresh, that had been pasteurized; and of lead in cows in barns or outdoors at different seasons. Surprisingly, cow's milk holds no lead; mother's milk does, especially if she smokes cigarettes. Lead is still used in the making of ceramics. I recall a case some years ago where a family was served orange juice in a ceramic container made by the mother. The acid of the juice caused a large amount of lead to be released, resulting in family illness and one fatality. The study of slow learners and children with seizures or violent behavior after an acute attack of lead poisoning was difficult to do because of sampling problems. We found that many factors influenced the safe amount. I persuaded a neighbor to give me the baby teeth of her children (only after a wish to the fairies had been made by each child with a tooth in place under the pillow). The reason for this trial lay in the known fact that lead follows calcium into bone and hence also into teeth. Measurable and varying amounts of lead were found in the teeth of all three children. This has proven a helpful fact to use in surveys of large populations in urban communities.

My work with lead effect led me to conclude that certain groups in the population have special risk from lead exposure: the pregnant woman, especially if she smokes cigarettes, which contain lead; the growing child; the worker with excessive exposure and/or such disease to cause anemia (for example, a chronic peptic ulcer with bleeding); those born with a defect in red cells as in so-called sickle cell anemia; and alcoholics whose iron is bound by lead in a "sick liver."

Control of lead use by law is difficult. This I know from the Lead Industry Association and its lobbyists. For example, when I was asked to do "research" for them, I was offered money. In addition, the Food and Drug Administration (FDA) was embarrassed because through a toy manufacture who called me for advice it was discovered that the standard for paint for toys and cribs was set by industry, while doctors and industry thought the safe level had been set by government. A pediatrician on the FDA staff visited me, and with the help of my staff engineer and chemist we showed him that the safe level of lead in toys and crib paints must be zero. But try as hard as the FDA did, Congress legislated a reduction in the allowable amount of lead but defeated our safe level of zero, so testifying to the power of the lead industry.

It would be unjust to write that all users of lead were careless; what is fair to note is that in all users' experience lead is expensive and difficult to control by engineering methods. In addition, the medical care of lead-poisoned patients, with rare exceptions, is inadequate, in part owing to lack of teaching of the subject by medical schools. I found and still find the problems of mild or subacute toxic lead effect of great interest, which offers the chance to study onset of disease. Older authors write of lead as a cause of aging and of joint disease, and some suggest that lead poisoning of the male may lead to congenital defects of his progeny. Lead is so ubiquitous and so useful that many research workers are currently at work to assess the harm of low-level exposure to leaded paint and fuel for combustion engines, among other uses. One unsettled question is how or if lead leads to shortening of life and/or fatal kidney disease, Thus, from the days of the Roman Empire up to and including the present, man has used and will use lead and must learn its subtle effects as it acts alone or with other toxic materials, following the same biological pathways for excretion, toxification, or storage.

REFERENCES

1. Schroeder, H. A., The Poisons Around Us, Bloomington, Ind., University of Indiana Press, 1974.
2. Selikoff, I. J., Churg, J., and Hammond, E. C., Asbestos exposure and neoplasia, JAMA, 188:22, 1964.
3. Hunter, D., The Diseases of Occupations, 6th ed., Boston, Little, Brown, 1978.
4. Pancoast, H. K., and Pendergrass, E. P., Roentgenological aspects of simple silicosis and silicotic tuberculosis, Am. Rev. Tuberc., 29:43, 1934.
5. Lynch, K. M., and Cannon, W. M., Asbestosis, Dis. Chest, 14:874, 1948.
6. Isselbacher, K., Klaus, H., and Hardy, H. L., Asbestosis and bronchogenic carcinoma, Am. J. Med., 14:721, 1953.
7. Selikoff, I. J., Churg, J., and Hammond, E. C., Occurrence of asbestosis among insulation workers in the United States, Ann. NY Acad. Sci., 132:139, 1965.
8. Stoeckle, J. D., Hardy, H. L., King, W. B., and Nemiah, J. C., Respiratory disease in U.S. soft coal miners: clinical and etiological considerations. A study of 30 cases, J. Chronic Dis., 15:887, 1962.

9. Hardy, H. L., Jeffries, W. McK., Wasserman, N. M., and Waddell, W. R., Thiocyanate effect following industrial cyanide exposure, N. Engl. J. Med., 242:968, 1950.
10. Hamilton, A., and Hardy, H. L., Industrial Toxicology, 2nd ed., New York, Hoeber, 1949.
11. Hardy, H. L., and Skinner, J. B., The possibility of chronic cadmium poisoning, J. Ind. Hyg. Toxicol., 29:321, 1947.
12. Hardy, H. L., and Elkins, H. B., Medical aspects of maximum allowable concentrations: benzene, J. Ind. Hyg. Toxicol., 30:196, 1948.
13. Vigliani, E. C., and Saita, G., Benzene and leukemia, N. Engl. J. Med., 217:872, 1964.
14. Hamilton, A., Industrial Toxicology, 1st ed., New York, Hoeber, 1934.
15. Gilfillan, S. C., Roman culture and dysgenic lead poisoning, Mankind Q., 5:1–20, 1965.
16. Aub, J., Minot, A. S., Fairhall, L. T., and Reznikoff, P., Recent investigations of absorption and excretion of lead in the organism, JAMA, 83:588, 1924.
17. Hardy, H. L., Elkins, H. B., Ruotolo, B., Quimby, J., and Baker, W. H., Use of monocalcium disodium ethylene diamine tetra-acetate in lead poisoning, JAMA, 154:1171, 1954.
18. Foreman, H., Hardy, H. L., Shipman, T. L., and Belknap, E. L., Use of calcium EDTA in cases of lead intoxication, Arch. Ind. Hyg. Occup. Med., 7:148, 1953.
19. Patterson, C. C., Contaminated and natural lead environments of man, Arch. Environ. Health, 11:344, 1965.
20. Hardy, H. L., What is the status of knowledge of the toxic effect of lead on identifiable groups in the population?, Clin. Pharmacol. Ther., 7:713–722, 1966.
21. Hardy, H. L., Chamberlin, R. I., Maloof, C. C., Boylen, G. W., Jr., and Howell, M. C., Lead as an environmental poison, Clin. Pharmacol. Ther., 12:892–1002, 1971.
22. Carson, R., Silent Spring, Boston, Houghton Mifflin, 1962.

CHAPTER 11

Travel Abroad (1950–66)

In 1948 Manfred Bowditch introduced me to two British doctors sent to study the status of industrial medicine in the United States. One was Dr. Trevor Lloyd-Davies, medical director of the great English drug company Boots. The other was a physiologist, Dr. Martin Wright, who was doing basic work on lung function tests for the British Medical Research Council. We enjoyed several occupational medical meetings and a party at the Bowditch's together.

It was Dr. Lloyd-Davies who considered the potential importance of my identification of beryllium compounds as toxic and launched my overseas experience. He wrote to ask if I would accept an invitation to tell my beryllium story before the Royal Society of Medicine in London.[1] At this time my chief for support and advice was Dr. Dana Farnsworth, director of the Medical Department at Massachusetts Institute of Technology (MIT). In a friendly way I boasted to him of the invitation and confessed that the English and I were without funds for such a trip. Dana outdid my highest hopes by finding money for the London trip plus enough more to allow me to travel on the Continent for a month. He, and later President James Killian, said the invitation was an honor to the institute. Although I had been abroad twice before, in 1926 and 1938, the prospect of telling my favorite and to me best-known story of a "new" work-related disease (beryllium poisoning) gave me a real thrill. In addition, I was to have an opportunity to travel, an occupation for which I have always had a taste, and this completed the delight of anticipation. Dr. Lloyd-Davies, a man of great vigor, was anxious that I see as much as possible both of the sights of London and of various industrial companies and operations. He knew most professionals in the field of occupational medicine in the United Kingdom and on the Continent, and so his plan for my travel was full and excellent.

This report includes mention of the many social, economic, and political views forced on my attention, fascinating as they were. Since poverty, ignorance, and malnutrition may be important parts of the disease process I went to study, these will be included as well. I started in London, where I was shown bombed-out areas and evidence of food shortages, a result of the short space of time elapsed since the active bombing of World War II. This was followed by a train trip to South Wales, refreshing because of great trees, open fields, and grazing livestock. I was billeted with three bachelor doctors wholly immersed in the work of the Pneumoconiosis Research Unit (PRU) set up by the British Medical Research Council to study the chest diseases of soft coal miners. The miners' output was poor, in part because many men could earn as much drawing welfare funds due them as they could by working in the mines. Coal production had fallen since the war. Studies of cardiopulmonary function, a variety of chest x-ray changes, dust count techniques, small animal experiments, and methods of dust control were the tools of the PRU. In addition, sophisticated epidemiologic and statistical skills were available to assess findings. There was a ward for sick workers at the Llandough Hospital near Cardiff to which the PRU was physically attached. Some early work was done by a mobile team for field study, including x-rays. One of the senior staff told me that much of the planning for this South Wales study drew heavily on the U.S. Public Health Service bulletin of the 1930s that described methods of study of coal miners' chest diseases.

During my three-day stay, I visited the famous Rhondda Valley to meet my host, Dr. Archie Cochrane, who was x-raying everyone with the intention of eliminating tuberculosis in the small Welsh mining town to see if this might not rule out death from coal workers' pneumoconiosis. If a worker has coal workers' pneumoconiosis, it is not necessarily damaging, but with tuberculosis superimposed the mortality rate becomes extremely high. Dr. Cochrane had had tuberculosis himself in a World War II prison camp. Very much interested in his project, he lived in this Welsh town, trying to persuade the Welsh miners and their families to be x-rayed, and, if tuberculosis was suspected, to go to the hospital. He had an arrangement with the government to make beds available; at that time the number of beds was very limited. He was much troubled by the fact that the Welsh miners were not all willing to be x-rayed, and he had begun a house-to-house canvass to see if he could persuade them with his own personal eloquence. When I visited the unit, he had x-rayed 86 percent of the population, a feat never achieved in the United States.

I heard a great deal about the political affairs of the miners, their living conditions, and their relationship with the mine owners. There has always been a great deal of emotion about the Welsh coal miners' work-related disability. The Silicosis Board in London could award a man permanent disability compensation, following which he could retire for the rest of his life. Many difficult problems naturally resulted.

There was jealousy on the part of the Welsh Medical School faculty of the work of the PRU, which had been set up by the British Medical Research Council. The historical differences between the Welsh and the English and the well-known Welsh nationalism were cause of much of this lack of communication. An unhappy feature of the South Wales coal miners' study, which covered a number of years, was and is the lack of rapport between the Welsh National School of Medicine and the staff of the PRU, located eight miles outside of Cardiff, which is the site of the Welsh Medical School. One result of this was that under the law there had to be an autopsy of a dead miner to determine the amount of compensation due the family. In Cardiff the pathologists, J. Gough, A. G. Heppleston, J. C. Leopold, and W. A. Thomas (those with whom I had contact), had access to the postmortem material from which they made important and original observations. But the results of the autopsies were not routinely made available to the PRU.

Many clues for research came from the Cardiff group; for example, an exciting discovery was made by Dr. A. Caplan, the pathologist who judged the extent of damage due to work in the mines and hence the amount of compensation. Dr. Caplan noted that coal miners with rheumatoid arthritis laid down the coal dust in their lungs in a peculiar fashion. This dust behavior resulted in what on x-ray looked very like small snowballs. Since Caplan's report, other diseases involving the lungs have been shown in patients with rheumatoid arthritis to produce the same x-ray, now called Caplan's syndrome. The syndrome is thought to show differences in the body's defense mechanism; this fact has led to further research in many laboratories.

The rewards to me of knowing and working with those on the staff during my 1950 visit (and again during visits in 1956, 1963, and 1966) were great. Of special help were Dr. Charles Fletcher, Dr. John Gilson, Dr. Martin Wright, Dr. Philip Hugh-Jones, and Dr. Peter Oldham. Dr. Oldham was a mathematician, a church-bell ringer, and the father of a daughter, Harriet, for whom I served as godmother on my 1956 stop at the PRU. All of these men have visited my home and have participated in professional meetings in the United States.

Returning to London to prepare for my paper before the Royal Society in 1950, I had the good fortune to stay with an old and good friend living near Hampstead Heath. Her flat at this time was surrounded by bombed-out areas; the building she lived in was so shaky as a result of war that each time the nearby underground train passed, the house shook and this awakened me. The nearby Heath provided me with a platform across which I pranced, rehearsing my paper. This was my first important and formal paper. Dr. Lloyd-Davies, my host, thinking he would comfort me, said, "You know, Harriet, this is the first session on Occupational Medicine sponsored by the Royal Society of Medicine, and perhaps only a few tramps who come in to be warm will be your audience." After this frightening or reassuring statement, however, when I entered the lecture hall every seat was full.

Before the session I was served tea to meet officials, fellow speakers, and the chairman, who proved to be a dermatologist. On impulse I told him of a few days past itching and scratching, which worried me for fear of leaving scabies in the mattress of my last hosts. The dermatologist-chairman was far more interested in my itch than in beryllium and told me to take off my jacket while he found his magnifying glass. After close study he said, "Have you been at the theater recently?" I replied, "Yes, I have seen Eliot's 'The Cocktail Party.'" "Well," he answered, "you have English midges from the red cushions of the theater seats." The cold of Stockholm, my next stop, would kill them, he prophesied. I scarcely had time to recover my jacket before the signal came for the lecture to begin. So I had little time for stage fright.

I began my paper as follows:

> I am very proud to be here. After a month in the British Isles
> visiting hospitals, laboratories, plants, and being so royal-
> ly treated in the homes of my colleagues, my previous con-
> viction that my boisterous, vigorous native land must look
> here across the Atlantic for mature counsel has been great-
> ly strengthened. . . . What I present today are my own
> opinions and observations, but the vast amount of material
> I have been able to study and use has been graciously made
> available to me by many colleagues — engineers as well as
> physicians.

New Knowledge — Wales,
Industrial England, Sweden, Holland

The day following my reading of the Royal Society paper, I had a
telephone call from Dr. Katharine Williams, who was in charge of
health and safety at Harwell, the English equivalent of the U.S.
atomic energy development laboratories. Would I travel to Harwell
to help her alarm her senior staff into accepting the facts of beryllium toxicity? This I did, using my frightening experience in the fluorescent lamp and atomic energy industries as examples. I saw her
again at MIT when she brought a beryllium-sampling device that
she had developed. In 1954 we had a day of sightseeing between sessions at an international meeting in Italy. Like all good tourists, we
went to Pompeii where I carelessly told the guide we were physicians.
This inspired him to show us everything that had to do with sex or
venereal disease.

Years later I met Dr. Williams at a so-called metal-binding
conference. Her interest was in methods of removing radioactive material from the bones. I was interested in removing heavy metals like
lead. We have corresponded on these subjects with great mutual
benefit.

I found London attractive medically. I talked to many people who worked in London hospitals, and I was taken through the
research laboratories of the Medical Research Council. I found congenial comrades in what is called the Factory Inspectorate, which
corresponds to our Department of Labor. This is an ancient and

honorable institution, with some laws ahead of ours and some not as advanced. At that time (1950), operating on a shoestring, the staff was first-class, with hard-working field people. They went into factories and rolled up their sleeves to find the hazard, then tried to persuade industry to mend its ways. If the companies did not, the British police had the power to call management into court. This group was not involved in post-World War II political changes.

I went next to Oxford where I visited the Institute of Social Medicine. This was not the first institute of social medicine to which I went nor was it the last. There were several such groups set up by the Nuffield Foundation, a rich nonprofit organization much like the Rockefeller Foundation in the United States. Lord Nuffield was the Henry Ford of England, a philanthropist who gave huge sums of money particularly for what is called *social medicine*. The use of these grants varied from community to community. Here in Oxford in 1950 the people at the institute held an academic appointment at Oxford University. On the staff was an internist who was doing somatotyping, a combination of Sheldonian skills and some studies he had developed himself. He was making psychological probings that were simple and straightforward, but he seemed rather astute, trying to correlate the illnesses of Oxford students with what he discovered by interviewing them. He had studied about 300 or 400 men, but because of the complexities of life at Oxford (1950), he could not have any women in his series. This doctor had not been able to see how he could undress women subjects and photograph them and how he could report his findings in conjunction with those of the men! I was not sure about the quality of his work, having participated myself in such work at Harvard College in 1943, but it seemed to me that he deserved to be noticed, and I encouraged my U.S. colleagues to consider his work. There was also a basic study of child health at Oxford, including the correlation of heights and weights by age, work I thought had been previously done. In addition, a tremendous amount of work was being done on the relationship of the incidence of tuberculosis to social and psychological conditions. I met irate defense of this work from some of the staff. They seemed to feel certain that I would criticize their doing this type of work, as I did — but to myself alone. I guessed the emotion I noted was due to "left wing" sentiment.

Next, I went to Nottingham, where my host, Dr. Lloyd-

Davies, had his headquarters. I stayed a week in his home and visited other centers from there. He was on the Dale Committee, a committee appointed by the prime minister to study industrial medical practice, that is, the problem of whether to absorb the area into the National Health Service or whether to let each plant appoint its own physician and pay its physicians' salaries. The problem of the Dale Committee revolved into an old scrap that was also going on in the United States and other countries, namely, the fact that public health authorities wanted to absorb any activity that could come under the heading of public health. In the United Kingdom the government was trying to absorb industrial medical activities into the Ministry of Health. In the United States the comparable authority would be the Public Health Service. People who have worked in industry and people like myself who have worked in departments of labor think it would be better for industrial medical practice to stay within a department of labor because of the need to enforce regulations concerning toxic hazards, safety, and radiation.

In 1950 England had an industrial phenomenon that we do not have in the United States — as a result of the law requiring further education. Children could leave school and go into industry from the age of 14 or 15, but they had to go to school one day a week. The industries arranged for the schools, and the bigger plants like Boots Drug set up what they called "continuation schools" in the plants. All types of studies were available, depending on the abilities of the individual pupils, from gymnastics and domestic science to classes in political affairs. At the time, the British were trying to get every person into some learning setting. A certificate for work accomplished was given, as required by law. In connection with these schools, Dr. Lloyd-Davies was collecting a tremendous amount of anthropological and psychological data, dating from the year 1935. Those in charge felt they were doing something helpful for the group by taking measurements and asking questions. It appears from what I heard and saw in 1950 that there was running through this company a fatherly attitude toward the workers, but this attitude was also governed by scientific or pseudoscientific discipline.

The plant doctors allowed their nurses to do a great deal more medical work than we do in either our factories or our college dispensaries. The doctor appeared only for an hour or two to sign papers and discuss whether certain x-rays should be taken. He might visit some work operation in which he was interested. For instance, when one plant was manufacturing substances such as stilbesterol, a drug used to treat endocrine problems, the male workers complained of painful breasts with an impressive enlargement of the breast tissue. Now women had been employed to do this work. I suggested that they employ postmenopausal women, a new idea to them. Young women on this job were having trouble with their menstrual periods. The stilbesterol was so fluffy and fine that it was almost impossible to control the air concentration. Workers inhaled the stilbesterol, it penetrated the unbroken skin, and it was absorbed through the nasal mucous membranes. With modern knowledge of malignancy due to stilbesterollike compounds, such work is currently done in completely protected work places. In summary, this big drug company, as other large British companies, handled their workers with a benign fatherly attitude. Many plant doctors I met were serving as sociologists and data collectors, as well as worrying about toxic hazards and first aid. I found this practice a debatable use of medical manpower.

I went from Nottingham to Manchester where there was another Nuffield-established department at the university, the Department of Industrial Hygiene. Professor Ronald Lane, head of that department, is very well known in most countries for his work on lead poisoning. He told me that occupational problems are broad and that doctors must learn that difficulties related to work have to do with group behavior. He urged me to take my attention away from mercury and lead and realize that all the problems are based on how workers behave in groups. He had a young internist on his staff trained as our internists with hematology as a specialty, good research experience, and war service. He came to realize that he most wanted to study the psychological adjustment of adolescents to adulthood in groups. He was spending much time and energy trying to get money for these studies.

To demonstrate how he was going about his studies, the internist gave me an example: "I was in a lead factory yesterday and saw a worker come along smoking near a lead-using operation, a practice against the rules. As I came along he put the cigarette in his pocket and I said to him, 'Look here, old man, you'll burn your pants!'" He did not say, "You shouldn't be smoking a cigarette." The man replied rather sulkily, "It's out." The internist explained to me that he would not consider speaking to him about his having broken the rule because it might create antagonism in the group toward the employers who were trying to set up a good employer-worker relationship. It appealed to me as an unreal way to tackle the problem.

To summarize the aims of the Nuffield projects: Many of these were set up in 1944. I congratulate the British, for — even with the bombs still dropping — the decision was made to set up constructive efforts in both academic and industrial settings. This appeared to be part of an important social attitude that was infiltrating the medical mind at the time. In the 1950s and 1960s changes in U.S. medical schools reflected a similar point. Many university departments previously called "public health departments" became "departments of social or community medicine." Such subjects as water purification were hardly mentioned. My British colleagues kept defending their actions and plans as though I had come to protest. I had not come for that reason — I had come to listen. I think the British employers felt, too, that workers might take matters into their own hands, so every effort was made to develop work satisfaction even on assembly lines.

When I got to Scotland and went to the Institute of Social Medicine, I met some hard-headed Scots who said that what I reported from Manchester was a lot of foolishness, as was the collecting of data at Boots in Nottingham. They were quite vocal about the National Health Service, much franker than some of the English. They felt it was not old enough to be judged yet. It was shocking to understand how it had lowered the level of practice of medicine from doctor to patient at that time. Several young men who had practiced for six months or so under this system said they were going to pieces, since they felt they could not do even the minimum for their patients. At that time for a doctor to earn enough to support his family, he had to have about 4,000 patients on his list. A conscientious man could handle about 2,000 — thus he would not be able to make ends meet because he was paid just so much per patient, regardless of whether the patient came to him 40 times a year or only once. A man with 4,000 cases per year would have to go at top speed all day long, and as a result he would have no time to examine his patients but simply to hear their symptoms and, if he dared, write a prescription. If he was not too happy about a particular case, he could write a tentative diagnosis on a piece of paper and send the patient to the hospital. As a result the hospitals were getting bogged down with a backlog of work and were suffocating.

When I was in Scotland, I visited another company, the William Collins Publishing House in Glasgow, where the doctor was conscious of the industrial disease of boredom from automation. He was interested in the psychological problems this presented and was reading Freud, studying deeply to try to understand all the sexual implications. He felt that sex was at the bottom of the personal troubles of the worker. There was such a mixture of doctors and managers telling me the same story of lack of work satisfaction, all emphasizing the urgency of some "cure." The doctor at the publishing company, however, felt that it was better for workers to get their social satisfactions outside of the job. He observed that young women would stay in the plant a certain period of time, get married and leave, and come back later after their children had reached a certain age.

In the groups I met, there was a good deal of controversy about how to produce work satisfaction. The faculty I talked to were studying the problem in the universities, and industrial medical officers were trying to improve matters in the plants. In contrast, in the years I know best (1945–70), I have seen little attention paid to work satisfaction in the United States until very recently. Our colleagues could well afford to copy some of the things that the English are doing. For some time in England, some large industries have used rest homes. Here a worker who had broken his leg, for example, would be cared for, even if the injury was not industrial in origin. The company bore the expense and arranged for a two- or three-week stay in the country. These rest homes held classes to teach such things as occupational therapy relevant to each case, and some of the larger and more elaborate had physiotherapy and gymnastics. These rest homes were impressive. I understood that they were a direct outcome of World War II. Workers staying there participated in maintenance and in decisions on policy. The place I visited had elaborate vocational planning and a full-time neurologist. These rest homes were often housed in the homes of wealthy people who had to get rid of them because of taxes and the high costs of maintenance. The owners had turned them over to industrial companies for nominal sums.

After World War II, perhaps in large part as a result of military research and atomic energy development, a number of persons from foreign government agencies and universities had visited Boston with mutual benefit by exchange of information. From Sweden came Drs. Sven Forssman, Lars Friberg, Axel Ahmard, and Sven Lundgren, while Dr. L. Noro and several industrial hygiene engineers came from Finland; all visited the Harvard School of Public Health. I was teaching there at the time and came to know Dr. Forssman and Dr. Friberg especially well. They urged me to visit them, and this I did on several occasions beginning in 1950. I went first to the Government Inspectorate headquarters for Scandinavia in Stockholm. From what I was told, their work sounded excellent. However, I was in Sweden for only one workweek at that time as a guest of the National Institute of Public Health, the state-supported bureau for all their public health and industrial health work. The Swedes are recognized for a high standard of work, especially in biochemistry. According to the Swedes, their plan of national compulsory health insurance works well. They direct the doctors less in managing their practices than was the case in England at that time (1950). The Swedes believed that all nations would come to such a plan sooner or later. All their hospitals were state owned, state run, and state supported. One trouble they admitted to was having too many buildings and equipment with not enough trained personnel to staff them — lots of material and not enough brains. This can be true anywhere.

Most urban buildings in Stockholm were marvelously designed and attractive in their use of glass, light, air, and greenery. We in the United States have come to this form of architecture somewhat later than they. In Sweden the countryside was lush, and the many grand new buildings were impressive. Suburbs had apartment-house complexes, even for people of very low income, with their own little schools, stores, and movies. Crowded conditions in Stockholm have been met by building self-sufficient communities of about 10,000 population each. Swedish physicians that I talked with said that since the end of World War II there had been an increase of 150 percent in criminality and also much sex delinquency among young people. There was a high divorce rate, much alcoholism, and a high suicide rate, which was puzzling to them. One man expressed the idea that the trouble stemmed from the Swedish abandonment of the church and the lack of an authority for which they might have respect. The state had made a study and found that 0.7 percent of the people went to church in Stockholm, and so abolished all but a few churches because it seemed impractical to support churches for so few people.

Many Swedes felt that they were caught up in a great web of regulations. Out of this they have received what Franklin Roosevelt sought for the United States: freedom from hunger and want. Therefore, they were baffled to know why they should be faced with great psychological and sociological difficulties. Literature, art, and drama in Sweden all reflected the existence of this state of affairs. I am amazed, in retrospect, at how much I learned. Talking with active investigators, I often found that we were interested in the same problem. For example, Swedish investigators as well as those in the United States, including myself, were all interested in the toxicity of cadmium, mercury, and "hard metal." This mix of cobalt, tantalum, and titanium makes such a strong metal that it is used for cutting diamonds — hence the tools made with these materials are often called diamond-cutting tools.

I had long talks with those concerned with social medicine, which taught me much of the social and political problems of postwar Europe. In fact, everywhere I visited medical groups or medical colleges, I discovered interesting investigations and the teaching of what was and is variously called "social" or "community" medicine. Our government began to have an interest in social welfare somewhat later than the Scandinavian governments. This interest has been a stimulus for medicine to study the sickness of groups or of a society as a whole, rather than to consider a sick individual as its sole responsibility. Sweden, neutral during World War II, was the first country I found to provide subsidized care from the cradle to the grave. Thus far, national health insurance laws in Sweden and England have suffered great legislative pains. I was told of many serious failures and saw miserable outcomes in a few individual cases. Perhaps wrongly, I,lay great blame on organized medicine. However, I can write dogmatically only of the United States. If organized medicine had at the start of various health insurance plans worked with, not against, government, the story today might be different.

A few days spent in Copenhagan with the late Dr. Aage Grüt and his wife — he with great experience in international occupational medicine — were both restful and fruitful. Dr. Grüt was in charge of Danish industrial health. His knowledge of variations in the ill effects of lead poisoning gave us much to discuss. We talked while sitting in his handsome gardens, drinking a beer called Hamlet, Shakespeare's heroic Dane. Aage took me to visit an ancient plant that had made the liqueur Cheery Heering since 1818. After walking through the old vaults, we were invited, at 11 A.M., to meet the president and have a refreshing drink which proved to be Cheery Heering plus a generous amount of gin!

Denmark was in poor straits in 1950 when I was there. The Danes did not have enough to eat. In my brief visit to Copenhagen, I met an English-speaking doctor, a Dane,who said his countrymen were gloomy and sad about the world and wondered what their economic future was.

During my 1950 trip my senior, Dr. Alice Hamilton, kindly arranged for me to visit the chief of the Dutch Factory Inspectors, Dr. J. F. Loutit. He was elderly and obviously not well, but he was determined to work as long as possible. We met in the Hague so that we might visit the great Phillips Eindhoven factory at Regendock, a fluorescent lamp-manufacturing plant. I was shocked at the casual attitude there toward excess beryllium contamination of workers and equipment. The chief medical official held the same conviction as did Scadding of London. According to him, all the abnormal chest x-rays — and I saw many — were due to tuberculosis or sarcoidosis, an atypical form of tuberculosis. To demonstrate his peace of mind concerning this theory, he had a young worker come to our conference table, his coverall quite white with factory dust. This doctor then used ultraviolet light to show the fluorescent effect on this man's clothes and lips. This showed up a recent kiss! I have not been able to get a follow-up report on this folly. My guess is that 25 to 30 percent of the workers are dead, based on the experience of the Massachusetts General Hospital Beryllium Case Registry, without benefit of correct diagnosis.

In the afternoon we traveled to Leyden where I had a quite different reception. I lectured to students on U.S. occupational medical problems; and I spent a helpful hour with two young investigators who had succeeded in reproducing, by using beryllium compounds in experiments with guinea pigs, abnormal changes in the liver very much like those found in autopsied beryllium workers. At that time in the United States, there were endless squabbles at endless meetings on whether the abnormalities in small animals were the same as those in human beryllium workers. This was, in my view, a sorry chapter in beryllium history, for it delayed finding safe substitutes or proper protection. To this day lawyers for companies facing litigation claims in the beryllium industry, using the history just sketched, protest that the companies were ignorant of the risk and that no government agency had issued warnings or orders. As a result, my patients suffered not only a miserable disease but also great financial hardship.

I came home feeling that we in the United States have great responsibility to make the most of our semibureaucracy and to hang on to our ability to make decisions, to improve things, and to make a fuss when we do not like the way public affairs are handled. I became quite emotional about the importance of voting.

The Dutch, the French, and even the Swiss apparently sold part of their souls to Hitler and were feeling depressed in 1950. In Geneva, where merchants scalped you financially, they would explain that this was necessary because of the world situation. In addition, there was much sadness, depression, and gloom. Everyone I met complained of regulations. In general, all believed that the only protection Europe had was that our country would foot its bills and solve all its military problems. At the same time they were very free in criticizing the United States. I lost my temper twice. I was told in three countries that the Soviet Union would not start a war, the United States would. This infuriated me. The second time I reacted was when I was told that we should have acted differently in Korea and that the Russians would have never started such a war. I discovered, in explanation, that the persons who told me this were "fellow-travelers."

I visited the Pneumoconiosis Research Unit (PRU) in Cardiff, Wales, again in 1956 for an extended stay. During this visit, I began writing a monograph on occupational lung disease that I had promised several of my MGH colleagues. The atmosphere was right, and the good company, new ideas, and foreign visitors resulted in many pages of notes from diligent use of the library but little writing. The end result did not go to the publisher until 1973 as part of a third edition of *Industrial Toxicology*.[2]

While in Sheffield, England, in 1956, I was privileged to visit the Mine Research Establishment. Dr. G. D. Nagelschmidt showed me electron microscope pictures of the particles found in the air on days of "smog," now a well-known entity in industrialized, heavily populated, gasoline-engine-using areas. John Pemberton, also in Sheffield at this time, invited me to his home where he described his original studies in patients of what has come to be known as *British bronchitis*, its diagnosis, outcome, and therapy.*

Back in London I visited the Brompton Hospital for Chest Diseases where Dr. Lynne Reid (now a professor at Harvard Medical School in Boston) was teaching. I had further lessons about bronchitis from her and her radiologist colleague, Dr. M. A. Simon. The Brompton group as well as others had made the observation that bronchitis correlated quite well with social class and residence. Quite foreign to me was the use of the term *social class* in medical studies. Class I was made up of the wealthiest; its members could afford to go to bed with a head cold, thus supposedly limiting its severity and duration. Class V, the least well paid, had to work although ill. This oversimplified explanation of social class and illness of 1956, however, is constantly changing in England and all countries.

An interesting London visit I had at this time was with Dr. Patrick Lowther, professor of medicine at St. Bartholomew's Hospital. He had a laboratory and various sampling devices on the roof of the hospital where his group was studying the chemicals in London air. He found the sulfur content from the burning of fossil fuel for heating of great importance. His studies led to the creation of smokeless areas of London, so that monuments and stone buildings now are the original color, and sufferers with bronchitis are relieved. The government supplied money where needed to convert buildings to gas or oil heat.

It is fitting to end my experience with coal dust and bronchitis with mention of this legislation brought before Parliament in 1661 by John Evelyn:

> She is to be relieved from that which renders her less healthy, really offends her, and which darkens and eclipses all her other Attributes. And what is all this, but that Hellish and dismall Cloud of SEA-COALE? which is . . . so universally mixed with the otherwise wholesome and excellent Aer,

---

*The PRU reports of Oldham (1956) state that British bronchitis was the second largest cause of death in England, corresponding in numbers to deaths in the United States from heart failure.

that her Inhabitants breathe nothing but an impure and thick Mist, accompanied with a fuliginous and filthy vapour, which renders them obnoxious to a thousand inconveniences, corrupting the Lungs, and disordering the entire habit of their Bodies; so that . . . Coughs and Consumptions rage more in this one City, than in the whole Earth besides.[3]

The book from which I quote was given to me by the late Dr. Andrew Meiklejohn, a professor in Glasgow, formerly a coal miner and a wonderful tutor to young and old on the history and currently known facts of industrial disease.

During this 1956 trip I had several visits of importance to my studies. The late Dr. Donald Hunter, chief of medicine at the London Hospital, had worked with Dr. Aub at the MGH on the subject of lead poisoning. Returning to London, he made the field of man-made disease a lifetime study of interest and joy to himself and a requirement for his students. I visited him several times at the London Hospital. He had collected a wonderful number of pathological specimens and illustrations from pamphlets and books picturing the plight of women and children at heavy labor in the mid-nineteenth century and men in dangerous trades up to the present. Dr. Hunter put his experience and his knowledge into a large compendium, *The Diseases of Occupations*,[4] now in its sixth edition. He and Dr. Ronald Lane, professor of medicine at Manchester, had been visitors at Massachusetts General when my studies in industrial medicine in outpatient clinics were just beginning. I am in great debt to both of these industrial medical chiefs, for they had encouraged me personally, had backed my plan to work within the Department of Medicine, and had spoken on my behalf to my hospital seniors. I also met Dr. J. A. Bonnell and Dr. G. Kazantzis, fellow research workers with Dr. Hunter, and I have been corresponding with them ever since; and we have met at several international meetings to exchange varying ideas on the toxicity of cadmium. Two incidents from my visits with Dr. Hunter stick in my mind. One, he insisted that I spoke biblical English, showing that my place of birth and environment was the U.S. Atlantic Coast. I was flattered but not convinced. Two, the modest paper I wrote with Skinner — published in 1947 — on chronic cadmium poisoning[5] had stimulated the interest of Hunter and his group. In the United Kingdom and Europe storage batteries for cars, trucks, and buses are made with cadmium. The Swedes and the English had begun to report lung changes, calcium abnormalities (kidney stones), and bone changes seen on x-ray.

At this time, at last, I was asked about my pet disease, beryllium poisoning, and how to distinguish it from sarcoidosis. This question was put to me by many people but none as important as Dr. J. G. Scadding, whose lifetime studies of sarcoidosis are known the world over. A few of the cases in his file I recognized as belonging to the Massachusetts fluorescent lamp-manufacturing epidemic. Politeness demanded silence, but I was relieved to know that my stolen goods had arrived at a place of honor! My host took me for lunch at a famous London club, the Atheneum. Here with fine food and wine Dr. Scadding worked mightily to persuade me that sarcoidosis was a particular form of tuberculosis. I learned much and enjoyed the Atheneum Club's storybook atmosphere.

That afternoon I visited the British Factory Inspectorate, which was very like the U.S. Public Health Service and labor departments in some states. Here I met the famous Dr. E. R. A. Merewether, who was first to report the high percentage of lung cancer in asbestos workers. One of the inspectors was Dr. Ethel Browning, well known then for her careful blood count studies in radiation workers and her phenomenal knowledge of medical literature. In 1961 Lloyd Tepper, Dick Chamberlin, and I published a monograph on the *Toxicity of Beryllium Compounds* at her request.[6] Dr. Sybil Horner, a senior inspector, and Drs. A. I. G. McLaughlin and Robert Buchanan joined us at the Savage Club where we gossiped about the varied problems of the United States and the United Kingdom in control of workers' illness. My last visit in London in the 1956 trip was to the London School of Hygiene and Tropical Medicine where I was able to talk to Dr. Schilling about byssinosis and to Dr. Guymer about medical education.

With the help of Dr. Cochrane of the PRU, who knew most of the investigators studying dust diseases of coal workers, plans were made for me to visit key centers in this field in Germany, Belgium, and France during my trip abroad in 1956, a trip financed by the U.S. Public Health Service. In addition, I was invited to be an observer at a meeting in Luxembourg of the medical section of the postwar Coal and Steel Community, forerunner of the European Economic Community. At this meeting a report was given of work done in each member country, followed by discussion. Dr. Enrico Vigliani of Italy, a leading figure abroad in the field of industrial medicine, was chairman. He was a trim, handsome man with continental manners who greeted me by bowing over my extended hand and giving a short speech on my "fame."

I was the only woman present and was seriously hampered by my schoolgirl grasp of the languages used, chiefly German and French. Some help came from two English-speaking members; the first was the late Earl King, known for his careful studies of the effect of infections (chiefly tuberculosis) and silicosis in small animals; the second was Dr. G. D. Nagelschmidt, a skilled, broadly educated, German-born geologist, now a citizen of England. A few quotes from my journal of December 1, 1956, are lofty in tone — amusing in view of my recent entry into occupational medicine.

> The Luxembourg meeting most educational. The Italians seem to me lacking in critical judgment; the Germans thorough and bright but not wise; and British good but hopelessly condescending; the Belgians careful, watchful, polite, enterprising. Policard of France, with whom I had corresponded on beryllium toxicity, far and away the best.

A short stay at Bochum, the coal-mining center of the Ruhr Valley between Cologne and Dusseldorf, gave striking evidence of war damage, which I was often told was caused by the United States. Housed in quarters used by the resident doctors, I learned more of their fear of the Soviet Union than I did of lung disease. When planes flew overhead, I was left alone at the table as my colleagues ran for shelter. I had equipment for recording, since I was hoping to get facts on tape in answer to my questions. But when I prepared the machine for recording interviews with the young doctors, they muttered "Big Brother" and were silent. I was shown elaborate laboratories for lung function tests and a great array of machines designed to help relieve — by sprays, exercises, and local massage — the shortness of beath of the sick coal workers of the Ruhr Valley. The best assessment I could get in questioning those qualified and willing to answer was that most of this therapy was of bogus character. No normal control values of lung function had been done. A series of chest x-rays of these crippled workers showed large shadows in both lungs. To me this meant a higher percentage of the dangerous silica dust in their exposure, surely of long duration, plus infection of varying causes. Perhaps it was because of my poor ability to speak German, but it was true also in other places I visited on that trip that I found the measurement of dust exposure in a muddled, unscientific state. I spent a useful afternoon with the pathologist at Bochum. As I guessed, the abnormalities showed the scarring effect of silica sand, which distorted normal lung anatomy including the bronchial tubes.

My visit to Belgium took me to the University of Louvain Medical College and to Hasselt, center for research on the effect of coal dust. Here was a team, engineer, radiologist, clinician and a physiologist, F. Lavenne, with whom I spent most of my time. I was touched by the fact that Lavenne quoted from *Industrial Toxicology* (2d ed., 1949),[7] frequently and carried a copy with him, perhaps to please me. I had met a Belgian company doctor in the United States, who exerts great influence on coal workers' research, this influence extending to what was then the Belgian Congo. Laboratory studies convinced him that finely divided silica sand particles were the greatest risk. He therefore suggested that aerosols of salt solution be sprayed into mine air to cause the fine particles to stick together, making a mass too great to be inhaled. As far as I can discover, no studies have been published by 1979 to prove or disprove this thesis. The same has proven true of so-called aluminum therapy to treat silicosis, tried in Canada and the United States. I include this here to illustrate the imagination and effort that has been used to fight this ageless enemy of man's determination to dig deep in the earth for coal, metals, and natural gas.

I returned in 1963 to the shelter of the London School of Hygiene, thanks to Dr. Richard Schilling, the dean, to use their good library and space given me when I began more seriously to write on the third edition of Industrial Toxicology, published in 1974.[8] Dr. Richard Doll, whom I had seen in the United States, and who is famous for the study of "cancer epidemics," kindly gave me time to hear about his work in developing a registry of nickel workers who contracted lung cancer. He had notes on every nickel worker in the United Kingdom and the cause of death in each case. Thus he could document cases due to nickel. The literature had named arsenic as the cause, but Doll's work ruled out arsenic and incriminated nickel. Since at the MGH we were painfully and slowly assembling a registry of beryllium cases, my meeting with Dr. Doll was of great help.

On this trip I spent a good day at Carshalton where the late Dr. John Barnes headed the national toxicology laboratories. I learned of the extremely toxic effects of organic tin compounds acting on the central nervous system.* We talked also of the cancer-producing behavior of a class of chemicals called nitrosamines, which are used in the chemical industry. In addition, Dr. John Barnes and I discussed what Dr. Gerald Wogan and Dr. P. M. Newberne of MIT, among other investigators, had learned of the toxins produced by certain fungi, a class of poisons called *mycotoxins*. Their importance lay in the fact that they grew on grain, the sole source of food in some countries. In animal studies these mycotoxins caused liver damage including cancer.

Sadly, Dr. Barnes died suddenly a few years ago, while alone in his laboratory. I do not know the final opinion of the cause of his death, but I feel that he may have been working on a deadly new or old poison without the controls he so thoroughly respected. I shall miss him and his always-active sharp mind. When I saw him in Geneva at the World Health Organization or in Washington and described some new facet of the beryllium problem, he welcomed a new question. He had raised a strain of mice that when dosed with beryllium, produced beryllium-containing progeny. However, the next generation he raised had no detectable illness. In humans we had shown that the children of mothers with severe clinical beryllium disease showed beryllium in urine but were not ill. Dr. Barnes's hypothesis was that beryllium changed some process vital to the body's defense, and this could be passed to the next generation. There are a few registry cases of beryllium disease in childhood. Such cases proved to be so-called neighborhood poisoning, based on the fact that their homes were in the path of plant discharge or that the child lived in the house with one or two beryllium workers.

---

*The difficulties of this field of medicine are illustrated by the fact that inorganic tin compounds are harmless.

Czechoslovakia

In 1959 I made a trip to the International Symposium on Maximum Allowable Concentrations of Toxic Substances in Industry in Prague at the request of the Permanent Commission and the International Association on Occupational Health. I made no notes at the meeting because I had clear evidence that my bag and briefcase were looked at daily. Whenever I tried to use the telephone, I was aware that someone was listening; my scrap basket was emptied often and my personal belongings moved around. Perhaps it was known that I and other members of the American group had security clearance for work with the Atomic Energy Commission (AEC). The professional proceedings took place in an interesting building with wonderful equipment for interpretation into the five languages of the meeting. We sat at long tables such as those used at a banquet, and each of us had his own equipment for listening in the language of his choice. There was plenty of opportunity to talk with colleagues in the halls and the coffee shop below; this was one of the most agreeable parts of the program.

  An amusing observation was that every time someone from the United States, Canada, or the United Kingdom spoke, his offering was greeted with silence, whereas when anyone from the Soviet Union spoke, there was enthusiastic clapping. In public the Germans were careful to be noncommittal about everything, although they were ready to talk in the corridors, pro and con, depending on whether they came from East or West Germany. It was clear that the Czechs were doing all they could to be polite to the Russians.

  While the Russian delegates seemed well informed and had done some original work, their whole plan was to turn the meeting to their political advantage. Whenever anyone from the West — especially the United Kingdom, the United States, and Canada — offered a number as a measurement of safe working levels, the Russians or the Czechs would immediately say this was wrong and give a much lower number without giving any supporting data. Several times, the leader of the Czech group apropos these differences, questioned, "How is it that the Americans are so rough in caring for their workers, and the Russians so very sensitive?" I am sure his job and perhaps more personal matters depended on the way he presented himself at the meeting. The Russians were cheerful and friendly but completely noncommittal. Professor August Letavet, the chairman of the Russian delegation, with whom Dr. Alice had been acquainted and whom I called the Russian Bear, not being very good at pronouncing his name, told me of a single neighborhood case of beryllium disease, although my correspondence prior to the meeting had suggested that we might exchange more of our experiences.

The member countries behind the Iron Curtain relied heavily on variations of the well-known work of Pavlov in setting safe worker levels. The laboratory tools in experimental animal studies of toxicity were the electrical tracings of the nervous system and evaluation of changes in the conditioned reflex. To set levels for workers, the flicker eye test and the testing of the sense of smell were popular at this time.

I was also told about what was called "fatigue" as a result of exposure to ionizing radiation at very low levels; certainly in this country we would find it very difficult to accept as correlated with any kind of gauge of biological harm. The events of 1977 at the American Embassy in Moscow with laser and microwave beams, used either to frighten the employees or for the detection of American movements within the embassy, may prove the Russians right. The Central Europeans had also worked out the fact that functional changes — and we all agree that this is true to a degree — lead to morbid changes. It was argued that the excitability, that is, the irritation of an organ or a system, may lead to its failure. Many speakers took the position that low-level exposures to toxic materials that can act as irritants may result in morbid anatomical changes (1959). This idea has been used and discarded by physiologists, but it was pressed hard by Hungarian and Yugoslavian delegates. We in the West are beginning to think along these lines (1980). In the Eastern European countries when scientific work is publicly described, care must be taken to put data to the greatest political advantage. Further, no knowledge that government wishes concealed should become public. The situation is miserable for the Czechs, personally and professionally. There was little to admire in the public scientific papers, even though many of the individuals involved were well trained and capable of first-class work.

In 1966 I returned to Czechoslovakia. I had the privilege of dining in the home of Dr. and Mrs. S.,* who had previously visited in my home in Massachusetts. We were told about the way the Russian occupation was affecting them and learned that they thought the situation had been better when the Germans were in control. Now, for example, they were taxed on the amount of floor space they had, and at least 50 percent or more of all earned income went to the Russians. In addition, their children learned both Russian and Czech, and they were personally under surveillance because they were teaching their children English and French at home after school hours. I learned that Dr. S. had had his license taken away from him so that he could no longer practice medicine. His wife, who was very outspoken in her criticism of the Russians when I was in their home, was a trolleycar driver to keep the family in bread and butter. Dr. S. went to the door more than once during our evening together to be sure that no one was listening to our conversation while his wife told of the difficulties of their life. I had been invited to attend this Prague meeting, which was concerned with safe levels of exposure in industry. People from behind the Iron Curtain appeared to be watchful of foreigners at this international meeting. Most members of the conference went to a sumptuous reception in the great hall of one of the castles.

Here we were greeted by the remarkable minister of public health, a defrocked priest who continued to wear his clerical clothes. He was defrocked because he joined the Communist party, but he went on saying mass just the same. When we offered him a cigarette, he refused, explaining that after six years of no cigarettes as a prisoner in Buchenwald he smoked so many of them when he was released that he was now quite sickened by them. He was an enormous man, at least six feet six inches tall, and had the appearance of a case of some endocrine disease. I am sure he could be a perfect museum for a psychiatrist, as well as for an endocrinologist; obviously, he did precisely as he was told, knowing probably very little about health matters but carrying out certain orders as they came to him from other sources. I was sorry for him but extremely interested as he shook hands with the late Dr. Baader, a German Jew who was known to

*Dr. and Mrs. S's names are omitted since they have fled Prague and are now living in another country.

have collaborated with the Nazis. Obviously, it was hard for the Czech to be friends with Baader. Baader was a small, obsequious man, a Uriah Heep character, with his head down, courteous and smirking, while this great giant of a man was shaking his hand in the reception line, probably thinking he would like to see Baader dropped in the ocean.

The Russians had invited me to go to dinner with them after the reception. They hoped to discuss certain matters concerning the excretion of strontium in the urine, even though I protested that I was a clinician rather than a chemist. My Czech friend, Dr. S., had warned that whatever was said at this meeting would be reported in two capitals, Prague and Moscow. Foolishly, I had in my purse a piece of paper with instructions from the AEC* telling me a number of things I was not to do, one of which was not to become separated from the main party. However, I felt the Russian request was such that it would be wiser to go. I reasoned that I would not be far from our large party, and there were a number of ways by which my whereabouts could be discovered. I managed to transfer my notes from the AEC document marked "Confidential" to the purse of Mrs. Boysen, wife of Col. John Boysen, a physician with our forces in Germany.

Then I went off with the same "Russian Bear" whom I had met in 1959 and with two younger escorts, one from the Czech government and one from the Occupational Health Institute in Prague. We drove in a tiny car a much longer distance than necessary, it seemed to me, to be shown the river in moonlight and various antique structures. In the end we drove so far that I wondered if I had been wise to go off with these people without more careful planning. Finally, we stopped in a dark street and entered a dark passageway; we went up some dimly lit stairs into a tiny restaurant, a single room that I sensed was in someone's house. We entered through a doorway covered by a red velvet curtain, and as we did so I could see a man in the kitchen acting as a cook while his wife distributed food. There were five or six tables, close together, and the people in the room seemed to know each other pretty well. All but one man were

---

*I and many of the other U.S. participants were consultants to the AEC and had security clearance from them.

in uniform. The Russian Bear and I sat on a sofa, our backs to an outside wall, with the two young men facing us. One young man sat up so straight that I felt sure he had a recording device in his lap. The Czech who had invited me to the conference was a physician who had been in Boston and had worked at the Harvard School of Public Health. This Dr. M. appeared to be extremely nervous, and I do not know why. The Russian Bear and I got on very well, laughing and talking, and when I had a little something to drink, he said that he was "afraid of acute toxicity" and refused to have any alcohol. He found this a great joke.

We talked about many things. I was asked questions that I could not answer about the detail and results of chemical assay of the urine for strontium 89, a measure of fallout from which the Russians guessed they might calculate the size of the current (1966) U.S. atomic bomb development. I characteristically felt it necessary to "lecture" my hosts on their questions and finished by inviting them to come to MIT where I assured them my colleagues could answer their questions. It was all very easy and pleasant for me, but I doubt they learned anything they wanted. In due time I was returned to my hotel quite safely.

The next morning Dr. S. came to my hotel, and we talked about the medical problems associated with uranium. Perhaps such talks might have been one of the reasons for his trouble with the Russian authorities. I sent him later, without identification, a method for the determination of uranium in urine, which he wanted. I hope that this was not a source of difficulty for him.

One day the group was taken to visit a factory and a cathedral and finally to have a dinner of international friendship in a castle in an old town 40 miles from Prague. We went in buses, grouped according to the language we spoke. Obviously, I went in the English-speaking bus where I found the Swedes, who were good company, as well as two strange Czechs who spoke very good English. As the day wore on, I realized these latter two were there to listen to our conversation. It was amusing to see the Russian delegation ride ahead of us in a 1950 American Chevrolet sedan, apparently afraid they would be contaminated, shot at, or ridiculed if they traveled with us. First, we went to an industrial plant where many hazards were apparent, especially from mercury and carbon disulfide. With the help of Dr. Lars Friberg of Sweden, members of the British delegation, and Dr. Elkins of the Massachusetts Division of Occupational Hygiene, we were able to see clearly that this plant was just as untidy and potentially harmful as some of the less well controlled plants in other countries including the United States. Therefore, the fine brave words of very low allowable limits used behind the Iron Curtain, stated at the meeting as true, might in fact be propaganda. In contrast, the medical program for the workers was very good.

As we finished our sightseeing of an ancient castle, Dr. S. came to me and said that the Czechs wanted me to make a radio broadcast. I agreed to do it, and suggested ten o'clock the next morning at my hotel. Dr. S. became red in the face and shook his head, saying "thank you" as he went to report. Later one of the group came up and said it just so happened that they had their broadcasting equipment along, and they asked if I could do it before dinner. Again I agreed, although I knew that by the rules of my AEC document I was not to give a radio broadcast without first talking to the American Embassy. When we arrived at the dinner, I saw no sign of the broadcasters until we were well along with the wine, the food, and toasts in five languages. Suddenly I was tapped on the shoulder and asked to make the broadcast. I was taken into a room away from the others. The two Czechs who had been on the bus with us were there, and I now think of them as spies. They had some equipment with them; whether it was directly attached to the broadcast equipment or whether it was simply a tape recorder I do not know. They asked me questions, such as, "How is it, Dr. Hardy, that the Americans are so rough in their care of their workers, while the Russians are so sensitive?" The combination of the good meal and the wine, and my own natural love of speaking, led me to give them a lecture on the attitude in my country toward industrial disease and safe exposure levels and the difficulty of arriving at correct safe working levels without data. The broadcasters (American, I decided from their accents — I asked them what part of New Jersey they came from) dismissed me politely, and I went back to the dinner table. I learned the next day that Dr. Elkins of the United States had been approached to give a broadcast after he was told that Dr. Hardy's broadcast did not come out very well. This was to me a great compliment!

Before I left Prague, through my persistent questioning and through the kindness of Dr. S., I was taken to the Pathology Department of the university where I was able to get some thick sections of the lung, said to be of the Schneeberg radium miners. These were men who worked in mines containing uranium and radium (Marie Curie used some of this ore for her original experiments) who later died of radium poisoning in the form of cancer of the lung. I was well treated, and the men to whom I talked impressed me as behaving independently.

Finally, I was driven to the Prague airport, and since there was a delay in departure, I went to the restaurant there. When I returned to my luggage and opened it to insert a book, I discovered that my two bags had been carefully searched while I was eating. It was fortunate, therefore, that I had the pathological slides in my purse; otherwise, this might have meant trouble for my Czech colleagues. I need not have bothered; when I reached MIT, delicate tests showed no radioactivity—our Czech hosts were amiable but were taking no chances.

Permanent Commission Meetings (1946-1966)

An international organization concerned with industrial disease was begun in 1911 by a group of Italian chemists. It is to be remembered that the Father of Industrial Medicine was Bernardino Ramazzini of Milan who in the eighteenth century wrote a long treatise on occupational medicine, *De Morbis Artificum*,[9] in which he included discussion of such hazardous jobs as, for example, grave digging, nursing, and barbering and laid a broad base for this field, neglected in these modern times of medical specialization. His single predecessor had been Hippocrates, who advised adding an additional question to the usual medical history taking, namely, "What is your job?" Thus it is not surprising that Ramazzini's countrymen founded the new-named Permanent Commission and International Association on Occupational Health. Meetings are held every three years (except for war years). At each meeting a host country is sought in a different part of the world. Between the large international meetings, small subcommittees meet from time to time if need be. I chose to be a member of the Committee on Carbon Monoxide Poisoning. The chairman was my old friend, the late Dr. Grüt of Denmark.

The first meeting I attended was that held in 1954 in Naples, where I read a paper on the then-new treatment for lead poisoning, chelation. I was asked to be moderator of the afternoon session during which time 14 short papers were to be read. Since all the papers were in languages foreign to me, I had an interpreter at my side. This proved to be a blessing, since not one of the authors listed on the program appeared. I learned later that for a delegate to have his expenses paid, his government required that a paper be submitted with the individual's name and the title of the paper printed on the program; but there was no requirement that the individual show up to present his paper! As I was preparing to close the meeting, an excited Portugese appeared and demanded to read his paper. I turned for help to my interpreter, who said, "From what he is saying, I advise you to let him speak." This I did, not even learning what the Portugese had said to the interpreter or what was in his paper. Next a ferocious-looking German pounded on my podium with a demand very like that of the Portugese. Again the interpreter advised permission to speak, and once more an almost untranslatable flow of angry words followed. I understand enough German to know only that his speech had nothing to do with the subject listed on the program. I was able to get back to my hotel finally about 7 P.M. and into the hubbub of a cocktail party. I made two visits to Milan, one at the time of this meeting and one in 1964. Milan is a great and old city, surrounded and influenced by industrial development. The Clinica del Lavoro in Milan is supported by funds from industry and devoted to diseases of workers. Dr. Enrico Vigliani, whom I had met in Luxembourg in 1950, is the chief of a large and busy staff having both clinical and research interests, including a team that can answer questions by going to a factory and making an inquiry. Dr. Vigliani showed me (1964) a few cases of mercury poisoning from the felt hat industry, cases of leukemia after benzene exposure, and a series of cases of carbon disulfide effect on the nervous system from rayon manufacture. I persuaded him to prepare a paper describing his cases of benzol poisoning followed by fatal leukemia. When I reached Boston, I persuaded Dr. Joseph Garland, editor of the *New England Journal of Medicine*, to publish the article, because I had seen a number of cases in Boston of leukemia associated with benzol exposure and felt this report was important for U.S. knowledge.[10] U.S. texts have rarely mentioned benzol as a single cause of leukemia or as one acting with other bone marrow-depressing agents as, for example, ionizing radiation. Field study, in my opinion, is of critical importance and not used enough or properly in the United States today. Studies of death certificates by computer have produced many statistics, but since death certificates are very often in error, U.S. literature in this field is becoming muddled.

I attended another meeting of the Permanent Commission in New York City in 1960. There were problems for the Commission at this session, especially of financial support. A scheme was evolved and discussed whereby industrial firms and various government agencies might belong after paying monetary contributions much higher than individual dues of $35. Ambitious plans were made for funds thus raised to be used by the commission.

In 1963 at the Permanent Commission meeting in Madrid, Spain, I reported on the MGH studies of U.S. southeastern coal workers.[11] The paper was well received by most and stimulated questions from others working with similar populations in other parts of the world. I believe that a paper is a successful contribution if it leads to questions, especially in a large audience where language barriers are present in spite of excellent interpreters.

The 1966 meeting of the Permanent Commission was held in the atmosphere of culture and national beauty provided by Vienna. This was a large session, many subjects being discussed at the same time in different lecture rooms of the University of Vienna. Samuel Levin, senior radiation protection officer of our Massachusetts Institute of Technology Occupational Medical Service, read a paper describing our MIT procedures, emphasizing the value of the team approach.[12] I read a paper on the beryllium registry, which we had updated for the purpose. In doing so, I and my associate Emily Rabe gleaned as much well-documented material as might suitably be presented in tables. Such data as years of illness, duration of exposure, and effect of engineering controls were recorded and shown in slide form. Several English colleagues asked if I would lunch with them and discuss our techniques in case finding, recording, and follow-up for help in deciding whether to set up registries of various industrial diseases. As far as I know, nothing came of the meeting, but we had good talk, excellent food, and a wonderful wine, the day happening to be my birthday.

On the same trip I traveled from Vienna to Prague to attend a short two-day meeting called by the commission's subcommittee on the problem of setting safe working levels for carbon disulfide, a chemical used widely in the rubber-manufacturing and viscose rayon industries. Dr. Hamilton had written in *Exploring the Dangerous Trades*[13] of reports of worker illness appearing in European literature as long ago as the early eighteenth century. She subsequently drew attention to cases in the United States in the 1930s, a sequence she repeated in several occupational diseases. The Prague meeting was an interesting mix of descriptions of clinical illness and results of basic research. Carbon disulfide attacks and inactivates certain essential enzyme systems with differing bodywide symptoms, mimicking other syndromes such as stroke, depression, or suicidal impulses. At this meeting my poor French was a handicap. Still, having seen Dr. Vigliani's inability to persuade physicians of the true nature of carbon disulfide poisoning, my trip was worthwhile because this is a widely used chemical.

The last meeting of the commission I attended was held at Brighton, England, in 1975. I was not feeling well and did not attend many meetings. I spent much of my time talking with friends from other countries, so learning a good deal about current work on industrial hazards. The formal sessions I did join were concerned with the asbestos hazard. Visiting England in 1979 I learned from Dr. Muriel Newhouse, a well-known authority on asbestos-related damage, that members of a community in Turkey suffered chest pain and lung damage owing to mining asbestos. This syndrome followed inhalation of certain forms of asbestos fibers. So widespread was the chest pain that the town was known by the Turkish words for "pain in the chest." A completely surprising report came from Israel describing disease similar to that suffered by asbestos workers. The surprise rests on the fact that no source of asbestos exposure could be found. This report caused much dispute and is not accepted as of 1980. Identification of various asbestos fibers is a difficult task.

There was some sadness for me as older members, friends of mine, had died or were too disabled to attend. I was affected by the death of Dr. Aage Grüt of Copenhagen, chairman of the Subcommittee on Carbon Monoxide Poisoning. At the 1975 meeting, Dr. Grüt's last, a most important observation made in the United States by study of a single case — followed by confirmation in small animal experiments — was reported. A patient with coronary artery disease had a hobby of refinishing furniture in his cellar, using the common solvent carbon tetrachloride to remove old paint and varnish. He died after a third acute attack. Important is the fact that his doctors advised him to continue his hobby during convalescence between attacks. Briefly, it was found that the liver, the organ attacked by carbon tetrachloride, converted that chemical to carbon monoxide, which takes the place of oxygen without which the heart cannot function, hence precipitating the patient's death. Attention to carbon monoxide effect varies throughout the world. Dr. Grüt wrote a classic monograph on the subject of chronic carbon monoxide poisoning (1943), a concept originally rejected by most.[14] During World War II wood was used for fuel in automobiles, which led to chronic exposure. I agreed with Grüt's concept and in later years at MGH had cared for two cases of chronic carbon monoxide exposure in work on and in cars with faulty exhaust systems. Both patients suffered irreversible brain and nerve damage. I believe that there are a number of such end results of chronic carbon monoxide exposure not identified.

The Brighton meeting of 1975 showed that the commission in the 20 years I had been a member had become a large, lively body with a real future of leadership in sponsoring new knowledge.

International Labour Organisation and World Health Organization

Dr. Luigi Parmeggiani, the medical officer in charge of Health and Safety of the International Labour Organisation (ILO), had been my guest in Boston in 1954. We had corresponded on matters of mutual interest, and I enjoyed learning the wide range of his problems, for example, trying to put an end to the employment of young children making handwoven Persian carpets. The reports showed that when the eyes of these child workers became so strained that they could no longer do fine needlework, they were put on the streets to beg.

A different but delicate job of statesmanship was done by Luigi in weaving together workers' problems that "belonged" to the World Health Organization (WHO) with those problems traditionally managed by the ILO, the older organization formed during the life of the League of Nations after World War I. It is sad to report that the U.S. Congress, pushed by the American Medical Association, temporarily withdrew its funds given in support of the ILO. I have recently learned, however, that labor groups are helping the ILO and that the U.S. government is again supporting it.

My work at the WHO, housed in the Palais de Nations in Geneva, once the headquarters of the League of Nations, was novel and taught me how large international bodies accomplish their work. A permanent staff member in the Radiation Health Unit, Dr. Lowry Dobson from California, a friend of mine from previous jobs, asked me to come to Geneva for one month as his expert adviser. I was to develop papers for use by a committee that would be in session for only one week. The title of the meeting was "Radiation Risk in Perspective"; its membership was to be widely representative.[15] This invitation came in 1961 while I was still in London, and although I should have returned to Boston commitments, I found the idea irresistible.

This ad hoc committee was formed to teach the officials of developing countries how best to use funds allotted to them. Lacking experience, some countries were using all their funds to control possible hazards from a nearly harmless isotope, carbon[14]. By so doing, much greater dangers from lack of sanitary engineering — for example, from badly contaminated water in India — were neglected.

During my month at the WHO I worked out definitions of terms for committee use, for example, *acceptable risk* and *acceptable calculated risk* for an investigator who knows the risk. Risk to a population must be weighed against the benefit. I used other terms to define such critical words as *harm, damage, risk, normal, safe margin*, and *recovery* to help committee members decide what would be useful in a final document for worldwide distribution. Many more subjects were covered, such as evidence at hand of radiation damage and relationship to other organizations working in the same field — in sum, radiation risk in perspective. This work was a rare treat and taught me much. The members of the committee had to be chosen with care to cover a subject completely, but choice also had to include representatives from various countries. For example, the genetic expert was from Holland; one toxicologist was from Italy and one was from Sweden; the chairman, the late Lord Adrian, was from England; a public health official with previous experience as a WHO adviser was from India; and an American represented the United Nations. The meeting proved to be a lively, stimulating week and left us friends, with much to think about and the certainty that considerable knowledge was missing. Later, a WHO pamphlet on radiation risk in perspective was published and well received in 1962.[15]

Travel in Africa

With the good offices of the late Dr. R.R. Sayers of the U.S. Bureau of Mines and Dr. A.J. Orenstein and Dr. Margaret Becklake in Johannesberg, I used some of my travel grant to go to parts of Africa in 1957; South Africa and the countries known then as Northern Rhodesia and French Equatorial Africa; to the cities of Brazzaville (French) and Leopoldville in the Congo (Belgian) to visit en route Dr. Albert Schweitzer in Lambarene; and finally to Dakar in Senegal.

    Because of the Israeli-Egyptian crisis at Suez and the fighting in Hungary, I was forced to spend two weeks on a large passenger vessel, the Winchester Castle, leaving Southampton, England. This voyage gave me an opportunity for reflection on all I had seen and heard as well as for some badly needed rest and sleep. The arrangements for dining, relaxing in deck chairs, playing games, reading, and drinking tea served by uniformed attendants gave a lovely nineteenth century glow that made one feel like a character from a Kipling novel.

    At the beginning, the crossing of the Bay of Biscay made the ship groan and creak with a sickening sideways motion. On the second day the ship's doctor, a dermatologist, asked me to see a patient with him. This man was a member of the House of Lords; he had diabetes and severe bronchitis and was confined to a wheelchair. He came aboard with a nursing sister, a butler, and his friend Lord H. – and also without the usual health certificate. With my faithful stethoscope, I joined my colleague to see a fatally ill man, very obese, his shortness of breath frightening, little helped by an oxygen mask and made worse by every plunge of the ship. Soon he died. His London family wanted him embalmed and the body returned to England. The ship's surgeon said that he understood that all American doctors knew how to embalm, but he was relieved when I refused to undertake this. They told me that the late Lord E.'s family had ordered the removal from the freezers of all the food stored for a month's voyage in order to be able to carry the body back to London. Heading for the tropics, the ship's captain took command and refused to listen to threats of lawsuits by the family. My Lord E. was quietly buried at sea very early one morning.

What did I learn on my visit to Africa? In Johannesberg I was welcomed by U.S.-born Dr. A. J. Orenstein, who had worked during the building of the Panama Canal and later as medical director of the great Rand Mining Company in South Africa. He briefed me on history, old and new, and showed me the dormitory compounds with armed guards and wire fences where black workers were housed while being trained for muscular work and where they were taught a little pidgin English so they might obey orders in the mine. Their food and Kaffir beer were prepared and doled out by the company in a fashion intended to make the natives fit for hard labor. When a black arrived from his home, he was usually not in good physical condition, because of poor nutrition, the heat, and local customs of living an inactive life. The black African who lived in great, shockingly crowded apartheid communities, as far as 30 miles outside the city where he worked, was quite different, often educated by missionaries and in racially mixed universities supported by charitable funds.

The natives who were being trained for work were cared for in a separate hospital. Each was examined and had a chest x-ray taken before he began work. The white miners' union, which was very strong, demanded this, even if the employers did not, as self-protection against tuberculosis exposure to the blacks.

I spent considerable time at the Silicosis Research Bureau where Dr. Webster, the chief, and Dr. Christopher Wagner, a pathologist, talked with me and showed me old and new examples of dust disease. It took me a while to realize I was being shown only the lungs of white miners. It takes 21 years of mine exposure to show silicosis in whites but only 7 years of mine dust exposure for the black.

Gold ore from South African mines contains an extremely high percentage of silica; this was of much interest to me because early studies had shown a different postmortem picture from more recent ones. No one knows why. Perhaps the use of ores with differing metal and silica content and modern machinery creating particles of different size and shape are responsible. Dr. Wagner showed me the unusual disease picture produced by asbestos (Cape Blue, crocidilite), both an acute pneumonialike reaction and after repeated exposure a chronic reaction leading to malignancy called mesothelioma. Now 30 years after the end of World War II, shipyard workers, among others, are found to suffer this lethal form of cancer.

I made one trip underground into a uranium mine, dressed in coveralls and a helmet and with an identification tag around my neck. After drinking strong tea, we went in a cagelike device, the bottom cage containing black miners to break our fall in case of accident! The shaft was a mile deep, the elevator without light, and I wondered why I had come. We tramped slowly about in humid air, viewing filtering and spraying devices to suppress and catch the respirable dust. We were shown a tank full of potassium permanganate, a chemical used to remove the carbon monoxide from the mine air. At last we reached the face of the rock where the drilling takes place. Here I discovered why the white man working in mines took 21 years of exposure to develop evidence of silicosis. He sat in a chair for 50 minutes of each hour, showed the natives where to place the drill, then returned to his seat after 5 minutes of effort; the black worker was exposed 50 minutes in an hour with 5 minutes rest.

I attended a Johannesberg medical meeting where white workers' records and chest x-rays were handled separately from the black. When the time came to show chest x-rays of blacks, the chairman spoke to me, "Dr. Hardy, you will want to leave the room now — we are going to show black x-rays." After catching my breath, I asked permission to remain. The x-rays shown contained extremely serious disease, large hearts, tuberculosis, or silicosis — all abnormal changes greater than I had ever seen elsewhere.

I was well treated by South African physicians Drs. Margot and Maurice McGregor and their two children. I learned much from them of the worry of liberal-minded people of South Africa. Margot, a specialist in chest disease doing first-class work on lung function, taught me about her findings of abnormalities in lung function due to blasting fumes, an observation I used in our Boston studies. Maurice is a cardiologist. They left Johannesberg in great sadness, each leaving a parent behind, and now hold academic posts in Canada at McGill University Medical School. Maurice expressed their final decision in these words, "I will not bring up my children in a land where one side has all the guns."

I was not sorry to leave the hostile, complex atmosphere of Johannesberg, although I had been well treated and I had learned a great deal. An easy air trip brought me to N'Dola in Northern Rhodesia. A black driver who paged me at the airport drove me in dark and rain through the jungle on a road like a cowpath. We did not speak until he asked me where I wanted to go! I had expected Dr. John Paul, a white, to meet me, and for a second I wondered about foolhardy behavior on my part. I said, however, "Dr. Paul's house, please," and soon I was settled with Dr. and Mrs. Paul and a glass of sherry.

Northern Rhodesia forms part of the copper belt, and Dr. Paul was in charge of the medical problems of the copper miners. I stayed for two days and saw endless chest x-rays of the familiar chest disease, silicosis with and without tuberculosis. A new observation, apparently common among black miners, is that they do not "cough and spit," a problem so troublesome to U.S. and British miners. Does this mean that there is a difference in the dust of metal ore and in mining practice? I think not. Is there a difference in air pollution, climate, or infection? Stethoscopic examination did not reveal bronchitis in these miners. Perhaps it is now known, 20 years later, why South African silicosis has changed over the years and why copper miners do not "cough and spit."

In 1957 there was much uneasiness in the Belgian Congo (Zaire since 1960). Shepherded by public relations men from the Sabena Air Company and the Unions Minères du Haut Katanga, I visited Elizabethville and Leopoldville, even though the Unions Minères had tried hard to keep me away. I believe they knew the Belgians were leaving, and they had great plans to continue their contracts under some of the black African leaders. Thus they did not want a critical report from me on health matters. The physicians who cared for the mine workers showed me many chest x-rays with a wide variety of abnormalities. Some of the changes, I was told, were present in preemployment films. I was expected to believe that such changes were due to the smoke arising from fires placed inside the small native huts in which blacks lived. Recent observers visiting nonmining areas, upon finding abnormal chest x-rays, believe this may be true. No studies except chest x-rays were done. If the x-ray changes were serious either before or during work, the man was discharged with some money and told to return to his village, thus bringing to a halt any chance of establishing the true diagnosis and perhaps carrying active tuberculosis to his village.

The Belgians, like the Rhodesians, arranged for the worker to bring his family to live with him near the mine. In South Africa, however, only the man was brought to the workplace.

A Week at Dr. Albert Schweitzer's Hospital

The trip across the Congo from Leopoldville to Brazzaville was fascinating. The water lilies, the strong current, the nonchalance of our black helmsmen, the talkative, brightly dressed native women with babies slung on their backs and goods stacked on their heads, my dignified porter at the Relais Hotel in Brazzaville, crews of many airlines, tired passengers, the arrogant but attractive Shell Oil Company couple calling me a "nice American," and finally a dogged tourist couple from Kansas City—all these made March 19, 1957, a full day.

March 20 was a hard day with an early start at 6:30 A.M., followed by a rough air trip. We arrived at Lambarene to be met by Homer Jack, a Unitarian minister from Chicago, who looked like a nineteenth century colonist in a sun helmet with a huge umbrella. We awaited our luggage in an ancient bus with a narrow seat, then rumbled to the river where we were poled and paddled upstream by four cheerful men, with Homer Jack pointing out Protestant and Catholic missions and the leper colony along the river bank.

I have mixed feelings about my visit to Dr. Albert Schweitzer (1957). My visit lasted five days during which I slept, ate, and worked as a member of the regular staff of Europeans—at that time there were about 25 with 4 doctors, 6 nurses, and the rest women of dedication who did household and administrative duties. Dr. Schweitzer ate at the table with us, but Mrs. Schweitzer, obviously very fragile, joined us briefly only for the noon meal. We each lived in a relatively narrow, screened-in, small bedroom, 6 by 12 feet, these rooms in rows of eight or ten, for the Europeans. There was a set protocol about every phase of our life, which was closely adhered to and guarded by two older female nurses who had been staff members and who sat one on either side of Dr. Schweitzer at the table. They looked sad, with yellow parchment skins, fragile in appearance, and always hurried and harrassed by detail.

Dr. Schweitzer was a tall, impressive man. He appeared well and, being a food faddist, ate enormously of various things the rest of us were not served. He often looked weary but became rested by the act of eating. He seldom spoke, being lost in faraway thoughts, but, occasionally, enthusiastically told stories in lively German of his travels and his acquaintance with Einstein or some other famous persons. In the jungle, dark came completely and suddenly about 6 P.M. By kerosene lamp after supper Dr. Schweitzer would announce a hymn from an old German hymnal. He played on the poor tropics-ruined piano as though he were touching a great cathedral organ, then would read two short bits from the Bible and repeat the Lord's Prayer in a French that I gradually grasped. Without a word he would leave the room. The rest of us, especially the physicians, would talk together for an hour or two into the night.

Except for simple social greetings, I had only one talk with Dr. Schweitzer — and because of my poor French and German and his unwillingness to talk in English, this was through an interpreter. We talked about atomic energy development, and it was not a satisfactory talk, although I caught a bit of his personal charm, which has rightly drawn to him so many people of all types and backgrounds. I was urged by a visiting American clergyman to tell Dr. Schweitzer of the peaceful uses of atomic energy, so through the interpreter I did what I could. Dr. Schweitzer's response was, "What harm has been done to the algae in the Columbia River which flows past the great Hanford Plant for atomic energy development?" With a sigh he continued, "I was in Paris in 1870 and saw the destruction. That must not happen again." The two world wars of the twentieth century were not even a memory to Dr. Schweitzer.

The concept of "reverence for life" is known throughout the world. At Lambarene it took a variety of forms, a few of which were inconsistent. Flowers could not be cut, and animals and their dung were everywhere; yet I was told (I do not know how reliably) that cats were drowned since Dr. Schweitzer did not like them. One morning as I left my cubicle to go to the clinic, the head nurse waved me to join her by Dr. Schweitzer's cabin. She showed me a column of army ants marching to the jungle from the cabin. She told me Dr.

Schweitzer had had a poor night's rest while the ants moved through his bed a number of times, and each time he got out of bed so as not to injure them. I suggested, perhaps in fun, that she should get a Flit gun. She did not disappoint me as she said, "For shame, 'reverence for life.'"

In the daytime, hustle and bustle prevailed, and everywhere animals of all kinds — gorillas, goats, antelopes, dogs, and hens — created endless trouble and mess but were very much a part of life. One nurse kept three young antelopes in her room at night; another had a four-month old gorilla plus an African baby who had been sick. Several nights the noises were quite wild. Dr. Schweitzer's plan was that sick people would come to Lambarene, brought by their families who would care for them and live at the African village located below the Europeans' living quarters while the patient received surgery or medicine. Dr. Schweitzer had natives on his payroll who cleaned the Europeans' rooms, did laundry, sewed, did carpentry, served food, and helped the nurses. All were paid with food that Dr. Schweitzer got for them, mostly bananas and rice, and a bit of money. The food for the Europeans was excellent and plentiful — native fruits and vegetables carefully cleaned, imported cheese, butter, and some meat. Dr. Schweitzer had built a new leper village about a quarter of a mile away with the money from the Nobel Peace Prize. I felt this was the most hopeful spot in the place.

My reactions: How can anyone judge or criticize such a legend or the man himself, an intellectual giant? However, I must also say that I personally could not set aside my professional and social standards, and so I must report that I came away dazed. The closer I got to Lambarene, the more people became scornful and condescending about Dr. Schweitzer's work and critical about the publicity, U.S. enthusiasm for him, and his endless visitors. I recorded my observations in 1957 after my trip, among them these. The medical work was shockingly bad, the worst kind of continental treatment of symptoms without diagnosis by endless drugs whose exact ingredients were unknown. Antibiotics were used so freely that there were then many drug-resistant organisms among the people. One valuable rule that Dr. Schweitzer enforced was that there must be an autopsy after each death. I carried tissue from a rare form of lethal heart disease to the Pasteur Institute in Leopoldville for study.

The daily clinic I attended was visited by a pathetic stream of adults and children suffering from tuberculosis, liver disease from malnutrition, kwashiorkor, elephantiasis, filiariasis, and other tropical diseases, until then only textbook diagnoses to me.

There were no hospital beds. Patients were taken from the operating room to the shockingly overcrowded dormitories of the village known as *casa*. No nursing care was given except a little that was initiated by one good Swiss nurse in the leper village, which was well run with modern treatment. There were all varieties of leprosy known to me both from textbooks and from having cared for a single case in New York City.

There was no use of knowledge to prevent the spread of enteric disease (dysenteries) in the African village. The Europeans used a privy open to animals and flies. I was told that Dr. Schweitzer had been offered money for a closed chemical privy several times but had refused it.

There deliberately was no education at Lambarene, as far as I could learn. The blacks could neither read nor write and had little knowledge of French, so communication was difficult. A few worked with the doctors and had become good at a single task, but they had not been taught any ideas or measures of prevention of disease. Surveys showed that most had venereal disease. I could not digest this part of Dr. Schweitzer's program. Why go to Africa to help the native and not give him weapons to help himself? Dr. Schweitzer instructed his staff not to trust the Africans, saying they were inferior and lazy. There was a rumor during my visit that Dr. Schweitzer had written to President Dwight D. Eisenhower, asking him to help the French cause against the Arabs in North Africa. How does one square these things with Dr. Schweitzer's writings and with what his interpreters, perhaps romantically, alleged that he said?

What do I think of Dr. Schweitzer, an intellectual giant, physically unbelievably strong, an individualist with a will of iron? His great contributions are his music, his books on theology and moral philosophy, the act of going to Africa to love the natives and atone for his and the sins of European society — surely this was enough for one man, and it overshadowed his arrogance and autocratic behavior, including the penury, the goat dung, the vanity, the love of "great visitors," and omniscience on all subjects. However, the mistrust of and failure to educate the natives, an important background for the great man, were hard to take. I do not understand his words and deeds being so separated.

As I review this material today, I find there is little left at Lambarene of his work. A variety of interpretations come to mind.

A widespread and probably nearly correct one is that Dr. Schweitzer was a nineteenth century continental who believed in nineteenth century colonialism and practiced nineteenth century medicine. His medical staff were not happy — at least the competent ones — and they would leave when they had finished their agreed-upon terms. However, Dr. Schweitzer, it appeared, had sharp clinical acumen and also in general left them alone in their work.

Dr. Schweitzer was at that time 83 years old, and his 44 years in the tropics must be considered. He had had to work hard to get buildings built and food for all, especially during the two wars, and this could account for the fantastic hoarding and miserliness on which he insisted.

Ideally, there should be no more Schweitzer publicity and no more Lambarene visits. Let this legend of self-initiated service to Africa act as a spur to moral conscience wherever there are privilege, ease, and domination, and let his great intellectual and musical achievements stand, as they well can, documented in his writings.

I then flew to Dakar in Senegal to await my plane to Lima, Peru, my last stop. I spent a day in Dakar with a working party of WHO nutrition experts and health educators whose job was to teach the local fish farmers how to handle and cook the plentiful fish they caught with ancient boats and torn nets. We drove to a beach where a great haul was being landed on a sunny and very hot day. The fish were laid on the beach and at once were covered with insects, and the air filled with the smell of rotting fish. French authorities and industry had provided refrigerator trucks, and the chore was to persuade the fishermen to use the proper techniques for preserving the fish for travel and sale. It was easy to see that the WHO had a problem working with an uneducated Muslim population and their taboos and lack of fear of disease.

Peru: High-Altitude Dust Disease

The trip to Peru by air is considered one of the most dangerous in the world.* The plane must remain at a height of at least 20,000 feet for nearly 22 hours at a stretch to go over the Andes. We flew

---

*I heard my host say this during one of those odd silences at a dinner party given in my honor at the storybook Rand Club in Johannesberg.

in a DC-8, and when the pilot was bored, he flew in a circle inside the rim of a dead volcano, a thrill I would have chosen to miss.

There were several reasons for the Peru visits. Under the leadership of J. J. Bloomfield, an engineer long in the U.S. Public Health Service, a team of doctors, chemists, engineers, and research fellows was formed to study dust disease in workers at high altitudes.

My time was well spent. I compared chest x-rays with work histories. I taught several sessions. I visited Dr. Hurtado, a graduate of Harvard Medical School, then dean of the medical school in Lima; he was a research physiologist with a high-altitude laboratory for special studies. I learned from Dr. Hurtado two fascinating facts. First, because of altitude the lung cannot expand, so there can be no emphysema. And second, presuming this important fact to have been proved at autopsy, I asked for a bit of tissue to take to Boston for study; Dr. Hurtado replied calmly, "I have never seen the lung of high-altitude metal miners as we do no autopsies in Peru." For once I was silent.

My Peruvian host took me in his official car to a metal-mining village 14,000 feet above Lima. We saw miners being examined (I worked, too) and saw chest x-rays with large heart shadows and mottling in the air spaces. These changes were all due to altitude and vanished when the worker returned to sea level for a few days. The life histories of these metal miners were grim indeed. They came at age 14 from hillside farms, already infected with hydatid disease due to the parasites in their animals (chiefly the llama) whose dung was used for farming. At the mine they inhaled metal and silica and — because of its prevalence — might acquire tuberculosis. By age 40 the shortness of breath prevented hard work. Lawyers who knew the story came to the camps with a truck; they coached the ailing miners as to how to describe their symptoms and drove them to a court, while promising great money awards. The miner, quite ignorant, was turned out of his job and, sick as he might be, received about $100 (in 1957) and returned to his farm for the rest of his short life.

These metal mines were chiefly U.S.-owned and run, but the politics of workers' compensation were in the hands of Peruvians, many of them university faculty. A U.S. hygiene engineer tried to double the disabled workers' final compensation. He was in serious trouble as local owners and bosses wanted the profit to come to them.

Weary as well as stimulated by all I had seen and heard, I was glad to reach Boston in springtime.

What had I learned during this period of visiting other centers of occupational disease study abroad? Much of this period was just after World War II, and I learned almost as much about social and political change as I did about industrial medicine. This experience, however, taught me what literature to follow and where to get information that might lead to cosponsorship of a project for ideas I had. The wide variety of medical and pathological material I saw in 1956/57 helped me to interpret our Boston findings as well as to know what was lacking and how to judge the work of others. Further, I learned that our MGH-MIT team did not suffer the restraints that many colleagues abroad had to accept.

The Colombian Teaching Experience

I taught one week in Bogotá, Colombia, South America, in 1959 as guest of the government, with initiative and technical help from the United States supported through our programs variously named Point Four and International Cooperative Administration. Professor Theodore Hatch, an engineer with long industrial hygiene experience in academic institutions, Dr. Donald Birmingham, chief dermatologist of the Public Health Service, and I were invited by the Colombian government through Jack Bloomfield of the U.S. Public Health Service to be the guest lecturers at the first seminar in occupational health in Colombia. We met about 120 Colombian physicans, engineers, and politicians in a comfortable classroom of the Faculty of Chemical Engineering of the University City, a Colombian government establishment. The Phillips Company of the Netherlands supplied equipment for simultaneous translation, which was extremely good.

The introductory speeches of the U.S. authorities seemed unnecessarily boastful; the Colombian, flowery and without substance; but I guess this was to be expected. South American physicians told me that the U.S. talks were not offensive, so I suppose this means I was self-conscious about our countrymen. U.S. policy is to keep administrative and technical staff moving from one country to another — two years minimum, eight years maximum in one place — so that the U.S. staff does not get involved in local problems. There was some grumbling because of language difficulties, but it was generally agreed that mixing professionals from different countries is wise.

As is the case in most Latin American countries, industrialization brought on by war and U.S. desire for metals and cheap labor has disrupted the feudal way of life that was accepted until recently. As one Colombian physician put it, "We have been sleeping in a hammock for 400 years." Now there are revolutions and meaningless laws that cannot be enforced. All national money was in the hands of one bank in Colombia. By 1959 the government was completely bankrupt. Bank interest was 11 percent — the situation was so poor that U.S. friends had been advised not even to have a checking account in Colombia. U.S. contracts that were expiring were not renewed. Rockefeller support was ending, partly by earlier arrangement, allowing Colombians to take over public health positions. The same was true of jobs in public health and industrial health that we had developed with Point Four (now International Cooperative Administration) support.

There was a certain unreality to the prearranged program because of the discrepancy between what we suggested and what the countries involved would be able to accomplish. We were taken to several factories, two of them less than one year old — clean and beautiful but full of potential hazards. One factory was a chemical plant that used a German process identical with that used in an old plant I saw outside Prague. The hazards of mercury, hydrochloric acid, chlorine, carbon disulfide, and sulfuric acid are very real. We were told about (but did not see) coal and sulfur mines where children aged 8 to 12 years were employed, of a mercury mine causing severe poisoning, of lead exposure causing abortion and sterility. An oil company physician told us that one of his chief problems was attending to wounds inflicted on workmen by the arrows of primitive, untamed Indians. The company has tried to woo these Indians without success. As far as can be learned, they are very low in native intelligence. Several of their children have been purposely captured, carefully reared, and educated but with little success.

We had a command visit with the Colombian minister of health to receive his personal thanks. He asked our advice on a pressing problem — a kind of fireworks in Colombia is made with yellow phosphorus and at that time was popular as an instrument of suicide. Adolescents disappointed in love swallowed the "firework" and would die painfully of liver failure! Such fireworks were cheap and widely bought, so the minister's problem was that in suppressing the sale he would be putting many people out of work. Jack Bloomfield suggested a high tax to force the manufacturers to find a substitute chemical, but the general shrug of the shoulders and sigh of the minister left one with the impression that not much would change.

I was impressed with the freedom of speech of the Colombians in telling us their problems and talking back to their politicians in the question period. For example, they asked me if excessive heat in industry caused tuberculosis. I said that I knew of no good studies to suggest that this was true. Then they turned to the physician-politician and asked how it was that the law said boilermakers should be given compensation for tuberculosis because of the heat when there was no scientific evidence — and was it possible that judges and politicians knew more of medicine than the physicians — with other comments in this vein.

Our lectures (mine, Ted Hatch's, and Birmingham's) went well. The audience was wonderfully attentive and asked endless questions. The translators were incredibly able at their job after having seen our manuscripts only once. The great compliment we received was, "I learned a great deal." The Colombians seemed hungry for information. One afternoon I worked with them for four hours showing x-rays.

One day we were taken to "Bavaria," a very old, well-run brewery. When we had seen all the operations in making the beer, we were given all the beer we could drink and entertained by dancers and musicians. Another day we were taken to ancient salt mines that have been worked from very early times — the actual date unknown. It is known that these mines were being worked by Indians when the Spaniards arrived in the late fifteenth century. The mines were still being worked but were gradually being abandoned since it is now cheaper to make salt from seawater. A big bank in Bogotá was paying to develop a cathedral undergound in several connecting caves. There was already a great wooden cross, a crèche, an altar — very impressive. We were told that 10,000 people could easily be housed in the "salt cathedral."

On our last night we were given a dinner and made members of the local industrial medical society. U.S. colleagues left it to me — without warning — to make the thank-you speech, which I muddled through in spite of wine and food. The food was pretty shocking — overcooked, tasteless, and often attacked by flies. Enteric disease is taken for granted in Colombia.

Foreign Visitors

In 1953 I left Cambridge where I had lived since my illness of 1939, always a countrywoman at heart. I was lucky to be able to buy an old house in Lincoln, Massachusetts, built in 1772, in an ancient apple orchard. It had once been a small dairy farm, was perfect for gardening, and was shielded by a century-old lilac hedge on one side and a rise of rock and tall trees on the other. I persuaded myself that I was too busy to keep house even if I had known how. So began a procession of housekeepers. There were many entertaining adventures associated with the comings and going of this panoply of humanity.

Established on two acres in a roomy house furnished with inherited familiar objects and equipped with a sound housekeeping department, I began entertaining. This is only novel because of the international character of the guests. Before I began my travels abroad, we received much pleasure and education as a result of the local custom of entertaining for a weekend foreign students attending one of the many nearby universities. We did this especially at Thanksgiving and Christmas. The use of the word *we* became real by 1958 when my only sister, Jane, and her seven-year-old son, with a dog as well, joined our household.

While we were having dinner one noon, the wife of a student excused herself, went into a nearby room, knelt down facing east, and said her Muslim prayers while her husband continued eating. Several medically trained women from India who visited us told of their frustrations in public health work, especially in trying to teach acceptable methods of contraception. Two families, the husbands studying in New England for two years, almost belonged to our household during their stay, so close to us they became.

The year 1960 was busy since the International Commission on Occupational Health met in New York City. Many of the colleagues I had met during my traveling in the 1950s came to this meeting and took time to see parts of the United States, of course including historic Boston. I was moderator at one session of the medical section, which gave me the chance to take the role I enjoy so much, that of challenger and advocate of opposing views; this time the subjects were beryllium toxicity as well as dust diseases of the chest. After the meeting a number of the delegates visited my home in Lincoln.

We showed them the historic spots in nearby Concord, enjoyed long hours of talk about professional proposals or our own work, or had happy, lazy days of talk of current events or of the natural beauty around us, while comparing differences between countries. Peru, South Africa, Sweden, England, Scotland and Wales were among other countries represented by these visitors of 1960.

In other years, several Czechs and two Yugoslavs, an Italian, a Finn, and a number of British physicians working in occupational health stayed with us for a meal, a day, or several days and nights. My young nephew, Will, aged 8 to 13 during this period, and his mother enjoyed these invasions and learned much of other opinions and other cultures. Will, knowing our house was built in 1772, took pleasure in saying to the British guests, "This house was here before we beat you!"

A visit never to be forgotten was a "command" visit one Sunday by five Russians with a UN interpreter guide. These visitors had been shepherded all over the United States for 30 days, visiting groups and individuals working in industrial disease and its control. Except for one doctor, the Russians were silent, and the interpreter did all the work of changing my questions into Russian and vice versa. We had lunch together, before which I tried to persuade the Russians to try a drink of bourbon whiskey. This was a real failure, so we nobly and sniffingly produced vodka. After lunch, a somewhat stiff ceremony, we settled down for more talk. The interpreter, obviously Russian born, took me aside to say that if this Russian group did not leave soon, he was going to be ill. At last I hurried their departure by asking which industrial disease Russia had most trouble controlling. The leader, the doctor, replied in broken English, "Russia has no industrial diseases." Having seen hazardous workplaces behind the Iron Curtain, I had to speak. I asked, "How do you know you have industrial diseases under control if you have none to study?" I had managed to make enough confusion to end the meeting.

REFERENCES

1. Hardy, H. L. The character and distribution of disease in American industries using beryllium compounds, Proc. R. Soc. Med., 44:257, 1951.

2. Hamilton, A., and Hardy, H. L., Industrial Toxicology, 3rd ed., Littleton, Mass., Publishing Sciences Group, 1974.
3. Evelyn, J., Fumifugium: Or the Inconvenience of the Aer and Smoake of London Dissipated, first published 1661, reprinted by the National Society for Clean Air, London, 1961, p. 17.
4. Hunter, D., The Diseases of Occupations, 6th ed., Boston, Little, Brown, 1978.
5. Hardy, H. L., and Skinner, J. B., The possibility of chronic cadmium poisoning, J. Ind. Hyg. and Toxicol., 29:321, 1947.
6. Tepper L. B., Hardy, H. L., and Chamberlin, R. I., Toxicity of Beryllium Compounds, A Monograph, Amsterdam, Elsevier, 1961.
7. Hamilton, A., and Hardy, H. L., Industrial Toxicology, 2nd ed., New York, Hoeber, 1949.
8. Hamilton, A., and Hardy, H. L., Industrial Toxicology, 3rd ed., Acton, Mass., Publishing Sciences Group, 1974.
9. Ramazzini, B., De Morbis Artificum, reprinted, Rome, Colombo Publishers, 1953.
10. Vigliani, E. C., and Saita, G., Benzene and leukemia, N. Engl. J. Med., 217:872, 1964.
11. Hardy, H. L., and Stoeckle, J. D., Disabling respiratory disease in U.S. soft-coal miners: value of intensive study of a small series of cases, Proc. XIV Int. Cong. Occup. Health, Madrid, 1963.
12. Hardy, H. L., Rabe, E. W., and Lorch, S., United States Beryllium Case Registry 1952-1966: review of its methods and utility, Proc. XV Int. Cong. Occup. Health, B III-4, 49-55, Vienna, 1966.
13. Hamilton, A., Exploring the Dangerous Trades, Boston, Little, Brown, 1943.
14. Grüt, A., Chronic Carbon Monoxide Poisoning, Copenhagen, Mundsgard, 1949.
15. World Health Organization, Radiation risk in perspective, Geneva, WHO, 1962.

CHAPTER 12

Teaching and Speaking

My younger sister was the first person to learn of my pleasure of speaking with the aim of teaching, persuading, and convincing. She patiently brought her chair to the small railed balcony outside our bedroom, while I stood pounding the rail to make a point. My speeches covered a wide range of topics brought from school or from our parents' talk on public affairs. Once, on a warm summer's evening when I paused for breath, our neighbors from their porch burst into applause, an event that curbed my enthusiasm for a time.

In 1934, when I began to practice medicine in Northfield, I was asked by the American Cancer Society to speak to people living in nearby villages. The questions I was often asked were: "Is cancer catching?" and "Should I burn Aunt Mary's clothes and bedding?" These questions seemed ridiculous at the time, but new knowledge of virus-induced cancer in animal experiments may shortly make the answers to such questions very different. I also attended a Lions Club luncheon and heard their friendly though noisy club roar. I was there to beg money for a clinic for poor children and hoped to persuade the Lions to help change this neglected problem.

My best and favorite teaching has always been to a single patient alone, with a setting like that of the famed Mark Hopkins on a log. My concept was and is that if the doctor (Webster's Dictionary says that *doctor* means "teacher") can explain simply the mechanism of the production of the patient's illness, therapy will be more effective. The wise physician does not dodge questions but, with understanding of the patient's education, temperament, and legitimate fears, gives some reasonable answers. In my experience, because it takes time and sympathy and may require "lies," too few practitioners are willing or able to use this kind of individual teaching for the support of his patient. A better word than *lies* to explain what I have in mind is the word *circumlocution*; for example, in a patient with a serious disease of the spinal cord that will be progressive, is it not possible in discussion to avoid the use of the word *progressive*?

During my years in student health work, I had to develop a different kind of teaching. For ages 12 to 18 at the Northfield School, the biology teacher and I put together a short course in anatomy. The students, after they knew us well enough, began to ask questions freely. At Radcliffe with students aged 17 to 22, greater sophistication was required. Using my title as head of the Department of Health Education, I asked for and received permission to test the students for their knowledge of human anatomy and function. Many colleges in these years gave a required term course entitled "Hygiene" and called by Wellesley students "organ recitals." Believing that Radcliffe students had adequate basic knowledge (not good judgment), I borrowed a Wellesley hygiene examination and gave a copy to Radcliffe students who had had no lectures. All passed with at least a C grade, and 85 percent had a grade of B or better, which confirmed my belief that the intelligent young woman of 1940 had learned at home, at school, at Red Cross courses, at summer camp, from reading but chiefly from each other enough of the "facts of life" sufficiently to rule out the need for lectures. I did two things to supplement the knowledge of the Radcliffe students. I used a movie and a few talks, with attendance not obligatory, on such subjects as venereal disease, which, I was informed, was totally unknown to this group. During the question period, as a result of discovering an odd mix of curiosity and slow maturation, I asked some students to come to my office for a long, private talk. The second step I took, after some consultation with experts and some reading, was to purchase for each dormitory a set of books on anatomy, sex, and the psychology of sex. Radcliffe paid for these books, and to judge by marked passages and the number of replacements required, this plan found a real reception among the students. In the senior year I taught each student how to obtain and judge medical care. These few steps were recorded in such a form that President Wilbur Jordan of Radcliffe included this in Harvard's postwar document, *General Education in a Free Society*.[1]

After I joined the Massachusetts Division of Occupational Hygiene (DOH) in September 1945 and had had a few months of field experience, Professor Phil Drinker of the Harvard School of Public Health asked me to lecture to his class of physicians and engineers on beryllium poisoning. Most of the teaching I did early in the 1950s was in schools of public health to engineers, military doctors, or older physicians disabled by illness or not interested in general practice. The picture has changed now because of greater interest in potential hazards of environmental insults. Unfortunately, in many cases attention to man-made disease rests on litigation and exaggerated media reports, and this is hardly the path to disciplined scientific inquiry.

As I gained knowledge of a variety of industrial operations, the critical data needed to make a correct diagnosis became clear to me. No medical school courses had covered this material. The data to which I refer may be summarized: a good occupational history including jobs and hobbies at all ages and quality, quantity, and duration of exposure. Also one needs to know the rate of exposure, that is, to discover if the exposure is a single short-peak exposure (acute) or a low-level, long-term one — such as 40 hours per week, 8 hours per shift for a lifetime. Currently government agencies are having difficult problems setting safe levels; these are confusing to all for a number of reasons. For example, how short is a short-(acute) term exposure? And to what other possible hazards is the worker exposed at home or at a second job? May there be errors in the worker's defense mechanism, either inborn or acquired, making him or her more vulnerable to a dose harmless to his fellow workers? As myriads of new and man-made materials are introduced, are the results of small animal experiments reliable as judges of toxicity in humans? Experience has shown failure of the investigator and those who interpret results in both over- and underestimating results. New techniques for assessing toxicity must be found, and legislation must be more flexible as our aggressive, greedy society plunges onward.

The study of all these questions, plus critical knowledge of the literature, plus experience in the clinic, hospital, atomic energy laboratories, and the DOH made up my assets for teaching. Once started, I would handle the format as asked for either a single lecture, a series, or a seminar for a wide range of students. Groups to whom I lectured included medical students (Harvard School of Public Health, Harvard Medical School, Massachusetts General Hospital, Tufts University School of Medicine, Boston University School of Medicine, Veterans Administration hospitals, and University of Massachusetts Medical School), nurses, lawyers, medical examiners, and MIT students (in metallurgy, chemistry, physics, civil, chemical, mechanical, and electrical engineering, nuclear reactor staff, and nutritionists). Occasionally, an industrial company would ask me to lecture to their senior staff, especially when beryllium was to be used in a process.

Thinking back, I suspect that some of my pleasure and success in teaching and speaking was a well-exercised genetic gift from my lawyer father and grandfather, from their skills in court or on the political platform. My mother was not as pleased with my easy flow of words while I lived at home. Her remark was, "Harriet, will you stop! You do go on and on like a babbling brook!"

Launched by the 1946 beryllium paper,[2] I received a number of invitations to speak in different parts of the country, at institutions or before organizations such as the College of Chest Physicians, Women's Medical College in Philadelphia, University of Utah, American Tuberculosis Association, Massachusetts Medical Society, and University of Colorado. I found this life exciting, exacting, and fatiguing. Moving about the country, I learned items great and small of value in my work.

I was honored by the request that I give the first lecture of a Harvard series financed by friends in honor of Dr. Alice Hamilton. I entitled this lecture "Beryllium Poisoning: Lessons in the Control of Man-Made Disease."[3] Some senior faculty who attended thought my words too critical of big insurance and big industry, but thinking of lessons that Dr. Alice and Dr. Aub taught me, I consider my words true and temperate. It is satisfying to report that this paper is now used for teaching.

An additional honor came from my local medical society to be orator at the annual Massachusetts Medical Society meeting in 1975. As orator I named my talk "Risk and Responsibility."[4] In it I traced briefly the history of industrial medicine as reflected in the writing of poets, novelists, and men of public affairs, rather than in physicians' articles. In strong words (judged by letters and comments to me) I argued that most doctors as a result of narrow education both in premedical and medical college years lacked knowledge of history, great writing, and philosophy. And as the number of specialty boards increases certain areas of medical knowledge of the physician, perhaps his interest in wider areas of his life becomes narrow. If judged by the number of requests from abroad, as well as from the United States, for reprints, once the article was printed in the *New England Journal of Medicine*, its contents struck a congenial note to many.

Princeton University was the site of two of my most interesting assignments. The first, in 1962, was a session arranged by the American Tuberculosis Association to help teach newspaper reporters terminology and content of medical writing. We worked steadily for two days and evenings, answering and asking questions after brief formal presentations of each participant's special medical field. For instance, I described in outline, as previously arranged, my knowledge of occupational respiratory disease. These sessions were lively and produced real mutual education.[5] The second meeting, an unusual few days at Princeton in 1966, was engaged in attack on the subject for the future of physicians in industry. The fewer-than-100 people who attended had varied interests. There were American Medical Association representatives, full-time industrial physicians, insurance company doctors, government officials, labor and management members with authority, and a handful of those like myself deeply engaged in the field of occupational medicine (doctors and engineers) working under the protection of an academic institution. Rereading today bits of the proceedings, I realize how much I learned in this two-day session about the "bad patches" of occupational medicine at that time. I was struck by the stark admission of several young company doctors that their titles often were or should be "corporate medical director." This was because of the fact that their responsibilities were to management, not to the workers. Further, usual practice dictated that worker's medical findings were to be made available to management without permission from the individual worker. Another shock to my notion of medical ethics was the description of a pool of medical findings shared by insurance companies, including such private matters as domestic troubles and past credit losses. It is fair to write that today Big Brother's Internal Revenue Service and Social Security programs are fast making the lives of all of us more public. The Princeton meeting opened my eyes to much that appeared pure mischief, ill-becoming to professionals. It further helped me to understand the heavy-handed behavior of some labor leaders as they sought to imitate their management opposites and to stamp out past inequities. As it has been my privilege to travel in various parts of the world, I conclude that what I write here in criticism is not unique to the United States but is, rather, a further reflection of man's greed.

A final, entirely different Princeton assignment was my appointment by a former MIT colleague, Dr. W. Dalrymple, to be on his staff as consultant. Dr. Dalrymple was chief medical officer for college health at Princeton and needed advice in the control of hazards in research and student laboratories. Princeton is set in a lovely old town on grassy slopes. This was a happy job, and as I heard the chatter of arguing students, I was almost homesick for Radcliffe.

Professor Rolf Eliasson, professor of Civil Engineering at MIT, had convictions about the need for engineers to know some human anatomy and physiology to work out proper controls to protect against work and environmental hazard. Prophetic of the outcries of the 1960s, Professor Eliasson arranged an MIT faculty appointment for me in 1951. In return, I planned a course that proved worthwhile to his students, including outside reading, lectures by others, and examinations. Feeling lack of interest in the whole subject in Boston, Professor Eliasson moved to Stanford University in California where he began a similar course. I continued for a number of years teaching MIT civil engineers. I did a similar job for Space Agency engineers in their Texas headquarters. Again I was praised by the students and rewarded by their questions. Teaching students without background in biological subjects made two points clear to me. First, it is possible (with effort) to put across the subject matter of one's profession to students educated in other subjects. Second, the hunger and thirst of all men for knowledge of their physiology and its possible deviations from the normal are very real, and this desire I found quite moving.

In retrospect, however, my best and most fruitful teaching was at the bedside or in the clinic when a sick worker provided the teaching material. This was especially true if the clinical clerk or house officer responsible for the case of the patient being discussed was present and interested in the future of his sick worker.

REFERENCES

1. Conant, J., General Education in a Free Society, Cambridge, Mass., Harvard University Press, 1945.
2. Hardy, H. L., and Tabershaw, I. R., Delayed chemical pneumonitis occurring in workers exposed to beryllium compounds, J. Ind. Hyg. Toxicol., 28:197, 1946.
3. Hardy, H. L., Beryllium poisoning: lessons in the control of man-made disease, N. Engl. J. Med., 273:1188–1199, 1965.
4. Hardy, H. L., Risk and responsibility. A physician's viewpoint, N. Engl. J. Med., 293:801–806, 1975.
5. Hardy, H. L., Correct diagnosis of environmental lung disease, Proc. Seminar on Resp. Dis. for Science Writers, Thoracic Soc. and Natl. Tuberc. Assoc., Princeton, N.J., 1962.

CHAPTER 13

Harriet Hardy and the Workers

Work with Labor Unions

My knowledge of the background and current character of the U.S. union movement was nil in 1945 when I entered the field of industrial medicine. Now in 1982 after real-life experience with members and leaders, I have a clear-enough picture to give me great interest in union activity.

Working with Dr. Alice Hamilton and reading her autobiography, I learned of the early struggles of the U.S. union movement, some of which took shape through the settlement houses, as, for example, Hull House in Chicago. Dr. Alice became active in urging formation of unions and aggressive action by them to gain better working conditions, shorter hours, and higher pay. She encouraged unions of women, especially the International Ladies Garment Workers Union, as a consequence of visiting the sweatshops in this trade in the early twentieth century. Child labor laws were either nonexistent or ignored. Her effort was not in vain. In addition, Dr. Leo Price — and his father before him — developed fine world-recognized medical care for the garment workers. A fact not generally known is that the workers of a garment factory headed for bankruptcy voted a gift to save the factory and their jobs, a practice that has been repeated by some other unions. By the 1970s variations on such action have been widely tried. And some unions developed their own medical advice.

In sharp contrast with Dr. Alice's early experience, present-day unions have varying degrees of power, including political influence, but they also have new and different problems. My experience (1945 to present) allows me to venture a few opinions. First, the unions with rare exceptions dislike, and some fear, influence from the Soviet Union. This is in contrast to workers in many countries. Second, my private view is that, aside from perhaps the late George Meany and John L. Lewis and a few others who behave like industrial executives, union leaders wish to justify their existence by making constant and, in some cases, unreasonable demands. The result is that in the same way as in the employers' ranks, the unions in part appear to be building pressure; this includes political pressure for industrial power, demand for personal profit. Beside this black picture of union and industry failure to behave rationally must be the fact that many unions and companies behave honestly, faithful to their promises to union members and shareholders.

Two examples of the problems posed by legal advice to unions are these: Two Greek brothers suffered lead poisoning, sustained while spray painting structural steel. With an interpreter's help, since they spoke little English, we learned that they had paid considerable sums of money to the union for sickness benefits. Neither they nor we could get that money for the sick workers. Eventually, these two and their families, without jobs because of absenteeism and exhaustion of savings and welfare, returned to Greece, penniless and ill. Such tragic and shameful tales might have been prevented if the union lawyers had allowed our Division of Occupational Hygiene (DOH) staff to get blood and urine samples, which, if abnormal, should lead to a safer job. Another union practice based on legal advice arose in Massachusetts during the time of the exposure of men to dust in a stove factory. The workers were told to refuse to have chest x-rays on constitutional grounds. Gradually, there has been, and is currently improvement in such practices, forced by the U.S. government's Occupational Safety and Health Act of 1970 and the Massachusetts DOH.

So-called Communist "infiltration" to an unknown degree forced on the electrical workers union isolation from other unions. Because of beryllium disease in Massachusetts fluorescent lamp workers, I was asked to talk during an annual meeting of member unions held in Boston in 1947 and also to have my picture taken with the electrical union leaders. I was considered very brave because

Communists were present, and the McCarthy Committee witch-hunts had begun. Years later, in 1970, a national union committee plus local leaders met at the New York Academy of Sciences to hear me and others lecture on occupational disease. I was awarded a first Dr. Alice Hamilton Plaque by the unions. The presentation was made by an older, short man with tears in his eyes while he told of my courage by speaking in Boston. While I suspect that my colleague Dr. Irving Selikoff helped to arrange the event, I was touched by the warm thanks and had trouble expressing my gratitude because of my own emotions.

I enjoyed teaching union stewards and members. One winter I gave a series of lectures to the American Federation of Labor and Congress of Industrial Organizations (AFL-CIO) foundry men. It was a new problem to stretch and constrict my vocabulary of medical terms to make my knowledge more understandable. The men, most of them modestly educated, asked good questions and persisted until our very different vocabularies were worked to the point of mutual clarity. I was stimulated by the picture of my grandfather, Judge Hardy, in his robes, on the wall just behind me. The room in a Boston hotel, the Parker House, near the state capitol, had been used for years for meetings of the legal profession. I thought the combination of the workers, the judges, and myself a hopeful sign of future trust — the thought perhaps a bit naïve. A memorable evening was spent in Providence, Rhode Island, again lecturing on work hazards. The plans were made by Larry Spitz of the CIO, a highly educated man with a Phi Beta Kappa key on his watch chain. A massive bunch of flowers was in my hotel room when I arrived, and after my talk Larry handed me a generous check. Among other lectures were occasional ones to Massachusetts Institute of Technology (MIT) employees who were also members of unions. The lectures of special interest to them were those on radiation damage and beryllium exposure. Often I felt the best sessions were those in which I answered whatever questions were asked.

I was twice approached by union officials asking for technical help, both times in 1971. The first time was by the legal adviser of a large countrywide union whom I had met at several industrial meetings. In a company with prior history of employer neglect and hostility, the union leader reported to me the fact of worker illness in spite of the company's claim that safe levels of the hazardous material were recorded by them and by the state. My resourceful senior engineer at MIT, Richard Chamberlin, went to this plant and discovered inaccurate techniques or purposefully erroneous recordings plus spillage and errors in sampling the air near the workers. This short high exposure could account for the illness. After endless conferences the company and the union agreed to share the cost of a first-class study of *all* exposed workers and the plant. Our Massachusetts General Hospital (MGH) team took careful histories, chest x-rays, and lung function tests. The MIT group sampled the air for the toxic material in a variety of workplaces in the plant. Some elevated levels were found and correlated with cases of medical abnormalities. Mr. Chamberlin then initiated a novel plan that I believe will become common practice. Based on past experience, the union had no confidence in the company's procedure. Mr. Chamberlin coached two engineers in sampling, one man from the union and one from the company. He stationed them in a potentially hazardous place, stood between them, and had them take samples in the same place at the same time. The results checked precisely. Three years later, after proper controls were in place, the Massachusetts General group found definite reversal toward normal of the lung function of the exposed workers. This work has been published,[1,2] and I believe it is a model for handling obstructive employers' behavior and/or exaggeration by union members.

Another difficult problem for unions of today is presented by new materials of unknown toxicity that are introduced hurriedly. A union member from a nearby town asked to see me. He brought a tale of asthmaticlike cough and wheezing among workers, severe enough in some cases to require emergency hospitalization because of apparent suffocation. The unpleasant side of the story was the curious action of the allergist to whom the company sent affected workers. The doctor examined and tested the men and sent his report to the company, telling the patients nothing nor disclosing the company report to the men or their doctors. About this time (1971) Dr. John Edge, working in an English factory using the same material, stopped to see us in Boston. He reported the same clinical picture to be well known in France and Holland, and he himself had suffered an attack and had left his job. We at the Massachusetts General studied the Boston men and some workers from New York and

Maryland factories with the same symptoms. I was impressed that in the group I studied, there were a number of men who had nose-bleeds or blood-stained sputum. By this time, because of the work of the Massachusetts DOH we knew the exposure was to a finely divided detergent containing an enzyme that attacked protein, hence the advertisement: "It will get blood off your husband's shirt." I telephoned a research chemist in a company making enzymes from meat for use as drugs. He said that in their company no work with enzymes was done without complete protective clothing. They had had several severe bleeding episodes before they realized the hazard.

As in the case of other harmful materials, technical change in the operation eliminated the risk. Medical follow-up showed 100 percent improvement when exposure stopped except in the case of a few older, already asthmatic men. There is no question but that nowadays unions, especially those whose members are younger and World War II veterans, force the companies to make safer operations once job-related illness is established.

In summary, my experience leads me to conclude that unbiased teaching will best bring the greedy employer and suspicious worker together toward mutual trust. Unions and industrial medicolegal lawyers who seem hungry for profit and power must be identified and forced by their colleagues to change their ways.

Worker Compensation Problems

For me, educated in the humanities and medicine, the job of get-ting for the worker-patient the compensation award due him under the law was one of my most interesting and frustrating duties.

This work began for me in 1953 and continues in the form of writing position papers and giving advice by telephone to patients' lawyers and doctors. One day a sheriff came to my home while I was away to deliver a summons for me to appear as a witness at a so-called hearing before the Industrial Accident Board. My mother, living with me at the time because of ill health and awed by the legal papers, took them. This was a mistake. For a fee of $2, such sheriffs are ex-pected to give the summons only to the witness named. Without legal advice that time (but never since), I went to the hearing as a witness. This means that I was legally bound only to read out of the record (the worker was dead) specific facts such as pulse rate and laboratory findings, but I was not expected to interpret or give an opinion of work relationship, the crucial factor. Not knowing this, I answered questions put to me by the insurance company lawyer who had a medical text open on his desk and asked me to discuss cirrhosis of the liver, the worker's disease. I began, but he interrupted, saying "Dr. Hardy, that is not what it says in this book." I promptly lost my temper, which had been oozing away for the past few hours. In a loud voice I mentioned that my medical education at Cornell was far superior to his use of a sentence in a text. On and on it went until the commissioner ordered us to stop. In the end my side, that of the dead man, won. I, like a winning prizefighter, went to the opposing lawyer, shook his hand, and invited him to lunch with me at the MGH to discuss the case. He said, "I wouldn't dare, Dr. Hardy — you would give me liver to eat." My father was a lawyer, and my grandfather was a judge. Their clerk was alive in 1953 and had his own law practice. I went to see him for a bit of tutoring. After exploding at the advantage that had been taken of my ignorance, he explained that I should have insisted on being qualified as an expert witness because of training and experience and set my fee if it had not already been done.

The Industrial Accident boards are part of state government in most states. In 1948 I learned that some states (New Mexico, for example) had no board (one has since been established). The members are called commissioners and are appointed by governors. They need not be lawyers; indeed I have appeared before commissioners who had been undertakers and newspaper reporters and all war veterans had preference. Legislation governing the boards' actions varies from state to state. In one state the occupational disease must be diagnosed within three years of the last exposure claimed as cause. Cancers of occupational cause, silicosis, beryllium disease — all have latent periods of more than three years, so this law rules out the coverage of much job-related illness. In some other states, compensation is not awarded unless the sick worker has a disease that is on an accepted list. In the case of beryllium disease, for example, and those diseases caused by recently introduced chemicals, new knowledge of toxicity makes the idea of teaching the worker a so-called safe list of exposure difficult.

This subject of liability and compensation is large and growing rapidly. I can speak of a few of the evils of the process with which

I am familiar. While some states have moved in the right direction, and the federal government has attempted to pass a uniform mandatory national industrial accident law, there are still many problems. I have worked to improve the patient's chances of greater rewards.

It is reprehensible that a company is defended by a "stable" of lawyers on salary, while a patient must find a lawyer and pay his fee out of his worker's award. Some lawyers who have workers for clients, knowing the sophistication of the company or insurance carrier's lawyer, ask for consultation from an experienced colleague. Others, ignorant of the complexity of the compensation process, fail to do this and simply delay the patient's award. I have a patient with beryllium poisoning who has used the services of three lawyers and is in her sixteenth year of delay. The doctors, some of whom know better, are part of the evil — some work with lawyers, companies, and liability insurance carriers; of course, not all take the devil's side. Some physicians make trouble unintentionally because they fail to make a job-related diagnosis if one exists or fail to tell a worker of the so-called industrial accident process and the fact that he must report this to his supervisor at once. Serious pressures on Industrial Accident Board commissioners arise because in many states they work on a part-time basis, hence their own back work accumulates and worker cases must wait.

Hopeful signs that lawyers can and will defend workers' cases have come to my attention. In the early 1950s I came to know Sam Horowitz, the author of a well-known text on the subject of workmen's compensation written for lawyers. One member of his staff and I did two forward-looking jobs. First, I persuaded the lawyer, Larry Locke, that in many cases of industrial disease not one but two or more exposures may be present in the worker-patient causing the illness or death. Mr. J., a patient of mine, had worked with two materials, both toxic to the liver, of which the second, at an interval of the time separated from the first, caused fatal liver failure. Because my legal colleague agreed with me and worked hard to establish the concept with the Industrial Accident Board, the patient's widow received the award. We used this procedure in other cases if there were supporting facts. The second project that Larry and I developed was to have him invited to physicians' groups, small or large, to teach them what the doctor needs to know to protect his patients before the law. Alas, enthusiasm lagged unless either I or Larry was present at the meetings. Such teaching of one profession by another, each with differing educational backgrounds and experience, is most valuable.

In American business the standard way of life is, first, loyalty to shareholders. The corporate medical director and the corporation lawyers must prostitute or adapt ideals of care of workers and appear in court prepared to protect the companies and their secrets no matter what the hurt to an industrially ill worker. My travels in other countries led me to conclude that compensation problems are complex everywhere and not settled in industrialized and developing companies.

My actual appearances before the Industrial Accident Board were not too frequent because of the amount of work at the MGH and MIT that I was bent on accomplishing, together with teaching and travel. However, I did go to the board in defense of patients with beryllium disease and dust disease due to talc and asbestos. I gained a reputation for fierce and sarcastic argument; in addition, as time passed, it became known that I never acted as an expert unless the evidence showed clearly the diagnosis of the worker's disease I proposed to support. An amusing and telling episode reflects the value of such a reputation. Because the delays preceding board hearings were often as long as a whole morning — and then the case might be dismissed owing to lack of time — I arranged with each patient's lawyer to telephone me at the hospital as to exactly when the case would be heard, and I would hail a taxi to the hearing, a very short ride. One day, following this routine, I arrived at the board room to discover that when the company's insurance lawyer learned that I was actually in the taxi, he settled the case with the patient's lawyer without a hearing. Thus my genetic inheritance of outrage in court helped the patient and made it possible for me to get back to my own work.

Fortunately, my associate, Dr. John D. Stoeckle, full-time internist at the MGH, has found compensation work of interest and has gradually taken over this part of my work and performed it with distinction. We both felt keenly the inequities of the political regulations governing workmen's compensation. With the encouragement of Professor Robert Keeton at Harvard Law School and the help of a graduate student, we wrote a paper on the subject that has been published.[3] Twice I spoke at national organizations of lawyers, trying to put in precise language the obstructive difference between law and medicine, quite apart from the mischief caused by trade secrets and worry about shareholders' demands. Appearance before a judge and jury is frightening—to me at least—and very different from answering questions before an Industrial Accident Board at a state level. My chief experience was in the case of Ruth Heck. This woman lived in Reading, Pennsylvania, near a beryllium extraction and alloy manufacturing plant. Her husband and a cousin boarding with her worked there. After two pregnancies Mrs. Heck developed the cough, shortness of breath, and abnormal chest x-rays characteristic of beryllium poisoning. In time it was agreed that she was suffering from a neighborhood case of beryllium poisoning acquired from air pollution caused by the proximity of the plant and the powdery dust from the clothes that the two workers brought home. In addition, she visited her mother's grave daily for a year, which we discovered to be in line with the chimney that exhausted the plant fumes of beryllium compounds. The plant's lawyers were determined to defeat the Heck claim, which was large because of her age and her children. The case was put in the hands of a Philadelphia law firm of great experience, which took three years to prepare Mrs. Heck's case. One lawyer was sent to me to be tutored in what was then, in 1967, known of beryllium poisoning, the past medical literature, and U.S. and foreign treatment. I examined Mrs. Heck and took her chest x-ray twice to my expert, Dr. Alfred Weber.

At last the jury was sworn, and reprints and books on the subject were shown to the judge. I sat with Mrs. Heck when she was not on the stand and glared at those (many of whom I knew) sitting in another section on hand to defend the company. Unhappily, by elaborate drawings one of "our" experts placed the Heck home outside the range of plant fumes. One of our lawyers flew to Pennsylvania State College and brought back a meteorologist qualified to correct the findings in favor of the Heck case.

I would liken my examination by our lawyer and the cross-examination by the company's lawyer as very like what is implied in the phrase "Hell on earth." My lifelong gift for appearing calm and cool stood me in good stead, but I was inwardly frightened and angry. I sat in an armchair, a platform holding the judge's armchair and desk raised above me on the right, the jury at my level on the left. The company lawyer, Mr. Williams, obviously excited, pointed his finger at me and said, "Dr. Hardy, I wonder if you know how serious the outcome of this case is for industry." I, too, was angry and spoke, but luckily only the jury heard. "Mr. Williams, I wonder if you know how serious this is for Mrs. Heck. She is going to die." If the judge had heard, I suspect he would have declared a mistrial, so devious are the laws. Eventually, after a retrial ordered by a higher court on a technicality (not due to my behavior), the Hecks won $110,000 — this could not give her back her health, but it could help educate her children.

After the Heck case I decided there should be no more such stress for me. From then on I gave conference time to lawyers and patients and agreed to have depositions taken. If I had another life to live, I might study law and join with civil rights groups already hard at work trying to correct injustices.

Once, a television camera was brought to my home, and the opposing lawyers asked their questions. After two years preparing reviews of the subject, examining two patients, and attending many teaching conferences, I agreed to appear before closed circuit television in Boston in a citizen's action suit against 14 companies, all involved with the manufacture and use of asbestos. In a fair-sized room I sat behind a table — on my left 14 lawyers from the companies being sued, ahead of me the television camera, on my right the two lawyers defending the sick asbestos workers and questioning me to present the case against the industry. I was stimulated by the scenario, but by midday I was ready for a rest. This television conference was to be made availabe for a jury when the case reached that point. I was impressed by the behavior of the two lawyers defending the asbestos workers. They worked hard and used their private funds, not the patients', in preparing the case.

REFERENCES

1. Kanarek, D. J., Warner, R. A., Chamberlin, R. I., Weber, A. L., and Kazemi, H., Respiratory illness in a population exposed to beryllium, *Am. Rev. Respir. Dis.*, 108:1295-1302, 1973.
2. Sprince, N. L., Kanarek, D. J., Weber, A. L., Chamberlin, R. I., and Kazemi, H., Reversible respiratory disease in beryllium workers, *Am. Rev. Respir. Dis.*, 117:1011-1017, 1978.
3. Stoeckle, J. D., Hardy, H. L., Ling, B. Chang-Wai, The compensation experience of patients with chronic beryllium disease, *J. Occup. Med.*, 17:167–170, 1975.

CHAPTER 14

Unusual U.S. Committees

I hazard the guess that scarcely any adult American has not been a member of some committee serving club, church, village, town, or city affairs. Here the word *unusual* is used to give a clue to rare needs of the U.S. government and how they are handled.

During and after World War II, the Atomic Energy Commission (AEC) stockpiled U.S. and foreign supplies of beryllium, ignorant of its toxicity through bad advice from the U.S. Public Health Service. During the war years and for some years longer, the AEC had contracted to handle problems of health and safety of those working with beryllium. And to try to prevent further beryllium-induced illness, in 1948 I was made chairman of a committee by Dr. Shields Warren, head of the AEC health program. The committee was muzzled by investigators who had drawn the wrong conclusions from experiments with small animals. In addition, I could not persuade the committee to demand more work on beryllium in air and near beryllium operations and neighborhood contamination in homes or to repeat old experiments with improved techniques. In fact, no action was taken in the ten years of the committee's existence. I disbanded it after talking with Dr. Charles Dunham, who in 1958 held Dr. Warren's post. I wrote the presidents of the national organizations that then represented occupational medicine, asking them to pick up the unfinished business. Little action has been taken to collect data to support or deny these 1948 untested so-called safe levels of beryllium in spite of litigation, a congressional hearing, and Occupational Safety and Health Administration pressure to lower the safe level.

Sadly, I write that the Beryllium Case Registry that I started in 1952 at the Massachusetts General Hospital (MGH) is being used to "prove" that beryllium is cancer-producing in humans as it is in monkeys and mice. The data at hand are inadequate and many are in error. To date so far as I know no case of beryllium disease or lung cancer has been documented in any person exposed at or near the presently allowed worker or neighborhood levels. I have really learned more than I wished (had I had advance knowledge) of the devious, self-serving ways of greedy management, jealous investigators, consultant engineers, and government authorities afraid of criticism. So I appointed myself, conceitedly, a one-man watchdog on beryllium problems. I have appeared before endless committees with and without invitation. An assistant secretary of Health, Education and Welfare who admired my 1965 article[1] on beryllium disease encouraged my effort. I came to know of U.S. plans, now discarded, for using beryllium as a rocket fuel (4,000 tons needed for one stage). I wrote protests, sending them here and there with help from some Massachusetts Institute of Technology (MIT) professors. The air force telephoned me for advice about the manufacture of a beryllium-fired device; another call asked my advice about moving a population before test firing. I was able to "scare" two industrial mangers in my office at the time with these true stories. Beryllium has such excellent properties of lightness and resistance to strain that I expect beryllium committees of all sorts to continue to form, perhaps act, disband, and reform.

However, in the year 1983 a great change has come about. Except for its use in various alloys, usually in small quantity, the use of beryllium and its compounds has fallen off markedly, but a number of new uses have been found, for example, in the space industry.

Engineering and Living Systems

My life at MIT was never dull. It was my good fortune to be asked a medical question by the Electrical Engineering Department, which led me to Dean Gordon Brown's office. He was dean of the School of Engineering in 1962 and administered the use of the Caspary Fund for research. Two technicians had developed scabies (a nasty, itching skin disease) while helping with research on some aspect of hearing, using alley cats. From then on Dean Brown asked me to review all applications for Caspary research money that had to do with looking for health hazards.

From this pale beginning developed a small committee called the Engineering and Living Systems Committee, made up of engineers known to be working on medical or biological problems. To begin with, the secretary of this committee listed departments and individuals falling in these categories. The group spent some weeks listening to individuals from various departments tell us of their experiments. The number of staff and students involved, the variety of their interests, and the collaboration with hospitals, medical schools, and other academic institutions came as a surprise to me. I will list the titles of a few projects as examples of how lively and complex this mix had become: Sensory Aids for the Blind, Ultrasonic Neural Sensory Man-Machine Systems, Life Support in Manned Systems, Experiments in Human Control, Control Systems Modelling of Creatures on Machines with Sensors (Project Transport), Research on Surgical Implant Materials, and many, many more. As a member I learned a great deal and always put in a word for prevention of work-related illness. I could help from time to time with my greater knowledge of physiology (biological function) and the mechanism of disease production. There were a number of changes in membership and goals, and the Engineering and Living Systems Committee grew. In coordination with Harvard Medical School in 1970, this committee was absorbed into a Harvard-MIT program called Health, Science, and Technology with Dr. Irving London in charge.

SuperSonic Transport

By telephone I was asked in 1971 if I would become an active member of a small committee advising the Department of Commerce on the wisdom of the proposal that the United States build a fleet of more than 100 supersonic transports (SSTs). My role was to learn what was known at the time of the danger of the SST to human health. There were only a few meetings of this committee because the Senate rejected the proposal later that year.

The work of this committee involved physical chemistry, mathematics, and physics beyond my comprehension. But the skills and talk of the members, among them industry representatives, were fascinating. The "observers," sitting in chairs behind us, were from all departments of the military, the AEC, the Congress, the Weather Bureau, and others not identified but adding special knowledge and unusual questions. The main committee was made up of a professor of physical chemistry, a vice-president of an airline not competing for the SST contracts, a meteorologist, two academic professors in various branches of ecology, an administrator representing the government, and myself.

My appointment was triggered by the action of a university-based physicist who had distributed to members of Congress and the media a memorandum prophesying the number of cases of skin cancer that the SST would cause. My job was to get the best possible medical "state of the art" (current knowledge). This I did by consulting with my colleague Dr. Tom Fitzpatrick, professor of dermatology at Harvard Medical School. I learned that the skin cancer caused by ultraviolet radiation would be increased by the SST through disruption of the ozone layers between the earth and the sun. Such cancers are well known to appear on the skin of sun-exposed ranchers, sailors, and excessive sunbathers, among others. Fortunately, such skin cancers are the least malignant and most easily treated of all cancers. Further research by Dr. Fitzpatrick's MGH group has developed an ointment that if applied before exposure, will prevent solar-produced skin cancers. A second potential hazard of SST development in which I tried to stimulate interest was the hardly considered fact that there is a natural diurnal variation in body chemistry (circadian rhythm). By the SST speeds and distant destinations of varying temperature, and with changes in barometric pressure among other pressures, surely the body's time clock would be confused.

The final meeting of this particular committee was held at Boulder, Colorado, the site of the U.S. National Weather Station. Each speciality presented its conclusion and recommendation. Even a novice like me could look at the handsome equation each speaker put on the blackboard and see the numerous X's (unknowns) and conclude that if the SST fleet were to be built, its path would be like that of Columbus sailing not knowing the location of the horizon. Our immediate troubles were over with the announcement that Congress had voted overwhelmingly to reject a U.S. SST plan — in large part because of the great cost. Perhaps the threat of ill-defined health hazards also played a part. This kind of assignment is much to my liking because of the uncovering of unknowns and the opportunity to work with colleagues from other fields. Surely this was a dividend from my choice of occupational and environmental medicine as my profession.

Committee on Marine Protein Resource Development

Under the Food and Nutrition Board of the National Academy of Sciences in Washington, the Committee on Marine Protein Resource Development was created in the early 1960s. The purpose of the group working under this grand title was to study a fish-protein concentrate for feeding underprivileged infants and preschool children at home and abroad to fight malnutrition, improve mental development, and combat the dread liver disease, kwashiorkor. The U.S. Department of the Interior through its Bureau of Commercial Fisheries provided federal backing, funding, and staff.

The membership of the committee included both academic and commercial experts on fish supplies in different parts of the world, chemists, nutrition specialists, and physicians. I was asked to join this group to help assess the toxicity of materials used in the process. Briefly, the plan was to extract fat from the fish and — through drying and other steps — produce a fine powder, fish meal. This meal was to be incorporated into a nation's food, a far-from-easy process since some countries like bland food, while others preferred food with a somewhat rancid or spicy flavor. A duty of our committee was to taste samples of fish meal, sometimes in tomato juice, occasionally in native foods, and usually in breadstuffs. The original plans called for the extractions to be made on the boat from which fishing was done. Infants and preschool children in South America and various Asian countries were the most needy populations. Dr. Nevin Scrimshaw, head of the MIT Department of Nutrition, a member of our committee, had devised a vegetable protein while working in Central America. From him came many important suggestions because of his own research and also because of his great knowledge of investigations in laboratories throughout the world. Dr. Scrimshaw also knew the difficulties and possibilities of help or hindrance from the innumerable U.S. government and international agencies involved.

I found the meetings fascinating because of the new knowledge presented, which confirmed my conviction that physicians must be able to adapt to, and to help with, new problems in the "real world," as my social scientist friends call it. Gradually I crystallized what help I might supply. First, how toxic is the fat solvent to be used? This proved to be isopropyl alcohol, used in homes and hospitals, and I could be reassuring since this alcohol, while irritating to workers, has caused no documented biological damage. Further, the solvent was to be washed out of the fish meal long before it was ready as a food. Second, since the fish were to be whole fish as they came from the water, the problem of fluorine from seawater deposited in the skeleton was a real one. It was my job to work with the head dentist of the Public Health Service and several members of the parent committee to reduce the fluorine in the finished fish meal to a level acceptable to the Food and Drug Administration. There had been a great hue and cry over the Public Health Service recommendation of one part per million of fluorine in drinking water of the United States. From the cry that this was a Communist conspiracy to the complaint by affluent mothers upset by the chance that so-called mottling of the teeth would mar their children's beauty, fluorine to prevent tooth decay had hard going at every town meeting. The background truth is that workers exposed to fluorine at high doses over long periods do show x-ray changes and, after further exposure, pain and deformity. Animals grazing in fluorine-contaminated pastures may lose their chewing ability and die of starvation. Finally, at low doses in drinking water, some but not all children do show a spotty distribution of mottling of the teeth. On the other hand, where natural waters contain relatively higher percentages of fluorine, bone fractures are fewer and heal more readily. The engineers of the Bureau of Fisheries, with my encouragement, found ways to reduce the fluorine in fish meal.

The final consultation help I gave this committee was uninvited. No plans had been made to discover whether any amount of potentially harmful metals might be in the fish meal since the fish were to be caught in a variety of waters. Only lead content had been assayed and had been found to be within acceptable limits. I mentioned the need to study mercury, arsenic, cadmium, and also the mycotoxins (poisons elaborated by fungi especially harmful to the liver and for a while thought at least in part responsible for a frequent liver tumor in Africa). Finally, I urged more clinical study, such as blood counts and liver function studies, in both those fed with fish meal and those not so fed so as to assess both value and subtle toxicity of the fish meal. This last suggestion had little appeal to those who knew the desperate situation of the malnourished.

I do not know enough of the various reasons for the formation of a committee, such as political loyalties, funding, and industrial bias, to understand the slow pace of this group working to fill so obvious a need to feed the malnourished and mentally retarded a fish protein to help develop body and mind. Such groups with title and initials as Food for Peace, AID (Agency for International Development), FAO (Food and Agriculture Organization of the United Nations), and FDA (Food and Drug Administration) were bringing a variety of pressures. Certain lobbyists tried to persuade Congress to vote for Viobin, a commercial fish meal for animal feed, as a substitute for our fish protein concentrate. Rumors came to us that AID departments overseas used the money intended for use in making fish meal to build macadam roads. I learned that the Viobin process used ethylene dichloride, a known liver poison, but this did not impress the Viobin company and their lobbyists.

Regretfully, I left the committee in 1969 because of ill health. Those deeply involved, Dr. Scrimshaw, Ray Pariser, and Dr. Paul St. Gyorgy pushed on as they found backing.

More Committees

For a number of years after I returned from Los Alamos at the end of 1949, I served on a Massachusetts General Hospital committee to guide the safe use of radioactivity at the hospital. The committee, in my view, was powerless from the start because the Radiology Department insisted on maintaining its own Radiation Health and Safety officer. The hospital administration could see no reason to interfere. Furthermore, radiotherapy was well represented on the committee, as was research, including a physics professor well known to want no lower levels for safety. These professionals served on the committee to see that no curbs were put on their work. Very little clinical help was available to ask about the risk to the patient, nurse, technician, or subjects used for research until the government took action.

What I write predates the Helsinki agreements on human rights. It is galling, however, to have to write what I believe is the truth—that physicians pledged to relieve suffering were and, in some places, are so careless of their ignorance and so ready to use radioactive materials improperly measured and administered that their "victims" have suffered radiation damage. I feel certain the committee was pleased when I resigned, pleading my MIT work in the same field as the reason.

By the late 1960s much about which I had complained had been set right. However, to complete the story, it is documented in the medical literature that some irradiated pregnant mothers gave birth to deformed babies, and children suffered thyroid tumors and leukemia as a result of medical or research use of x-rays and use of radioisotopes experimentally.

Senator Edmund Muskie was chairman of a group of senators reviewing job hazards in the 1960s. I gave the committee at its request a full account of the beryllium problem. After some questions, one member awoke from a short nap to ask if I knew of the Gaulley Bridge deaths. While I searched my brain for dates (these were in the 1930s), the senator, now awake, said, "Bless my soul, you were not yet in grammar school." A discussion of some aspects of lead hazards followed and then we had lunch. The vice-presidents of the two chief beryllium-manufacturing companies were present and asked me to lunch with them, promising not to put beryllium in my drink! I learned they really wanted the name of a case I had discussed at the hearing, not known to them. I was impressed with Senator Muskie, perhaps because he appeared to agree with my testimony, although little was done afterward to act on my suggestions for control. And I was more impressed with his staff, who did the homework and coached me.

I was asked by certain committees of the National Academy of Science to present my position. These included the group working on detergent soap hazards and the ad hoc committee appointed after I, among others, had blasted the United States for considering beryllium as a rocket fuel. I was flattered by media and government attention, and as far as I know, the idea of using beryllium as a rocket fuel has been dropped, not because of me, I surmise, but because of cost and technical problems. However, my share of the opposition includes writing and talking to the military, the assistant secretary of Health, Education and Welfare, the president's scientific adviser, the National Research Council, MIT faculty and administration, and of course the press about these hazards.

An interesting assignment asked for by a National Academy of Science committee was to be being an anonymous expert adviser for a report on lead toxicity that arose from exposure to naturally occurring lead, its industrial uses, and environmental pollution as well as the diagnosis of poisoning and adult and childhood treatment. The section of the report on which I was best informed was shockingly poor and correctly accused of bias toward industry. I telephoned an official of the academy and the chairman of the committee to protest. The answer was, "Harriet, we must have industrial input." Caught off guard by a *Science* magazine reporter, I complained that the academy must not be held to the pressures naturally generated in our profit-oriented society. I learned that the Lead Committee of the academy was using industrial doctors and scientists as members of this important committee. A protesting editorial was published by *Science*, and I continued to make adverse comments publicly, but I doubt that academy policy has changed. I conclude that an open, free-trade, industrialized society holds a number of greedy people in positions of power for a variety of reasons.

A ragbag of committees on which I have served through the years include a Harvard Medical School faculty committee to discover if there need be teaching in occupational medicine as a separate subject, a National Institutes of Health committee (to assess research), a search committee (to recommend a professor at the Harvard School of Public Health), a district medical society committee (insurance for disabled doctors, 1943), a state medical society committee (occupational medicine), a National Industrial Medical Association committee (education), various Tuberculosis Association committees, and, of nonmedical societies, the Library and Water Supply committees of my town.

What do I think of committee work? My experience tells me that they are of little use in decision making followed by action. The success of a committee depends on one or two individuals willing and able to learn the questions and the background of the goals and, in spite of domineering members, to persuade their fellow members to vote positive action and follow its results.

REFERENCE

1. Hardy, H. L., Beryllium poisoning: Lessons in the control of man-made disease, *N. Engl. J. Med.*, 273:1188-1199, 1965.

CHAPTER 15

Trials and Tribulations

Physical Trials

I am blessed, or cursed, by a strong drive to act, which I take to be genetic in origin. This has made my life a kind of twentieth century *Pilgrim's Progress*. Included here are a few paragraphs of the "bad patches," as the English say, of my personal and professional life. It is a narcissistic exercise, but I hope it may encourage my sisters in medicine who may have similar trials to carry on as taste, ambition, or thought directs.

The countrywide economic depression of the 1930s found our family hard pressed. I was in medical school; hospital training was made possible by a small inheritance and by borrowing and jobs such as camp doctor during holiday stretches. Thus began the accumulation of fatigue and the predisposition for anxiety. By September 1934, when I reached my first job at the Northfield School (see Chapter 3), I had lost nearly 50 pounds, had had four days abed for an appendectomy, was concerned by the family's woes, and had loans to repay. Prior to the two years of Philadelphia General Hospital internship with duty of 36 out of 48 hours, I had been tiresomely healthy and had won prizes for endurance, hiking, swimming, and varsity golf. I am certain this sequence is true of many students in the professions in the 1930s and now again in the late 1970s and 1980s.

A trigger to the onset of my illness was provided by a natural disaster, a real crisis that came in September 1938 when a hurricane of great fury swept up the Connecticut River to Canada, laying great waste en route. It passed through Northfield, blowing at a rate of 100 miles an hour, uprooting ancient elms and lifting roofs. When it reached our campus, it had torn the slates off the infirmary roof, then twirled them in such a way that they came straight at the glass windowpanes, smashing them. We protected the girls in bed with pillows. Just as this job was finished, a student, with blood and rain making her appearance frightening, rushed in to cry, "Dr. Hardy, go to G — — Dormitory at once." There I found that a two-ton brick chimney had toppled through the roof of the dining hall on at least 100 girls who were eating supper. The faculty present acted quickly and wisely, leading the uninjured girls to the cellar, where one member began to read aloud.

Upstairs we found 2 dead students, 1 unconscious, and some 10 to 15 with a variety of injuries. Not suprisingly, electric power lines were down, and all roads were blocked; other doctors were away or could not reach us. So my faithful nurse and I set bones; did lumbar punctures, looking for fractured skulls; and sewed up lacerations from flying glass — all by lantern light. This nurse and I had both trained at Philadelphia General, so we worked swiftly and silently, relying on knowledge of each other's style. Since the river had torn down bridges and flooded roads, there was no possibility of reaching a hospital.

Without phones or doorbells my village patients had to reach me by a path made by men who chopped fallen trees, first a footpath, later made wide enough for cars. The village was without phone or electricity for several months, and the nearest available hospital became 45 instead of 15 miles away. So when I was wanted, the light of a flashlight or lantern was played on the white of my bedroom ceiling. A single telephone was allowed the seminary to let parents know the safety of their children, some 500 girls minus the 3 fatalities. This episode predated transistor radios and other electronic devices, so that my mother and stepfather, en route from Vermont to see me and stopped by fallen trees, could not reach me. The ingenuity of ham radio operators succeeded in getting word to me of their safety, as they holed up with a family's chickens in a hospitable New Hampshire farmhouse.

The ferocity of the storm plus loss of telephone and electricity made every sick baby, patients with heart disease, and aged folk already confused develop new and worsening symptoms. It so happened that this period included the hunting season, which drew other doctors out of town for part of the time. As a result I was sometimes the only physician in this or nearby towns. I thought gratefully of my Philadelphia General Hospital experience — riding ambulance, working in the Emergency Ward where swift action based on knowledge and judgment without emotion was required. During this period I was able to do my work calmly and accurately. But when the crisis was over, I was limp and useless, although I am told by friends and patients that I performed my physician's work with every outward sign of calm. However, the truth is that never since September 1938 have I been able to speak or teach without some degree of apprehension, best known as stage fright. Several months of little sleep, snatched meals, and worry about the inadequate care I could give my patients triggered what biographers call a nervous breakdown; the military call it combat fatigue. My previous good health made the insomnia, poor appetite, apathy, and pounding pulse most difficult to accept. Because of a persistent afternoon rise in temperature, I had a thorough medical checkup. One kind colleague suggested psychoanalysis. At my second visit to the analyst, I asked the cost. In the year 1939 the charge would have been $3,000. My expected income (if I could work) was to be $4,000, some of which had to go to help my parents. Miserable as I was, I confess to some outrage (probably healthy).

It became clear to my senior adviser, Dr. Robert McCastline, and me that I was unfit for duty, and I was bundled off to the Massachusetts General Hospital (MGH), studied carefully, and found to be organically sound. An old friend and her family on Cape Cod patiently nursed me for a month, and when I was able to travel, I went on to Monterey, California, to a schoolmate's home. During this period of rest and freedom from responsibility in a completely new environment, with my friend and her husband and children and amid natural beauty, I studied the "art of convalescence" and began to heal. While there were "down" periods of depression and needless worry, there were stretches of joy in reading; listening to music; studying land and sea birds, sea mammals, and vegetation; sampling California-made wines; and reading nineteenth century novels. Most of all I learned the incredible therapeutic value of friends who support but do not fret. The good humor and patience of these friends cannot be too highly praised. When my appetite was still poor and I was apparently pushing my food about my plate but not eating it, my host said in tones of a teacher, "Harriet, that food has no maggots in it — now eat it." I did, and wonder that I was not sent home. My long walks alone on the Carmel beach studying the behavior of kelp with the tide and the friendly gestures of seals and the great tall larches and pines together with the good humor and goodwill of my friends made me quite healthy and strong enough to return East.

I dwell on this abrupt change in my health for two reasons. First, I believe that I am able to give better patient care as a result of this experience. Second, I report that I never again had the good health of the period from 1906 to 1938. Excess work brings back varying patterns of the original breakdown. And yet, even as I rest physically, my mind is actively conceiving better therapy on this or that patient, and what questions to look at next, using my continuing interest in clinical investigation.

A final reward during my early convalescence came in part from my Wellesley choice of English literature as a major, from the influence of a home full of books, and from the influence of the Chief. I refer to steady and widely varied reading of nonmedical books.

So the rest of my life has required attention to my health — on one hand, a bore, on the other, a resource leading to much satisfaction in books, other arts, and travel. Quickly told are the "big" health items. I had pelvic surgery in 1954, with incorrect preoperative diagnosis of cancer. A "stroke" diagnosed in 1968 proved to be the first sign of a large brain tumor, also benign, removed in 1972. This last exercise, at the age of 65 years, left me with periodic difficulty with speech and handwriting.

But the "drive" to continue is so strong that I write, teach, and consult as my disability allows. This ego-rich recital is in part a contribution to encourage my colleagues — although disabled in any way — to continue because there is so much in medicine that needs discovery or change.

Professional Tribulations

There have also been failures in my professional program. Many jobs remain that I believe need doing and are capable of being done. When I had had experience at the Division of Occupational Hygiene

(DOH) and had been writing with Dr. Alice Hamilton, and after a year spent at Los Alamos, I realized the need for the teaching of occupational medicine in medical school. With help from Dr. Joseph Aub, at the MGH, I approached Dr. David Rutstein, who had recently been appointed chairman of the Department of Preventive Medicine. For a few years he allowed me 10 to 12 hours per year for teaching "my" subject, a rich gift. A real bonus occurred when Dr. Alice came once a year to give a wonderful lecture on her work with the deadly poison benzol (C_6H_6) during World War I. In a soft voice she told of asking the Department of Labor for a list of benzol-using plants. She was told that she would have to find the plants herself, since their names and addresses were secret. The crowded amphitheater where she lectured was thoroughly roused while she reported that her job was like that of the children of Israel, told to follow a cloud by day and a pillar of fire by night. Unfortunately, as the medical school curriculum changed to permit more electives and fewer required lectures, occupational medicine became once more a stepchild, a fourth-year elective buried deep in the catalog. By 1971 my share had become one hour, although the Pulmonary Unit of the MGH had "adopted" this subject since industrial chest disease provided good teaching material for lung function testing research and pathological study as well as sophisticated patient care.

From questions I am currently asked — by letter and by telephone — it is clear that few practitioners have been taught even the fundamentals of occupational medicine. As the media find an interested audience, especially since the word *environment* has taken the place of *occupational*, citizen groups, professional organizations, and politicians needing an issue have taken a great interest in man-made disease. I feel that I failed by not being able to persuade Harvard Medical School and other medical schools at whose doors I knocked to require the teaching of occupational medicine. The American Association of Medical Colleges and the American Student Health Association, among others, were politely interested; the Massachusetts Medical Society formed a committee that rarely met. The American College of Physicians helped me give a one-week course open to 100 physicians; only 23 attended, although Dr. Means, Dr. Aub, and other seniors of the MGH staff plus Dr. Dana Farnsworth of the Massachusetts Institute of Technology (MIT) gave stimulating lectures.

Feeling overloaded and knowing that the new professor of

medicine at the MGH was not interested in my subject and was eyeing
the space that I occupied, and noting the decrease in my lecture time,
I talked to the dean of the Harvard Medical School, after sending
a letter to him resigning my faculty post. I planned to spend my energies at and for MIT, retaining the MGH clinical position to make
certain I might have hospital backing for the care of my patients.
The dean would not accept my resignation. Aware of my missionary
attitude toward the teaching of industrial medicine, he appointed
a professional committee to survey department by department what
the state of affairs was at Harvard Medical School in teaching the subject of "man-made diseases," the then popular term. At that time the
Harvard School of Public Health was indeed teaching this subject but
to postgraduate students, foreign students, doctors from the military,
and a few members of industrial medical departments. These groups
had chosen occupational medicine, intending to make it their specialty. There was by now available a certificate in the field of Occupational Medicine, a subspecialty of the Board of Preventive Medicine.
The reader will see that my actions were all directed toward stimulating the teaching of students in the undergraduate medical years.
The Harvard Medical School Committee on Man-Made Diseases had
David Rutstein as chairman, I as secretary (for which read "dogs-
body"). Like most committees this one died of inaction, each department head being satisfied with the status quo and unwilling to allow
time for more lectures.

Since Earth Day in 1970 and the rise of student and citizen
interest in a reasonable environment, teaching and action in and out
of medical school (some of it in poor perspective) are changing. Dr.
David Rutstein invited me to have lunch with him and Dr. Arthur
Fishman, professor of medicine at the University of Pennsylvania,
to discuss the future of teaching man-made diseases in the nation.
It is my view that because occupational diseases are often unidentified, much of what medical students, doctors, and policy makers need
for prevention is already to be found in reports of worker illness from
all industrialized countries beginning at the time of the Industrial
Revolution. Dr. Fishman's idea was that this field will not be recognized until "institutional commitment" of space, faculty, salaries,
teaching time, and laboratories is made.

The other big disappointment in this area was my failure to
persuade those in authority to permit me to establish a unit at the

MGH devoted to study and care of industrial illness. Between 1946 and 1966 with the backing of Drs. Nathaniel Faxon and Dean Clark (medical directors) and Drs. Means and Aub (professors of medicine), I did find space. With National Institutes of Health funds and Dean Berry's help, a stipend for a secretary and a medical fellow supported four different projects over a period of about 20 years. When I became ill in 1968 and when Dr. Means and Dr. Faxon retired, "our stock" declined. Fortunately, MIT welcomed us. But the loss of space at the MGH as well as of a clinical fellow with enthusiasm for epidemiological research meant the failure of this project and great disappointment to me. As I finish this section, I can report that the tide has turned and most of my plans for study of man-made disease have begun to flower in various fashions.

Through the years when I was active in visiting and consulting for industry and its lawyers, an idea — not original — occurred to me. Why not try to kindle the interest of business school students and also executives in the plight of sick workers? I learned early in my work with the fluorescent lamp industry that the manager of a plant located at a distance from the main administrative office found it best to solve his problems with sick workers by himself or with his local insurance agent. This was true in the beryllium epidemic (see Chapter 5) when my papers on beryllium disease were published. At about this time, 1947, a niece of the Massachusetts commissioner of labor died of beryllium poisoning, and the vice-president in charge of personnel for the plant hurried to the site of the epidemic and discovered how little of this industrial tragedy was known to the executives in the home office in New York City. From this experience I argued that if I could teach at the new MIT Sloan School of Industrial Management, I might reach the most influential group in American industry. I was able, through the kindness of the first deans of the Sloan School, Dean Edward Brooks and Dean Howard Johnson, to give a few lectures there regularly. The lectures were greeted (except by company lawyers) warmly, and good questions followed. Alas, change in deans and faculty resulted in gradual decline in invitations to carry on this teaching. Some of my colleagues and federal agencies (the National Institute of Occupational Safety and Health and Occupational Safety and Health Administration) are now bringing the facts of hazard control and the realization that humanity is needed in compensation settlement to the decision makers in management.

Finally, in the years from 1968 to 1973 I had real tribulation in getting the third edition of *Industrial Toxicology*[1] published. These years coincided with my "stroke," which proved to be a large benign tumor of the brain. I worked slowly, often having to do sections more than once, grateful that I had sensed my decreasing powers and had the help of competent younger colleagues for sections I could not manage. These colleagues were Drs. Asher Finkel, Clarence Maloof, John Stoeckle, and Lloyd Tepper.

I had a contract with a respected university press plus some financial support from the Commonwealth Fund and hoped that a low purchase price would enable medical students to buy the book. This press returned the draft and broke its contract because of a poor review. Without being told the name of the reviewer, I was pretty certain I knew my critic. On reading my contract with the publishers, I found their abrupt action perfectly proper. I next tried another press, having been urged to do so by one of its editors. After a long delay I was told that I would be personally responsible for soliciting sales! Refusing such an offer, I applied to a well-known New York firm (a now-dead uncle had been a senior partner, and I had known him well during my adolescent years). This company kept the manuscript for six months, and at the end of this period a polite voice on the telephone told me that the editors were interested but had decided an edition would not sell the 25,000 copies required by the size of the organization to make money.

This seemed a good time in which to throw results of more than five years' work into a nearby river. In fairness to my younger colleagues and to loyal secretaries, I hesitated and wrote a letter recounting the tale to my doctor coauthors. Dr. Finkel had taken a job with the American Medical Association that involved much writing and working with editors and publishers. He suggested that I see, among others, Dr. Frank Paparello, a former teacher who was on the staff of D. C. Heath, publisher of textbooks. He and a few colleagues were starting a new business, Publishers Science Group. At the time the Raytheon Company, a large, well-known company, was parent to the Publishers Science Group, now John Wright · PSG, Inc. My manuscript was taken to the Raytheon medical director for an opinion; he said at once, "You haven't a chance. There is a classic in this field, Hamilton and Hardy." Dr. Frank Paparello produced my manuscript, the third edition of Hamilton and Hardy. This tale ended happily. The Publishers Science Group published this much-worked-over-and-wept-over third edition in 1974. To date 7,500 copies have been sold in the United States and abroad, and a new edition, edited by Dr. Asher Finkel, has recently been published. My energies, meanwhile, are going into this memoir with the hope that others with medical training take a more kindly interest in sick workers and view the field of finding and preventing the human damage of new and old risks, the speciality of occupational or environmental medicine, a fruitful choice.

My zeal to inform the medical profession, industrial management, and insurance companies with the knowledge of the dangers to U.S. workers led to several of my flattest failures. My first priority was to establish an endowed unit within a teaching hospital. I wrote out careful plans to include an industrial hygienist (with chemical engineering skills), a physicist, and perhaps a part-time lawyer. I peddled these ideas to foundations and insurance companies, looking for financial and institutional backing. This appeared to me an ideal project, and I decided in the 1950s that my ideas were in error or (owning a comfortable ego) premature. An amusing episode ended this trial. Dr. K. invited me to give a seminar at the University of Pittsburgh School of Public Health. With the help of a wealthy patient of mine, I had previously applied for funds for such a project to the Mellon Foundation, located in Pittsburgh. Dr. K. drove me to the train after my lecture. He asked me if I recalled the request I had made at Mellon. After a pause, Dr. K. said, "I was asked to assess your request. I would be less than honest if I didn't tell you that I wrote 'This is what we want for Pittsburgh,' and shortly the man with the brown bag appeared. *We* have your million dollars." But as I read current medical literature, I am consoled by the thought that the 1950 "failures" probably acted as players in the wings, awaiting their cue. This chat about personal adventures has as its intention the aim of conveying that one should follow the odd path if it looks right. Thus I came from Radcliffe days where I began to crystallize plans for working at clinical preventive medicine (Dr. Aub's reaction: "What's that?" to which I retorted that it was the need to study clinical evidence of onset of disease and so to learn better how to prevent it).

I am aware that my wings have been clipped, my stamina diminished since the 1972 surgery. The discipline of undependable health has a lot to teach, perhaps very like the demands made on a person by tuberculosis before drug therapy. At all events my experience is, I suspect, common. I have found that disability in the course of a developing career has rewards. I learned to prepare my teaching sessions with enough slides to allow me to handle vertigo, tremors, and apprehension before I need speak again. Writing a medical article for publication with or without collaborators, I took more time and pains; second and third drafts resulted in less time for social pleasure. However, when the article was accepted by a medical journal, I was rewarded with great satisfaction, knowing the effort I had been making came to a good end. I gradually learned to rest even when not asleep, a great boon. In assessing how I have survived my depression and physical weakness (while working hard and being productive), I believe my life out of doors in the woods, searching for birds or the source of a small stream, and the ancient satisfaction of working a garden made the difference between a neurotic pace and a continuation of life as a doctor. And as if my life sap was very like the maple tree in December, a session with a patient during which I sensed I was being helpful provided me with an irreversible tonic causing the sap to rise.

REFERENCE

1. Hamilton, A., and Hardy, H. L., Industrial Toxicology, 3d ed., Publishing Sciences Group, Acton, Mass., 1974.

CHAPTER 16

Recognition

The title and contents of this section have given me much difficulty. The title seems to claim too much, while the contents that I review while lying awake at night appear too boastful.

To finish this offering I chose the title "Recognition" plus a bibliography as well as a few unpublished papers referred to earlier in the text. My aim is to inform the reader that I have been hard at work since 1932 — the year I entered medical school — and the work has borne fruit. The first — perhaps all — fruit is expressed by my marvelous sense of having reaped the harvest of my potential. As a great admirer of Charles Darwin, I like to think my childhood choice of playing at being doctor has evolved to mature decisions, the ability to assimilate new knowledge, and the will to adapt, for example, to my various illnesses. A few unusual awards are described to lure physicians, especially women, to work at some variation of medicine looking toward prevention and control of disease.

Women in medicine were honored when I was elected to the Association of American Physicians in 1957. This distinguished group of 250 (3 of us women) was known as the Old Turks. Not an attentive scholar at the right time, I was a bit awed to be given honorary membership in Sigma Xi, Phi Beta Kappa, Alpha Omega Alpha, and Delta Omega and a Distinguished Alumnae Award from Wellesley and one from Cornell Medical School. And my industrial medical colleagues saw to it that I received their chief prize (enormously heavy, perhaps meant only for men), the Knudsen Award, plus the Award of Merit of the Academy of Occupational Medicine. I was touched to receive a silver bowl from the society made up of my chemist and engineer friends.

A union award I have mentioned earlier, and the American Public Health Association honored me with their 100th Year Award. But exceeding that, the American Public Health Association gave me the Browning Award at their New Orleans meeting in 1974. This included a $5,000 purse. Considering that Edward Browning had died in 1934 leaving this award fund in trust until his adopted daughter "Peaches" Browning died in 1970, it seems very farsighted and prophetic of him. The sum of $5,000 was to be given to five different individuals chosen by the American Public Health Association. One prize was for distinguished work in the alleviation of addiction; a second was for agricultural research such as development of a new grain; another was to reward the propagation of the Christian gospel; and another was for discovery of ways to control pollution or air and water; mine was for prevention of disease. In view of the fact that Mr. Browning set up these prizes in the 1920s, his vision is to be admired. My plaque, with a profile of the donor, reads: For outstanding contribution to human welfare.

The list of my published articles is included (see Publications) to illustrate how wide may become the interests of one with an M.D. degree only. I also hope the list indicates the number of collaborators, not only to acknowledge their help but also to show my not-very-subtle missionary methods of attracting others to occupational medicine.

CHAPTER 17
Teaching at Dartmouth College (1971-73)

After returning to work in 1968 following a "stroke," I became aware of loss of endurance and the need for more rest. Since MIT has a plan to provide pensions if a staff member chooses early retirement, I reviewed my assets and liabilities with regard to health and finances and began to look for part-time work, preferably in the country. Fate continued to be kind and brought me to a medical meeting where I met and talked with Dr. Tom Almy, chairman of the Department of Medicine at Dartmouth Medical School in Hanover, New Hampshire. Dr. Almy was working to expand the clinical opportunities at the medical school. In addition, with great vision, he was planning, along with Dean James Horning of the undergraduate school, to join undergraduates and medical students for definite training in the field of environmental problems to produce a medical graduate broadly educated and equipped to ask important questions and seek their answers. The reader will recall that I, early in my carrer, had grasped at goals similar to those of Dr. Almy. Thus our talk led to correspondence and a visit to Dartmouth in 1970. Dr. Almy and I warmed to the satisfaction of mutual ideas and to each other's company. A 20-hour workweek was outlined, and I was interviewed by appropriate medical school officers, a process I found interesting since I had so often been the interviewer in the past.

One of the many "fringe benefits" of going to Dartmouth was the opportunity to spend time with Dr. Henry A. Schroeder and his wife Janet. Harry, as he was known to me, had a distinguished professional and personal career before his death in 1975. It was my privilege to have him sponsor my appointment to the Dartmouth faculty. Even greater privilege lay in talk on his lawn looking toward the New Hampshire mountains in summer or in winter before the blazing fire, with his sculptress wife popping in from the kitchen to make a useful comment. Harry was disabled by muscular dystrophy, but this did not slow his active mind. He often said to me as I arrived for a visit, "Come on, Harriet, charge my battery."

His muscular dystrophy and malignancy made Harry a wheel-chair invalid but not before he had achieved notable success in the control of hypertension while working at the Rockefeller Institute in New York City. He did inspired work on benefit and harm from metals at Washington University School of Medicine in St. Louis and in his own laboratory in Brattleboro.

I helped him frequently, with my often tiresome curiosity, and must write of one special occasion in our collaboration. I urged Harry, without success, to use his skills to study mercury. He had refused until the great mercury scare in the United States when former President Richard Nixon, in deep political trouble, appeared on the television screen in 1972 to call mercury in water supplies "a national disaster." The excitement arose because of Japanese reports of deaths and nervous system disability caused by mercury in edible fish, a disease called Minamata disease since the fish came from a bay of that name. Government agencies went to work, as did Harry. He and I collected water samples and fish from various sources. The Japanese had reported up to 40,000 parts of mercury per million parts of water. Since mercury is everywhere in soil, water, and air, U.S. workers found mercury but at levels as low as 1 mg or less in one million parts of water. Where mercury waste was allowed in drinking water, fishing was forbidden, and steps were taken to prevent further contamination. No human mercury disease was reported. Two lessons emerge: first, the harmful dose is high; second, Harry Schroeder was right in reporting the safety of naturally occurring mercury. This well-publicized episode was part of the great tide of interest in environmental protection sweeping the United States during the 1970s.[1]

The decision to leave MIT and to move to Dartmouth, however, was not easy. With much regret and real sadness I resigned my post in the Medical Department after 21 consecutive years of service and the satisfaction of buiding a unit, called the Occupational

Medical Service, later called the Environmental Medical Service, with a competent team that guarded the academic staff and students from the risks of the growing research interests of MIT. The change was hard on my sister, who was living with me, as well as on her son when he was home from school. My sister, who was teaching in the local school, had to move. The home that we three enjoyed and in which we had entertained and gardened had to be sold, a sad day. For better or worse, our beloved housekeeper Alice left, and the vans came and moved me to a newly bought house in Hanover, New Hampshire, and my sister to a Concord, Mass., apartment in June 1971. My MIT friends gave me a large, handsome party at the Faculty Club where I had spent so many hours at meetings, scheming with administration officials, entertaining foreign visitors, learning things I never had dreamed of before while lunching with professors of metallurgy, geology, nutrition, and aeronautical engineering, among others. I was given a beautiful gold wristwatch, heard laudatory speeches, and took home a large, framed handwritten list of the signatures of my well-wishers. And with the next mail came a handwritten note from President Jerome Wiesner, saying among other things:

> I have admired your efforts and integrity and believe that
> you have been a major force for good in the place.

My first days at Dartmouth were spent in the usual tiring unpacking and in meeting new colleagues. My titles were grand: visiting professor of medicine and adjunct professor of health sciences, the second so I might teach in the college, too, in courses being taken for credit in medical school.

Much to my disgust, although I could do my Dartmouth work reasonably well and spend time working on the third edition of Hamilton and Hardy,[2] the weariness I planned to leave behind in Cambridge came with me to Hanover. Since I was not due to begin work until the fall term, I talked with Dr. Almy and spent much of the summer of 1971 chasing here and there hoping for better health. I visited in London, Devon, and Cornwall in England and then went to my favorite solitary haunts in Vermont. By late 1971 I knew that some organic lesion in my central nervous system was established, perhaps a second stroke. My greatest torture was the fact that even when I had a typewritten page before me, I could not read nor articulate what I saw. There followed a series of torments: misspelling, inability to use the dictionary, failure to speak the wanted word while teaching, slurred speech (without alcohol), and limited periods when I could write legibly, plus trouble with walking and dropping things. All of these troubles were made worse, I suppose, because I continued to answer consultations, write out lectures, and force myself to work on the Hamilton and Hardy text. Naps, quick picnics in the woods, the return of our miraculous housekeeper, Alice, a few friends nearby, and our faithful dog saw me safely through this misery. But abruptly all signs of illness worsened — I could not sign a check nor speak understandably. There followed a few days in the Dartmouth Infirmary with the diagnosis of a second cardiovascular accident (stroke). A neurologist made the correct diagnosis. By using radioactive material for a scan of the brain, a large brain tumor was found. My internist, Dr. Robert Charmain, came to my room, sat on my bed, and hugged me, reporting it to be large but probably benign. Such a hug is mighty good therapy.

I chose the Massachusetts General Hospital for surgery so that I would be in a familiar place near my sister and our friends. I was lucky to have the doctors of my choice — Dr. Earle Chapman, competent and friendly, as internist; Dr. Miller Fisher, very experienced, as neurologist; and Dr. Robert Ojemann, widely praised, as neurosurgeon. Studies wanted before the operation were swiftly done. Of only one study did I (and still do) complain. For the purpose of outlining the brain's blood supply, an arteriogram is done by injecting a dye into the carotid artery, which can be found below the jaw. To make sure that the patient cannot move, he is strapped rather like a prisoner prepared for execution. I was strapped to a sloping, uncovered metal affair. My complaints were several. There was a long pause in a painful position before the radiologist came; when he arrived, a medical student asked him to discuss another case. When I complained of my discomfort, the medical student made my torment greater by twisting my restraints. Then the procedure followed. When the artery is punctured, the dye is shot in with a "gun," which produced pain and frightening lights (of which the radiologist had warned me). I protest that modern technology can and must find a less painful way to get the information that the neurosurgeon needs. On August 22, 1972, a large benign tumor (meningioma) was removed from my brain.

I had a prompt recovery during the 17 days I remained in bed. This period is framed by several things: the touching interest of my sister and brother; the early visits of the late Dr. Albert Seeler, my MIT boss and old friend, and of Dr. Gordon Winchell, my local physician, all with anxious faces. And lovely flowers and fan mail came from patients and friends. I recall sitting up on my stretcher to scold a patient of mine who was waiting outside my door to observe my safe arrival from the Intensive Care Unit where I had been nursed for two days after surgery. I was temporarily mentally confused but have vivid memories of the two hallucinating drunks in nearby beds in the Intensive Care Unit. One man saw the classic pink elephants, while his wife sat beside him weeping. The woman in the bed next to mine kept calling the nurses to take the poodle dog off her arm. Perhaps a partial return to normal function made me call out to a resident across the room who was misdiagnosing a man with occupational lung disease whom I felt certain I had seen in consultation in the Veterans Administration Hospital in White River Junction, Vermont, on my last working day as part of my Dartmouth duties.

Driven back to Hanover by my sister, accompanied by the incomparable Alice to keep house and by Suzie the dachshund, I wondered about my future. But it was still mild weather, the thrushes and grosbeaks were singing, and the woodpecker was apparently tearing down the house. My need was to drift, with no action. Gradually, unhappily, I slid into a depression so deep I could not guess at a way out — no sleep, no taste for food, profound apathy, no wish to read, reduced to playing solitaire on my bed tray. Then I met a psychiatrist, who diagnosed a postoperative organic depression; with the right drugs he watched me through this frightening malaise and accomplished this without any use of Freudian hunts. I recalled my 1938 depression and questioned again the value of psychoanalysis and in general the poverty of fruitful study and care of the disabled brain and its physiological function by practitioners and research workers. In the 1980s this state of affairs is changing.

My convalescence was slow but steady. It is fair to report that what I did for Dartmouth was a disappointment. A medical student worked with me during his elective period on the all-important subject of getting accurate data on the patient's work history. This was a critical time at Dartmouth since the medical history sheets were being prepared for computer storing. I helped coach those who were working on job-related illness for the Cancer Registry. A small but useful group of consultation requests came to me. For example, a woodsman came to the clinic complaining of indigestion and a skin rash. The usual laboratory studies were normal. I learned that he used a solution called Salvasol to circle tree bark to destroy it for cutting the tree. Salvasol, an arsenic-containing material, was very like Salversan, a discarded treatment for syphilis. We detected an abnormal amount of arsenic in his urine. Once he stopped using this material, his symptoms disappeared. Another case of skin rash made it possible for me to visit a nearby chemical factory. This factory used a method that generated certain deadly chemicals including cyanide. I had cared for four trainmen who had been stalled at this factory and unconscious owing to cyanide inhalation, so I was glad to visit it.

I visited the state departments concerned with industrial illness in Burlington, Vermont, and Concord, New Hampshire, attended some of their meetings, and was a speaker at one. I made plans with two pediatricians to carry out some of my and some of their lead studies by enlisting their pediatric patients to try for new knowledge of how lead affects the brain. Officials of the Dartmouth business school, Tuck, were cordial; they listened to me and dined me and allowed me to give a lecture. Much more selling was needed there, however, before any commitment to industrial medicine was made. The work of Health Sciences, a department developing within the college, was well supported by a few faculty members interested in the increasing number of environmental problems. My chief job here was to guide and support faculty until a formal structure took shape. The final job I did for Dartmouth was to give a series of lectures on man-made risks, new and old, in the summer of 1974. My recovery from the head surgery of 1972 was slow but steady if I took the rests and drugs prescribed. Dr. Fisher, my Boston neurologist, finds it puzzling that to this day at my age (over 70) I continue to improve.

REFERENCES

1. Schroeder, H. A., The Poisons around Us, Bloomington, Indiana University, Press, 1974.
2. Hamilton, A., and Hardy, H. L., Industrial Toxicology, 3d ed., Acton, Mass., Publishing Sciences Group, 1974.

CHAPTER 18

Retirement

Return to Boston

I returned to the Boston area from Dartmouth in mid-1973, and my sister and I bought a house in Lincoln where we had lived before, returning exactly two years after leaving. Foolishly, we had sold rather than rented the cherished home we had owned since 1954. Slowly, very slowly, I learned the new limitations imposed by my head surgery of 1972.

Much like the old fire horse who is drawn to the familiar sights and sounds of a crackling fire, I found a modest consultation job at the nearby old Middlesex County Tuberculosis Hospital; the late Dr. Doris Barber, medical director, looking to the future of fewer and fewer cases of tuberculosis, saw the possibility of diagnosis and care of occupational lung disease as well as some teaching of the resident staff as forming a part-time position for me with my experience. So I spent two half-days each week at the Middlesex at conferences and consultations as requested. It would be hard to exaggerate the satisfaction I derived from the diagnostic challenges, the proximity once again to patients, and the chance to put forward the concepts of industrial medicine to students and staff. Two active consultants, Dr. Gordon Scammell and Dr. John Moses, old friends from the Massachusetts General Hospital (MGH), made me feel welcome. In 1974 I tried to serve again in the MGH Clinic where I had served steadily except for travel since 1940 and was daunted to find I could not go the pace, my handwriting illegible and my speech slurred. However, the very warm greeting given me in the doctors' cafeteria at lunch was fine therapy.

In our Lincoln home one room was kept free for my recent files, my desk, and generous shelf space for my beloved books. Perhaps most precious were a first edition of Osler's *Textbook of Medicine* and the *Gray's Anatomy* that I had used in medical college. The walls were cluttered with a disorderly montage of framed and unframed pictures of colleagues I admire, travel pictures, and awards. Against one wall was a couch for napping and for thought. A small greenhouse, a gift from a college roommate as a reward for recovery, and an outdoor garden completed the scene.

My retirement, like that of most people who have been truly satisfied with their working years, was and is far from complete. With the increasing number of women choosing medical careers and the general interest of the public (hence, also the media) in medicine, I have been interviewed and questioned. I enjoy most the visits of premedical and medical students, male and female. Those medical schools that are building environmental studies into their departments, variously called prevention, community, or social, have asked for my help. Modern librarians or historians have interviewed me for archival purposes, and a few reporters have come with specific questions about beryllium, lead, and asbestos. By telephone, by conference, and by television cross-examination, I have helped lawyers defending sick workers.

It is hard to explain the new anxieties and foolish fears I have suffered since my 1972 surgery when I have agreed to speak in public, work that I used to take rather easily. The two "jobs" that proved a worry were serving as the Massachusetts Medical Society orator in 1975 and developing as novel a paper as possible about Dr. Alice Hamilton for the historical society of the Boston Medical Library in 1974. The oration I entitled "Risk and Responsibility"[1] and wove through the occupational disease sections many of the ideas that run through this present writing. The paper was published in the *New England Journal of Medicine*. The many requests for reprints from all parts of the globe and the laudatory personal letters I received were flattering and quite convinced me that Dr. Ojemann, my neurosurgeon, had left behind a reasonable amount of my mental faculties.

At the request of two members of the National Institute of Occupational Safety (Drs. Peter Infante and Joseph Wagonen), I reluctantly wrote in 1977 a historical perspective on a subject well known to me, beryllium poisoning. Whether beryllium causes cancer in humans (as it does in certain animals) is in my opinion not settled. There are too few data on all exposed workers and on the amount and duration of exposure. Quite understandably, the beryllium industry wants beryllium to be proved noncancer producing and the liability to be kept low. Certain government agency staff want the opposite answer to prove their pronouncements correct and to support their demand that presently used safe levels must be lowered. My paper was still in the process of being published, two years after it was submitted by request.[2] This tale of my requested article is a small model of the disarray in government agencies and the single-mindedness of industry. Some new device must be found, nongovernment and nonindustry, to referee such problems. The stakes are too high for the injured worker and for legitimate industrial interests to allow the present "numbers game" to be played concerning safe working levels. At present the finally decided safe working level is treated by unions, courts, and conservationists as one of the Ten Commandments.

My final industrial consultant experience, which took place in 1978, has a few worthwhile lessons. As far back as 1947, Dr. Sven Forssman of Sweden told me of worker illness in the so-called hard-metal industry, and I reported this in the second edition of *Industrial Toxicology* (1949).[3] In the mid-1950s British observers reported similar findings in men engaged in similar jobs. In the 1950s the medical director of a large U.S. firm, one of whose operations was very like those reporting illness in Sweden and England, had asked me to visit the plant and advise him. I did so and found a small but definite group of sick workers. I urged help of experienced engineers to control the potential hazard that was not then precisely identified. In addition, I argued without success that the medical findings should be published in full. I argued for publication to warn physicians who might be caring for sick workers without an identified cause of illness. An article concerning one small group of cases was published after I heard an internist speak at the Massachusetts Medical Society describing his cases as nonspecific lung disease. These cases were shown to have been exposed to similar material as were those I had recently seen at the large firm. In 1969 one of the medical consultants to this large firm was allowed to publish his clinical findings.

With this history I was surprised to be asked to have lunch with two senior corporate medical directors of one firm. Their request was that I head a team of MIT chemists and engineers and MGH chest physicians. The purpose was to find work hazards and worker illness, if such existed, in their hard-metal operations. Many meetings and phone calls took place, as well as a visit to the sites in question by my associate Dr. John Stoeckle and me to meet officials, look at jobs, meet lawyers, and describe how we proposed to carry out our studies. On the whole this was an unsatisfactory study. Each worker was asked to sign an informed consent form, and a surprising number refused. In addition, it was discovered by engineers that exposures similar to those abroad were no longer being used in this U.S. plant.

The reader may well ask two questions. First, What did the companies, one large, one small, hope to get from our projected studies? Both companies, although we were told they were asking us in tandem, hugged their operations as trade secrets from each other. Dr. Stoeckle and I had to sign long legal documents promising secrecy. At first reading, the legal papers seemed harmless to our work, but they prevented publication of our findings, a demand totally against our standards. The document was changed to read "may be published without deletion or correction after 60 days," time for company lawyers to find the type of problems the companies might meet in case of litigation.[4] The second question is, Why do I write a long history of events that took place prior to this recent MIT-MGH work? The answer to the first question is that the companies had learned that the government agency in charge of occupational health (Occupational Safety and Health Administration) was planning to reduce the safe working level to half the present standard. This would raise costs for engineering controls.

The second question is answered on the basis of experience. The reported illness (Swedish, English, American) was, in all fairness, controlled by proper engineering once the harmful agent was identified. As in the case of beryllium, the U.S. Public Health Service had published a bulletin reporting *no* illness in hard-metal manufacture. A fatal flaw in this study was the failure to investigate those workers who were absent or who had left the industry. In our studies we had problems:

1. Records of all exposures of men now at work were missing or incomplete.
2. More than one union represented the workers, and some unions persuaded their members not to participate for fear of losing their jobs.
3. Quite properly, the MGH team gave each worker a so-called informed consent form to sign before his testing. As many as 50 percent in one part of the study group refused to sign, reflecting, I suspect, mistrust of "scientists," the company's motives, and the union's official advice.

In summary, many of the facets of industrial disease-hunting serve to slow the progress of prevention of occupational disease to the pace of a snail. It must be true that in a number of instances the competitive spirit of free enterprise leads to greed for profit. Corrupt practice to make profit is condoned, and humane feelings are set aside. I am reluctant to write that these conclusions arise from my experience and apply to most private industries, some but not all insurance companies, consultants, and certain government agencies. I believe that many industrial medical laboratories and academic researchers are "used" by the greedy rather than that they are inherently corrupt. Some union leaders present problems to investigators and teaching units because in some cases they follow the examples of industry or are overwhelmed by pressures for funds or political power.

Rewards

What have I missed in life? My motherly instinct has been well satisfied in caring for infants, children, and adolescents. Born in 1906 into a home of comfort and convention, I did not suffer the pressure modern women feel for unhampered sexual activity. Seeing my parents and friends happily married, I did seriously consider the offers of marriage made to me, but none appeared just right. In addition, medicine is a jealous mistress. My medical training, my career at Northfield, Radcliffe, Massachusetts General Hospital, Massachusetts Institute of Technology, and Dartmouth, and wonderful relationships I have enjoyed with colleagues have made a very happy, rewarding life.

REFERENCES

1. Hardy, H. L., Risk and responsibility, a physician's viewpoint, N. Engl. J. Med., 293:801–806, 1975.
2. Hardy, H. L. Beryllium disease — a clinical perspective, Environ. Res., 21:1–9, 1980.
3. Hamilton, A., and Hardy, H. L., Industrial Toxicology, New York, Hoeber, 1949.
4. Sprince, N. L., Hales, C. A., Weber, A. L., Chamberlin, R. I., and Kazemi, H., Respiratory disease in tungsten carbide workers, Am. Rev. Respir. Dis., 117 (supp):260, 1978.

CHAPTER 19

Women in Medicine

Early History of Women in Medicine

It has not been easy to find correct and interesting data on the early history of women in medicine. Of four volumes of medical history that I have, none lists women as doctors until the mid-to-late nineteenth century, when Elizabeth Blackwell and Alice Hamilton became doctors. Social anthropologists from James G. Frazer in *The Golden Bough*[1] to Margaret Mead make clear that women have been tribal doctors, sorcerers, and witches with various healing skills. However, now a number of historians are at work on the subject. It is of interest that Elizabeth Blackwell (1821-1910) had to train as a nurse to be allowed to attend medical school lectures in France and Germany. A small medical school in Geneva, New York, allowed her to qualify for an M.D. degree. She later founded the New York Infirmary for Women and Children where I studied in 1930.

In 1910 the famous Flexner Report[2] on the state of medical education in the United States closed the small medical schools. Shortly thereafter, a change came about when the so-called land-grant colleges were required to admit women in return for tax exemption. Thus a small-but-steady flow of women students was admitted by Columbia, Johns Hopkins, Tulane, Cornell, and the University of Michigan, among others, during the early years of the twentieth century, and the flow steadily increased. During the World Wars, male physicians were called to active duty, and too few male students applied to medical schools to meet the schools' economic needs, medical education being especially expensive owing to the need for laboratories, large faculty, and access to patients. So *more* women were admitted.

For a few years during World War I, the Harvard Medical School catalog had noted in fine print as a footnote that women might apply. Since none did, the notice was withdrawn until the early 1940s, and in 1945 women were admitted. In contrast, Tufts University and Boston University had been educating women physicians since the early 1900s. The behavior of Harvard toward women has been a matter of interest and controversy, especially in the history of the so-called Annex, Radcliffe College. Not to be forgotten is the pioneering and steady progress of the Women's Medical College of Philadelphia. This college now admits men. Very recent reports from the National Organization of Women suggest that after a peak in the 1960s fewer women are applying to medical school, but the reason for this is not clear.

While I had "adventures" such as caring for black and white men with genital disease as an intern in 1932, both the patients and I made adjustments to the novel situation and got on with the job. When I first began practice in a small town, I had trouble gaining the confidence of new patients, especially because of my youthful appearance. But while in medical training and in the early years of general practice in Northfield, where I was the only woman physician in the county of 52,000 population, I was never treated unfairly because of my sex by fellow students, faculty, medical staff, or male patients.

A more difficult position arose when I reached Cambridge and Boston, largely because of the curious misogyny of the Harvard University authorities. I was appointed to the courtesy, not the regular, staff of Mt. Auburn Hospital because of my job as medical director at nearby Radcliffe. Dr. Arlie Bock of the Harvard Medical Department and Dr. Means, chief of medicine at MGH, did arrange for me to have the lowest rank possible within the MGH clinic, which began a happy association that is still alive. As the MGH unit moved to join European colleagues in caring for the casualties of World War II, we few women and the men turned down for active duty became a small busy corps at home. Dr. Helen Pittman, an internist with her own practice; Dr. Madeline Brown, a neurologist; and Dr. Marion Ropes and Dr. Ann Forbes, both clinicians also active in laboratory research, made up this group. We were asked to help teach part-time at Harvard. Dr. Wyman Richardson and Dr. William Breed were my sponsors. Dr. Richardson, who wanted my help, had trouble securing an appointment for me because of my sex. He got his way by first getting President Ada Comstock of Radcliffe to allow me the time from my full-time Radcliffe job. Various officials agreed, but before I could teach there, Dr. Richardson had to gain permission of the highest ruling body at Harvard, the Corporation. All such foolishness stopped in 1945 when women students were admitted to Harvard Medical School.

In the late 1940s the late Dr. Rita Kelley, a Cornell medical graduate and a distinguished oncologist at the MGH, was appointed chief medical resident at the hospital, the first woman to be given this rank. Gradually Harvard's policy toward women changed, and it and most other schools became coeducational.

Women Workers and Industrial Hazard

Militant feminists in the recent past have insisted that women can do any job that a man can do. This, in my view, is a foolhardy position. It is not true that women can do all jobs without injury. We all know of hazardous jobs where the risk of disability is expected and against which insurance is required by law. Our greedy society, perhaps unconsciously, accepts the fact that progress may lead to a variety of more or less serious injuries. Women are the childbearers, and risks to them must be weighed carefully. While both sexes carry genes, only the mother bears the child. It is no small matter that lead and ionizing radiation exposure at certain levels damage the gene-carrying semen of the male. But the threats in the early weeks of development of the embryo, while not known in entirety, are well enough known to prohibit women in the childbearing ages to work in certain jobs. Exposure to certain heavy metals, which can be internally deposited, to ionizing radiation, and to certain solvents such as benzene (benzol), which harms blood-forming organs, may at some levels be hazardous to pregnant women. Thus not only is it an error to state that any woman can take any job, but it is a risk that no society can afford. The great number of congenital deformities and diseases of the nervous system can only mean that those skilled in study of genes have not yet looked far enough to discover causes. Some of these are surely job related.

Conclusion

I feel there is no such physician as a man physician or a woman physician — there are only poor physicians and good physicians. If I was regarded poorly by men students, faculty, or colleagues in my years of medical training or practicing, I was blissfully unaware of it. I wish for my sisters in medicine the rewards that have been mine.

This volume must emphasize the responsibility of professional women to participate in community service not wholly medical. Outside of my clinical duties, I have served with local (as a library trustee), state (civil defense), national (SST hazards, U.S. Department of Commerce), and international groups (Radiation Risk for the World Health Organization). By accepting these civil duties, I found my horizons widened, my professional contributions increased, and my life made richer.

Physiologically reflected in her ovarian cycle, there is a mothering instinct whether or not a woman bears children, and a good woman physician is sensitive and perceptive of her patients' woes, which may be unspoken. Endocrinologists (in Boston, my colleagues Drs. Aub, Ann Forbes, Fuller Albright, Priscilla Benedict, and Ira Nathanson) have confirmed these observations of mine as true in a measurable fashion.

Finally, my frequent and sometimes lengthy periods of illness and convalescence brought me real dividends: time for rereading those books I most enjoyed. The novels of Tolstoy, Austen, and Hardy and essays of Darwin, Audubon, and Thoreau, some history and biography, and the many lovely unexpected volumes found in the home libraries of friends gave me much pleasure. The pure aesthetic joy of learning to know birds and their songs, walks in woods especially after a rain or during new growth, all these gifts came with or after illness — so while I would not wish anyone an illness, these experiences do bring rewards. I confess that I am jealous of the young, healthy premedical student, medical student, or practicing physician, or any

learning doctor, male or female. I will even make a bow to the research worker, the medical scientist without whose collaborative interest and achievements work in clinical investigation would be
impossible.

REFERENCES

1. Frazer, J. G., The Golden Bough, New York, Macmillan, 1922.
2. Flexner, A., Medical Education in the United States and Canada, New
   York, Carnegie Foundation, 1910.

Publications:
A Comprehensive Bibliography

Hardy, H. L., Clarke, H. L., and Brouha, L., Testing physical fitness in young women, R. Can. Biol., 2:407–415, 1943.

Hardy, H. L., The clinical significance of data accumulated in the medical care of young women, N. Engl. J. Med., 233:811, 1945.

Hardy, H. L., and Bullen, A., Analysis of body build photographs of 175 college women, Am. J. Phys. Anthropol., 4:37, 1946.

Hardy, H. L., and Feemster, R., Infectious hepatitis in Massachusetts with a review of present knowledge of the disease, N. Engl. J. Med., 235:147, 1946.

Hardy, H. L., and Tabershaw, I. R., Delayed chemical penumonitis occurring in workers exposed to beryllium compounds, J. Ind. Hyg. Toxicol., 28:197, 1946.

Hardy, H. L., New clinical syndrome: delayed chemical pneumonitis occurring in workers exposed to beryllium compounds, Bull. N. Engl. Med. Center, 9:16, 1947.

Hardy, H. L., Prevention of anthrax (correspondence), N. Engl. J. Med., 236:883, 1947.

Hardy, H. L., Pulmonary disease in industry. Present knowledge of delayed chemical pneumonitis occurring in workers exposed to beryllium compounds (abstract), Reprint Trans. XLIII annual meeting, Natl. Tuberc. Assoc., 1947.

Hardy, H. L., and Skinner, J. B., The possibility of chronic cadmium poisoning, J. Ind. Hyg. Toxicol., 29:321, 1947.

Hardy, H. L., Delayed chemical pneumonitis in workers exposed to beryllium compounds, Am. Rev. Tuberc., 57:547, 1948. Abstract also in JAMA, 138:1197, 1948.

Hardy, H. L., and Elkins, H. B., Medical aspects of maxium allowable concentrations: benzene, J. Ind. Hyg. Toxicol., 30:196, 1948.

Simeone, F. A., and Hardy, H. L., Chronic progressive infectious gangrene of the skin: a patient with exposure to cold wave solution, Ann. Surg., 128:1112, 1948.

Hamilton, A. and Hardy, H. L., Industrial Toxicology, Hoeber, New York, 1949.

Hardy, H. L., Acute and chronic beryllium poisoning, AECU 569, U.S. Atomic Energy Commission, Oct. 1949.

Hardy, H. L., Toxic effects of beryllium, Metals Industry, 18:23, 1949.

Hardy, H. L., Mercury poisoning, Phys. Today, 2:11, 1949.

Hardy, H. L. The beryllium problem: the chronic or delayed disease. Clinical and epidemiological aspects. Pneumoconiosis: Beryllium, Bauxite Fumes, Compensation, New York, Hoeber, 1950.

Hardy, H. L., Hazards of common solvents, Phys. Today, 3:15, 1950.

Hardy, H. L., Jeffries, W. McK., Wasserman, N. M., and Waddell, W. R., Thiocyanate effect following industrial cyanide exposure, N. Engl. J. Med., 242:968, 1950.

Hardy, H. L., and Maloof, C. C., Evidence of systemic effect of tetryl, Arch. Ind. Hyg. Occup. Med., 1:545, 1950.

Hardy, H. L., Beryllium (Sect. X, Industrial Toxicology Chapter), Oxford Loose-leaf Medicine, 4:42, 1951.

Hardy, H. L., Beryllium poisoning. Case records from the Massachusetts General Hospital. Am. Pract., 2:361–366, 1951.

Hardy, H. L., The character and distribution of disease in American industries using beryllium compounds, Proc. Soc. Med., 44:257, 1951. (Paper read before the Royal Society of Medicine, October 20, 1950.)

Hardy, H. L., Bartter, F. C., and Jaffin, A. E., Metabolic study of a case of chronic beryllium poisoning treated with ACTH, Arch. Ind. Hyg. Occup. Med., 3:579, 1951.

Hardy, H. L., and Maloof, C. C., Treatment of lead poisoning with sodium citrate, Arch. Ind. Hyg. Occup. Med., 3:267, 1951.

Hamilton, A., and Johnstone, P. T., reviewed by Hardy, H. L., Ionizing radiation, Oxford Loose-leaf Medicine, 21:150–177, 1952.

Hardy, H. L., Clinical evidence for the latent and addictive action of benzol with other toxic insults: report of two cases, Arhiv. Za Higijenu Fada (Yugoslavian journal), 3:1–6, 1952.

Hardy, H. L., Experience accumulated in 3 years of occupational medical clinic. Ind. Med. Surg., 21:9, 424, 1952.

Hardy, H. L., Progress report: occupational medicine, New Engl. J. Med., 247:473–483, 515–524, 1952.

Foreman, H., Hardy, H. L., Shipman, T. L., and Belknap, E. L., Use of calcium EDTA in cases of lead intoxication, Arch. Ind. Hyg. Occup. Med., 7:148, 1953.

Hardy, H. L., An M.I.T. enterprise in occupational health, Technology Review, 55:3, 1953.

Hardy, H. L., et al., Use of calcium ethylene diamine tetra-acetate in treating heavy metal poisoning. Report of conference held at Massachusetts General Hospital, Arch. Ind. Hyg. Occup. Med., 7:137, 1953.

Isselbacher, K., Klaus, H., and Hardy, H. L., Asbestosis and bronchogenic carcinoma. Am. J. Med., 14:721, 1953.

Hardy, H. L., Elkins, H. B., Ruotolo, B. Quimby, J., and Baker, W. H.,

Use of monocalcium disodium ethylene diamine tetra-acetate in lead poisoning, JAMA 154:1171, 1954.

Sprague, F. B., and Hardy, H. L., An unusual case of joint pains and fever. Berylliosis and pulmonary hypertension mistaken for rheumatic fever. Circ., 10:129–132, 1954.

Hardy, H. L., The disability found in persons exposed to certain beryllium compounds, Arch. Ind. Health, 12:174, 1955.

Hardy, H. L., Epidemiology, clinical character, and treatment of beryllium poisoning. Progress report, Arch. Ind. Health, 11:273, 1955.

Ahlmark, A., Friberg, L., and Hardy, H. L., The solubility in water of two cadmium dusts with regard to the risk of chronic poisoning, Ind. Med. Surg., 25:514, 1956.

Hardy, H. L., Differential diagnosis between beryllium poisoning and sarcoidosis, Am. Rev. Tuberc. Pulmo. Dis., 74:885, 1956.

Hardy, H. L., Toxic hazards: current hazards of toxic beryllium compounds, N. Engl. J. Med., 256:715, 1957.

Cogan, D. G., Fricker, S. J., Lubin, M., Donaldson, D., and Hardy, H. L., Cataracts and ultra-high frequency radiation, Arch. Ind. Health, 18:299, 1958.

Hardy, H. L., Case 420: beryllium poisoning, cases from the medical grand rounds of the Mass. Gen. Hosp., ed., J. H. Knowles, Am. Pract. Dig. Treatment, 9:2029–2041, 1958.

Hardy, H. L., Current knowledge of beryllium intoxication, Occupational Safety and Health (Official publication of ILO, Geneva), Apr.–June, 1958, pp. 77–80.

Hardy, H. L., Technological advances and their relations to industrial and public health, Reminder, 16:1–10, 1958. (Speech to Biol. Sci. Div. of the Special Library Association.)

Hardy, H. L., Cyanide poisoning, N. Engl. J. Med., 261:619, 1959.

Hardy, H. L., Editorial: Honoring Dr. Alice Hamilton (90th birthday), New Engl. J. Med., 260:560, 1959.

Hardy, H. L., Editorial: Journal of Occupational Medicine, N. Engl. J. Med., 260:610, 1959.

Hardy, H. L., Man-made disease of the nervous system, prepared for the Commission on Mental Health, Boston, 1959.

Hardy, H. L., Medical control of beryllium, Arch. Ind. Health, 9:203, 1959.

Hardy, H. L., South American teaching trip, June 19–29, 1959, published for private circulation, Occupational lung diseases, Bogotá, Colombia.

Hardy, H. L., and Stoeckle, J. D., Beryllium disease, J. Chronic Dis., 9:152, 1959.

Hardy, H. L., and Tepper, L. B., Beryllium disease: a review of current knowledge, J. Occup. Med., 1:219, 1959.

Lead Hygiene Conference, Lead Industries Association, Nov. 6–7, 1958, Chicago, Ind. Med. Surg., 28:93–133, 1959.

Hardy, H. L., Pulmonary irritants (toxic hazards), N. Engl. J. Med., 263: 813, 1960.

Hardy, H. L., Beryllium disease: a continuing diagnostic problem, Am. J. Med. Sci., 242:150, 1961.

Hardy, H. L., Case 40-1961. Case records of the Mass. Gen. Hosp., N. Engl. J. Med., 264:1154, 1961 (Discussion).

Hardy, H. L., The definition of sarcoidosis. Am. Rev. Resp. Dis., 84:2, 1961.

Hardy, H. L., Experience in the United States with proposed safe levels of exposure to toxic beryllium compounds. Pure and Applied Chemistry, 3:33, 1961.

Hardy, H. L., Farmer's lung, N. Engl. J. Med., 264:1313, 1961.

Hardy, H. L., Hazards to health: criteria for diagnosis of occupational disease, N. Engl. J. Med., 264:1046, 1961.

Hardy, H. L., The choice of a medical career, Occupational Medicine, Essays on the Fields of Medicine, J. Garland and J. Stokes, III, eds., Philadelphia, J. B. Lippincott Co., 1961.

Hardy, H. L., Problems in the diagnosis of beryllium disease, Beryllium Workshop, Kettering Laboratory, Cincinnati, Ohio, Jan. 5–6, 1961, p. 48.

Hardy, H. L., Section on dangerous occupations, Encyclopedia Britannica, 1961.

Hardy, H. L., Use of chelating agents in lead poisoning. Discussion. Clinical experience with use of calcium disodium ethylene tetra-acetate in the therapy of lead poisoning, Fed. Proc., 20:199, 1961.

Tepper, L. B., Hardy, H. L., and Chamberlin, R. I., Toxicity of Beryllium Compounds, a Monograph, Elsevier, Amsterdam, 1961.

Hardy, H. L., Beryllium Case Registry progress report: 1962, Arch. Environ. Health, 5:265, 1962.

Hardy, H. L., Correct diagnosis of environmental lung disease, Proc. Seminar on Resp. Dis. for Science Writers, Am. Thoracic Soc. and Natl. Tuberc. Assoc., Princeton, N. J., 1962.

Hardy, H. L., Editorial: The will to survive, N. Engl. J. Med., 266:788, 1962.

Hardy, H. L., Occupational health program in a large research institution, J. Am. College Health Assoc., 11:78, 1962.

Hardy, H. L., Reaction to toxic beryllium compounds: terminology, J. Occup. Med., 4:532, 1962.

Stoeckle, J. D., Hardy, H. L., King, W. B., and Nemiah, J. C., Respiratory disease in U.S. soft coal miners: clinical and etiological considerations. A study of 30 cases, J. Chronic Dis., 15:887, 1962.

Hardy, H. L., Beryllium disease — experience with investigation required to establish etiology of occupational disease, Ann. NY Acad. Sci., 107:525, 1963.

Hardy, H. L., and Stoeckle, J. D., Disabling respiratory disease in U.S. soft-coal miners: value of intensive study of a small series of cases. Proc. XIV Int. Cong. Occup. Health, Madrid, 1963.

McDermott, Wm. V., Jr., and Hardy, H. L., Cirrhosis of the liver following chronic exposure to carbon tetrachloride, J. Occup. Med., 5:249, 1963.

Hardy, H. L., Beryllium Case Registry, Am. J. Clin. Pathol., 42:409–410, Oct. 1964.

Hardy, H. L., Beryllium Case Registry, Letter to Physicians, 1964.

Kranes, A., and Castleman, B., (discussion by H. L. Hardy), Dyspnea in pipefitter 6 years after amputation of leg for sarcoma. N. Engl. J. Med., 270:789, 1964.

Hardy, H. L., Asbestos related disease, Am. J. Med. Sci., 250:381–389, 1965.

Hardy, H. L., Beryllium poisoning: lessons in the control of man-made disease, N. Engl. J. Med., 273:1188–1199, 1965.

Hardy, H. L., Editorial: Asbestosis and malignant disease, N. Engl. J. Med., 272:590–591, 1965.

Weber, A. L., Stoeckle, J. D., and Hardy, H. L., Roentgenologic patterns in long-standing beryllium disease, Am. J. Roentgenol. Radiat. Ther. Nuc. Med., 93:879–890, 1965.

Hardy, H. L., What is the status of knowledge of the toxic effect of lead on identifiable groups in the population? Clin. Pharmacol. Ther., 7:713–722, 1966.

Hardy, H. L., Rabe, E. W., and Lorch, S., United States Beryllium Case Registry 1952–1966: review of its methods and utility. Proc. XV Int. Cong. Occup. Health, B III-4, 49–55, Vienna, 1966.

Levin, S., Chamberlin, R. I., and Hardy, H. L., The occupational medical service of the Massachusetts Institute of Technology, Proc. XV Int. Cong. Occup. Health, B XI-2, 303–312, 1966.

Boylen, G. W., Jr., and Hardy. H. L., Distribution of arsenic in non-exposed persons (hair, liver and urine), Am. Ind. Hyg. Assoc. J., 28:148–150, 1967.

Hardy, H. L., Current concepts of occupational lung disease of interest to the radiologist, Semin. Roentgenol., 2:225–234, 1967.

Hardy, H. L., Editorial: Respiratory disorders among textile workers, N.

Engl. J. Med., 277:209–210, 1967.

Hardy, H. L., Review of beryllium: its industrial hygiene aspects, H. E. Stokinger, ed., New York, Academic Press, 1966. J. Occup. Med., 9:203–204, 1967.

Hardy, H. L., Rabe, E. W., and Lorch, S., United States Beryllium Case Registry 1952–1966: review of its methods and utility, J. Occup. Med., 9:271–276, 1967.

Hardy, H. L., Boylen, G. W., Jr., Cyanide-poisoning Encyclopedia, Geneva, Occupational Health and Safety, International Labour Office, 1968.

Hardy, H. L., and Chamberlin, R. I., Beryllium Poisoning Encyclopedia, Geneva, Occupational Health and Safety, International Labour Office, 1969.

Hardy, H. L., and Leahy, J. E., Recognition of occupational lung disease, Clin. Notes Respir. Dis., 6:3–11, 1968.

Redding, R. A., Hardy, H. L., and Gaensler, E. A., Beryllium disease: a 16 year follow-up case study, Respiration, 25:263–276, 1968.

Andrews, J. L., Kazemi, H., and Hardy, H. L., Patterns of lung disfunction in chronic beryllium disease, Am. Rev. Respir. Dis., 100, 1969.

Hardy, H. L., Dr. Alice: first lady of Harvard, Harvard Med. Alumni Bull., 43:4–5, 1969.

Hardy, H. L., Lead and health, Scientist and Citizen, 10:80–82, 1969.

Hardy, H. L., Toxicological appraisal — lead, discussion, J. Air Pollut. Control Assoc., 19:701–703, 1969.

Kelly, Wm. N., Goldfinger, S. E., and Hardy, H. L., Hyperuricemia in chronic beryllium disease, Ann. Int. Med., 70:977, 1969.

Stoeckle, J. D., Hardy, J. L., and Weber, A. L., Chronic beryllium disease. Long-term follow-up of sixty cases and selective review of the literature, Am. J. Med., 46:545–561, 1969.

Freiman, D., and Hardy, H. L., Beryllium disease — the relationship of the pulmonary pathology to clinical course and prognosis based on the study of 130 cases from the U.S. Beryllium Case Registry, Hum. Pathol., 1, 1970.

Hardy, H. L., Chamberlin, R. I., Maloof, C. C., Boylen, G. W., Jr., and Howell, M. C., Lead as an environmental poison, Clin. Pharmacol. Ther., 12:982–1002, 1971.

Hardy, H. L., Guest Editor: Alice Hamilton, M.D., What price safety, tetraethyl lead reveals a flaw in our defenses, J. Occup. Med., 14:132–134, 1972.

Hardy, H. L., and Chamberlin, R. I., Beryllium disease, The Toxicology of Beryllium, I. R. Tabershaw, ed, Washington, D. C., U.S. Public

Health Service, 1972, Publication no. 2173 (revision of PHS no. 181, 1943).

Hardy, H. L., Leahy, J., and Kazemi, H., Impaired pulmonary function following an unusual railroad accident, Pracovni Lekarstvi, no. 2-3, 70–73, 1972.

Hamilton, A., and Hardy, H. L., Industrial Toxicology, 3d ed., Publishing Sciences Group, Acton, Mass., 1974.

Hardy, H. L., Talk on Dr. Hamilton, Boston Medical Library, May 15, 1974.

Hardy, H. L., Annual Discourse — Risk and Responsibility, a physician's viewpoint, presented at annual meeting of Massachusetts Med. Soc., Boston, May 28, 1975, publ. in N. Engl. J. Med., 293:801–806, 1975.

Hardy, H. L., Risk and responsibility. A physician's viewpoint, N. Engl. J. Med., 293:801–806, 1975.

Stoeckle, J. D., Hardy, H. L., and Ling, B. The compensation experience of patients with chronic beryllium disease, J. Occup. Med., 17:167–170, 1975.

Hardy, H. L., Correction on the number of presumed beryllium-induced osteosarcomas in humans. Correspondence, N. Engl. J. Med., 293: 624, 1976.

Sprince, N., Kazemi, H., and Hardy, H. L., Current (1975) problem of differentiating between beryllium disease and sarcoidosis, reprinted from Ann. NY Acad. Sci., 278:654–664, 1976.

Hardy, H. L., Beryllium disease: a clinical perspective. Environ. Res., 21: 1–9, 1980.

Hamilton, A., and Hardy, H. L., Industrial Toxicology, 4th ed., A. J. Finkel, ed., Littleton, Mass., John Wright • PSG, 1982.

Stoeckle, J. D., Oliver, L. C., and Hardy, H. L., Women with asbestosis in a medical clinic: underreported women smokers, delayed diagnosis and smoking, Women & Health, 7:31–36, 1982.

Index

239